How Did I

Get My Foot In My Mouth

When I Can't Even

Touch My Toes?

ISBN 978-0-6151-3916-6

Dedicated to Alexis, Irene, and Jarod for a life filled with laughs, tears, hugs and love.

I pray you will all continue to grow into lovely people who love the Lord as much as He loves us!

Foreword

Have you ever put on a pair of gloves, or even a pair of jeans for that matter, and had them fit so well, you hardly knew they were on?! Well, that same perfect fit is what Jayne has going on with her writing.

Jayne and I met several years ago through a Christian magazine website, became fast friends, and have yet to see each other in person, but that doesn't matter at all because we type so frequently back and forth to one another in e-mail messages we know each other as well as if we spent all these years sitting across from each other at the kitchen table sipping hot cups of chai tea. It is through these years of e-mail correspondence that I first became acquainted with Jayne's "gift." We're all given at least one gift from God above that He wants us to use for His glory and honor and Jayne's been blessed with the gift to gab....with keystrokes that is! Well, you can rest assured that she is not like the person in the Bible that buried his talent, to save it for another day. No way! She's been recording her shared experiences with family and friends for years now and after being encouraged by so many more than just me, she finally acted on her deep desire to become published. Do I ever feel so sorry for her kids and grandkids now! No longer will they be able to keep their guardian's "secret" life under wraps. Instead, Jayne has allowed us the pleasure of joining her as she reminisces about so many of her precious, hysterical, and often times poignant memories.

So great is her talent from the Lord, Jayne's words will not only make you laugh and cry (or cry while laughing!) along with her, but you will see as I have these many years, how God blesses others through her and her gift. Not everyone uses their gifts as effectively as she does and, no doubt, after reading through this first book ever from her, you will be grateful not only for the time you spent reading it, but for the time she spent putting it all together for us.

Jayne, thank you for putting aside the demands of daily life long enough to open yourself up to be used in such a mighty way by God. May His blessings continue from one reader to the next just as the ripples play on in the water after something connects with its surface. Prepare yourself to see firsthand, with each turn of this book's pages, the perfect fit Jayne's gift of writing is to God's plan for her...and for you as the reader. As the lyrics to a popular Christian song by singer Sandi Patti goes, "The Gift Goes On!"

~Katy B. Ludwig

Introduction

Thank you for reading my book! It is my sincere hope that you'll enjoy reading my stories as much as I have enjoyed living them. Everything you'll read within is true, and I had a wonderful trip down memory lane as I wrote and edited. I have been writing about and sharing my memories over the past ten years and had forgotten some, but memories flooded back as I worked to prepare them for this book. I laughed and I cried as I recalled each event. The following pages contain stories from my own childhood to funny things that my kids and grandkids have done and said over the years. Of course I have included some serious memories. How else would we recognize the rewards of laughter without tears?

There is no chronological order to the stories so allow me to introduce my family. My husband Paul Ernest (AKA Ernie and Bapa) and I have been married for a fast and fun twenty five years. Mistie is our oldest daughter and is mom to Alexis who is 11 years old and Jarod who is 5 years old. Middle daughter Brooke is mom to 9 year old Irene. Stacie is our youngest daughter, and of course Aunt to all three kids. Though the stories span the past ten years or so, they all remain cherished memories.

All three of my grandchildren are a delight and constant source of amusement with Irene and Jarod vying for position as lead comedian. Alexis is the oldest and more serious. All three offer me living proof that God has a wonderful sense of humor. Christian author and humorist Liz Curtis Higgs encourages us to look for the funny in each day, advice that I take seriously. With these three I don't need to look far to find the fun.

No author is a success without support, and I have always had a wonderful support system. I have been blessed with friends who have encouraged me to "write a book!" and by family members who have been amazingly patient with me when all they seemed to see was the back of my head as I sat in front of the computer writing,. Though there are far too many to mention by name (and you know who you are) I do want to thank a few extraordinarily helpful people. Thanks to Mistie for suggesting the title of the book. I had so many suggestions that I held a contest and hers was the winning submission. Thanks to Lori Kelly for suggesting the runner-up title. Thanks and hugs to Brooke for the cover design (even though she voted for the title "My Kids Say I Talk Too Much"), and thanks as always to Stacie for her grammar assistance. Mom is never too old to learn from the best. Sincere thanks to Leslie, Delores and Katy for scripture search assistance. Katy also has my heart felt thanks for being my biggest fan and supporter over the years. I've always known I can count on her for honest and loving feedback. Most importantly, loving thanks to my wonderful husband who has been the best assistant anyone could ever hope to find. He has been incredibly patient (even when I was at my wits end and so frustrated with the publishing process that I wanted to quit) and is wonderfully smart. I could never have done this without you. In fact all of you are all true blessings.

The proceeds from this book will be divided between American Family (Christian) Radio based in Tupelo, MS. (www.AFR.net) and my home church, East Tenth Street Church of Christ in Roanoke Rapids, NC. Both have been tremendous ministries and I can never say thank you enough for all that they have done and continue to do.

A Cookies And Ice Cream Summer Treat

Irene, who was 4 months old at the time of this tale is now nine years old and Alexis who was days away from two is now eleven, so this is not a recent story. It is nevertheless a very strong memory and one that I enjoy taking out of my memory vault and playing back like a video, over and over to this day.

This particular summer my family and I planned to go to my parent's 50th wedding anniversary celebration in Arkansas but were forced to miss it because Mistie and I were in classes at the college and were taking exams the week of the party. As soon as we finished our final exams we made plans to go. Unfortunately by this point my husband Ernie, at that time an Army accident investigator was on call, and Brooke had changed jobs and couldn't go, so Mistie, Stacie and I just tossed Irene and Alexis in the back seat of my Jimmy and took off from Alabama for the drive to Arkansas. The actual trip is another story in itself, with a plot of a screaming baby nearly every mile of the 13 hour trip (BOTH ways) and hilarious conversations about favorite cartoons. However, the main plot is about an innocent trip to an ice cream parlor one hot Sunday evening after church services. If you care to join me as I trip down memory lane, I'll do my best to describe events as they evolved.

This trip felt doomed almost from the beginning when it became clear that four-month-old Irene was not going to be a happy traveler. Then within the first two days of arriving, Alexis fell and busted her little top lip open and Mistie had to be rushed to the emergency room with what turned out to be kidney stones. She (Mistie) spent Sunday morning in the ER being diagnosed and given pain medicine, so when my sister mentioned that their family was planning to meet at Braum's Ice Cream Parlor that evening after services and asked if we'd like to join them, we eagerly accepted the invitation. We hadn't had much fun so far so we were all looking forward to it. She and my mom rode into town with us, arriving well ahead of the after —church crowd. Braum's is a reasonably large place but was going to fill up fast, and we were expecting a fairly large gathering. We staked out our territory using baby, kids, purses and adults to secure enough seats for our gang. That alone, caused a few curious stares. But when you toss in a cute young child with a fat lip, and a young woman who is in obvious pain, well…you can just imagine. We took over an entire section just inside the door. We thought it was obvious to all that the area was going to be used but one middle-aged couple either wasn't very observant or just plain didn't care, because they took two of our seats directly inside the doors. Little did they know that they would soon become a part of the drama about to unfold…

By the time we arrived, Mistie was starting to feel rotten again. In fact was barely able to sit up. We had just decided to take her to the hospital ER when my brother-in-law, Chuck walked in. He told us that some folks from church would be there soon and that Joshua, my youngest nephew, was coming with my dad in a few minutes. I was sitting pretty much wedged in on the bench along the back side of the table, so I ever-so-sweetly asked Chuck to drive Mistie the two blocks to the hospital and even assured him he didn't have to get out. "Just drive her to the door and give her a shove" I said. He nicely agreed to take her but said he wasn't going to shove her out. Shortly after they left, some of the folks from church showed up and slid into the bench beside me. We were all in high spirits. Sue and I were laughing while getting acquainted when I whispered that the couple at the stolen table may be sorry because our crew can get kind of rowdy. She whispered back that she knew the couple and didn't really care for him. He's some sort of business man and not very nice and to top it all off, he permed his hair. We were still giggling over that fact when someone looked out the window and noticed my dad's truck pull into the parking lot so we were all watching the door as he and Joshua walked in. What happened next unfolds like a perfectly choreographed comedy sketch, and though took only seconds to transpire, is permanently burned into my memory bank.

Josh preceded my dad through the door. He was just even with the couple in the absconded booth when he paused, then spewed forth like a fountain. A yellow stream shot from his mouth straight out into a huge puddle in the floor. Our group of course saw it happen, but few others in the place did so they were clueless as to the sudden pandemonium. Joshua's mom, my twin sister, is one laid back mom. (In other words, nothing like me). She just watched and immediately said (and I quote) "He had animal crackers at church didn't he? That looks like animal crackers to me!" That was all it took for Sue and me to burst into sidesplitting laughter. It's a good thing I was wedged into the back bench because that's the only thing that kept me from falling onto the floor. The harder I laughed the harder Sue did, and so on. Then Shane, who is also a very laid back kind of person and Josh's big brother, starts hollering in his best born-and-raised-there Arkansas drawl, "Someone get a mop!" over and over. By this time we are pounding the table in hysterics and we're barely able to catch our breath. It's at this point that we realize that Mr. & Mrs. Table Thief are leaving and that Mr. TT has a definite greenish tint around his lips. This just set us off even more. A young man from Braum's rushes up with the much-requested mop and bucket and we look up to see another couple walking towards "the puddle". They are walking slowly yet straight ahead. They are turned to speak to another couple in a booth they are passing. I am near desperate for air at this point so I nudge Sue and gasp "LOOK!" and point at them. We are laughing so hard we have to hold our sides now as we watch them oh so innocently advance towards the animal cookie tragedy in the floor. Mere inches from disaster, Mrs. Gabby looks down and sees the mess and barely stops in time. The look on her face was priceless and of course set us off into new fits of snorts, guffaws and table slapping. Let me tell you, we had the attention of the entire ice cream parlor by this point but were too far gone to care. It's really quite a wonder that the management didn't politely, or even not so politely ask us to leave. I did notice a few other customers grinning so we apparently weren't the only ones who enjoyed the show.

I of course had to go get Mistie at the hospital, so I sent my little ones home with the family while I drove over to retrieve her. She was still in an examining room when I arrived so they allowed me go back to her. I was still hurting from laughing so hard and started telling her about the chain of events, reminding her of how we took over the section, Alexis' fat little lip and how she was hanging on the table in pain. The more I got into it, the harder I laughed and the louder I got in the telling. I finally hollered, "We looked like a scene out of the Exorcist!" Mistie nearly lost it as she reminded me "Shhhh! Mom, we're in a CATHOLIC hospital!" I don't know about her but I nearly needed sedating at that point.

To this day I still wonder about the unintended participants in our little drama. Do the Mr. and Mrs. Regret misappropriating our table? Can he still eat ice cream or even look at animal crackers? Is Mrs. Gabby now more attentive when she's walking? Did that poor kid at Braum's look for a job that didn't require mopping the next day?

Does he still perm his hair..........?

Proverbs 4:25 Let your eyes look straight ahead, fix your gaze directly before you.

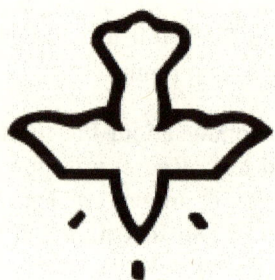

A Different Kind Of Veggie Tale

The year was 1997 and we had just moved into our new home in Alabama. Ernie was stationed there with the Army and had been there for four years. We had rented a nice home for those first four years but grew weary of problems with the also-military landlord so decided to buy. The home we found was beautiful; we quickly fell in love with it and ultimately moved in the week of Thanksgiving. We weren't quite settled but we managed to have a very nice Thanksgiving in spite of some unpacked boxes.

Before I go on I must share a detail with you. I was (still am actually) a pro at clogging sink drains. I had to call the plumber to our house on three separate occasions while we lived in the rental house. The last time I had put a roast down the disposal that no one would eat. I have no idea how it happened but I somehow managed to get the thing down the throat of the disposal, whole. It jammed it up but good. I tried everything I could think of but nothing, and I do mean nothing, was budging it. When the plumber came (we were on a first name basis by this point), I told him what had happened . He said it was no wonder no one would eat it if it was that tough. As it turned out, even he had trouble dislodging it. Finally, after several trips to the roof, he managed to push it on through. That clog was so bad it cost extra. It was during his trips to de-clog us that I learned that there is a vent on the roof for the plumbing. Interesting.

So, it's Thanksgiving Day in our gorgeous new home and we're ready to clean the kitchen so Ernie and I wander in to start loading the dishwasher. Bad news; the sink was clogged. This time however I was innocent! Ernie had poured turkey drippings down the drain while cooking and apparently hadn't run lots of hot water after it. We tried running the disposer but all it did was swirl the water around and back up into the other sink. Out came the trusty plunger which, due to previous experience we always had on hand, and we took turns plunging. We plunged and plunged and plunged some more but that clog was as stubborn as that roast beef had ever been. Finally one of the kids, as I recall it was Brooke, had the brilliant suggestion to try using the wet/dry vac in blower mode to push it through. "Hey! That is a brilliant idea!" we all agreed. So out comes the wet/dry vac and into the disposer hole it goes. Ernie turns it on and it appears to be working or at least the water is leaving. About that time Mistie looked out the window and said "I didn't know it was supposed to rain!" Rain? There isn't a cloud in the sky! We run outside to look and sure enough vegetables and water are shooting straight up through the plumbing vent, into the air and down the roof. It was like a volcano erupting; only it was food. We laughed so hard we could barely breathe and said we sure hoped the neighbors weren't looking outside at that moment. Talk about new meaning to blowing your stack.

The worst part was it didn't fix the clog. We ended up going next door to the new neighbors and begging for some Drano which they thankfully had. We went through nearly the entire can but still it wouldn't dislodge.

The next morning I called my plumber buddy and explained the situation. He said he'd try to make it but had a lot of post-holiday plumbing problems to clear up, and to complicate things, it was pouring rain. He didn't relish the idea of climbing up on our roof in the rain but if it quit he'd try to stop by. I was sick of looking at crusted plates and greasy baking pans so finally, in desperation I grabbed the can of Drano and dumped the last of it down the drain, saying a prayer that it would clean the clog. Glory Halleluiah it worked! I was fairly dancing a jig of happiness as I ran to the phone to call the plumber to let him know that he was off the hook for climbing the roof.

Too bad though. I was sort of looking forward to showing him my new kitchen complete with three sinks.

Job 5:10 He bestows rain on the earth; he sends water upon the countryside.

Ah Kids Wonderful Kids!

I truly believe grandkids are a gift from God. They keep us young, make us laugh, give us an opportunity to spoil as we couldn't with our own, and are a wonderful incentive to exercise.

Jarod is now walking and has been since he was 81/2 months old. I had forgotten how busy a baby can be when they learn to walk. He is into, on top of, underneath and around everything within his reach and some that aren't. He can barely reach the drawer that my keyboard sits on but this doesn't stop him from playing havoc with my typing. I have corrected his "additions" three times since I started. Yesterday his mom left him with me while she and her younger sister Stacie, went to Wal-Mart. During the time they were gone he took off with my jug of fabric softener (he's also very strong!), dumped over our cross-cutter paper shredder, emptied my bottom kitchen drawer of all measuring cups and pushed the screen out of the side door twice. For some reason he found my having to go outside and put it back to be very funny and belly laughed while I was standing on the porch replacing it. I suppose it could have something to do with all the funny faces and noises Nana made while struggling to get it back in place. He loves to help me do laundry and stands in front of the dryer while I try to load it assuring that Nana gets some additional exercising in while trying to bend and twist to pick up the clothes that miss the mark because he's standing in front of it. I think he may have a future as an athletic trainer. He makes up for all the messes though by being one of the most affectionate babies I've ever known and just soaks up the loving and cuddling.

Alexis, who is 6 years old now was going to spend the night last night but changed her mind at the last minute. She has stayed many times before so wasn't afraid of being away from mommy. No, she couldn't stay because she forgot to bring Baby with her, something that rarely happens. Baby is a stuffed cat that meows and wiggles her tail when you smack her on the back. The older Baby gets, the harder you have to smack her to make her work. Poor Baby, she's kind of like me. I bought this cat at a yard sale for her when she was 18 months old and it was the best $1.50 investment I'd ever made. She and Baby are inseparable, as is evidenced by the brown color of her once cream colored coat. Baby comes to spend the day with Nana every school day and Alexis will often ask me to make sure Baby is happy while she's gone. I have to get creative to make sure she knows I did my job too. Some days I'll set her on a chair so she can look out a window, place her in the baby swing or set her on the coffee table so she can watch TV. She loves that cat and was nearly in tears at the thought of being away from her last night. Baby is a lucky stuffed cat to be so well loved I think.

Our **Irene** got the notion in her head this weekend that she wanted her ears pierced. She talked about it all evening Friday so her mom told her if she still felt the same way the next morning then she would take her to the mall to get holes in her ears. Her Aunt Stacie who has never had her ears pierced, told her how much it would hurt. Irene got enough, looked at her Aunt Stacie and declared, "You're the evil sister!" Saturday morning she was still excited at the prospect so off they went. Brooke said she was fine on the first ear and only whimpered a little. They were afraid she would try to chicken out and had told her she couldn't stop with one ear unless she was looking at a life as a pirate, so she sat very still and bravely allowed the second ear to be done. When Brooke looked up there were several women standing around watching, and all holding their breath. They all breathed a collective sigh of relief when she made it through. As for Irene, she was so excited and proud of the new earrings that she couldn't allow her mom to shop any longer. They had to come home so she could show off her new look for Bapa and Nana. She went around all afternoon saying, "Aren't they precious?" Yes they are and so is she. (BTW, she is taking great care of them cleaning and turning them several times a day without being told!)

Both little girls love to play in my make-up so it's not unusual to find smears on my bathroom sink that are telltale signs of their snooping in my makeup case. I've noticed that as I get older I wear far less make-up and I go out with nothing more than eye liner on most days. Getting old is very freeing since you just don't care what other people think of your looks anymore. (Apparently you also get smarter as you get older). I have had some of this make-up for years now so I decided to clean out my kit and gave it all to Alexis and Irene to play with. I also happen to be a perfume/scent addict. It's a real sickness with me and I have more bottles of perfume than I can wear in a lifetime, so I tossed in some bottles of perfume as well which cleared some of the old stuff out and made room for new. Those girls had a ball with that make-up. Anyone who sat still long enough got a makeover. So far Bapa refuses to play with them but we're waiting to catch him napping. I tend to be their favorite victim since being Nana and always tired from chasing Jarod, will sit still for most anything. Alexis did my hair and makeup one afternoon after school and spent quite a bit of time on me. When she was finished Ernie took one look and said, "Gee baby, you look nice." I should have picked up on the sarcastic note in his voice. Mistie came in after work to pick the kids up and doing a double take when she saw me, asked what happened to me. I told her that her child had made me over. She just smiled and kept going. I noticed during dinner that everyone kept looking at me funny but didn't think much of it since they often give me funny looks. Later that night while getting ready to brush my teeth before bed I finally saw myself in the mirror. I now understood why I had heard Ernie mutter something about Bozo the Clown while looking at me earlier. I had the biggest and blackest eyebrows I've ever seen! I also had streaks of green eye shadow on my cheeks, lipstick smudged everywhere but my lips and for some reason black smeared all over my neck. She has quite a knack for.....inventive hairstyles but I don't think she has much future as a Merle Norman consultant.

I'd better run now. Jarod just knocked the paper shredder over again. I just finished vacuuming up the mess from earlier and I guess he got the idea that Nana was having fun unclogging the vacuum head every 15 seconds. He sure has a lot to learn about Nana and vacuum cleaners.

John 5:2 This is how we know that we love the children of God: by loving God and carrying out his commands.

Alexis And Nana, Students Together

Mid-way through Alexis' fourth grade year, her mom made the decision to remove her from public school to homeschool her. There were several reasons for this decision, chief among them being a conflict with one of her teachers. Another teacher confided in me that Alexis' teacher was nearing retirement and was simply holding on until she could do so in two years. Unfortunately, possibly from being tired and beyond ready to retire, she was rigid and unwilling to accept any responsibility for the problems between Alexis, her mom and Alexis' needs.

Alexis is not, never has been, and will likely never be a morning person. We have discovered, through tests at Duke University that she suffers from night time brain seizures called "Rolandic Seizure Disorder". These are unwitnessed seizures, in no way affect her intelligence, and will resolve by the time she's a teenager. They do however, cause attention problems as the day goes on and as she tires. Unfortunately, she went to this teacher's classroom after lunch just as the fatigue and focus problems would set in. By law, any child with learning needs is entitled to extra time and assistance in the classroom however, the teacher was adamant that it wasn't her problem so an impasse was reached. Making matters worse, Alexis is very petite and several boys would pick on her, sometimes physically. We saw little results from our complaints to the administration so the decision was made to remove her, which her mom did after Christmas break 2004.

I had agreed to help homeschool so Mistie and I divided teaching duties. I took History/Geography, Language Arts, Spelling, Reading and home economics. Mistie would teach my much dreaded math and sciences. We bought our first curriculum and jumped in feet first and we all nearly drowned. Having never done this before and unable to find anyone in the area who also homeschooled, we struggled through the rest of the school year, sighing with relief when summer break arrived.

We searched, and finally found a homeschool support group at Lake Gaston, a twenty five-minute drive but Mistie was more than willing to take Alexis so every other Friday did just that. I would occasionally fill in when she had to work.

Realization finally hit home one day as we struggled yet again in the fall, to find a workable routine. She is *one* student and we are *home*schoolers yet I had been attempting to structure our days as if we were in a classroom. We were far less stressed and delighted when it finally dawned that we didn't need to spend X amount of time on each subject with scheduled breaks. We could start working when we were ready, stop when we were done or needed to and still get all subjects covered in a few hours as opposed to an entire day as in a classroom of twenty plus students. We are bound by law to have 180 days of education just as public schools are but are free to use those days for any education we choose. We often turn grocery shopping into math lessons and home ec classes and can do these seven days a week, not just Monday through Friday. We can also teach bible related lessons without fear of school interference. We can choose our curriculum, form of learning, and often use crossword puzzles from a free homeschool site. Alexis finds that she retains more when it's fun and she enjoys crosswords so I simply use her test questions and enter them into a crossword to print for her exams.

We also found a homeschool group in town that we simply adore. The drive to Gaston was getting costly with the rise in gas prices and making matters worse, our cell phones got no reception on the trip; we may as well have been carrying rocks in our purses. Now we meet every Tuesday morning and I get to socialize with a wonderful group of Christian ladies while Alexis gets to play and socialize with kids from two to sixteen. All play well together and none of us parents has to worry about what and who they are being exposed to with regards to language and behavior.

We are still trying to find a curriculum that we all like but there are so many choices that we know we'll find one. In the meantime we have seen Alexis go from a struggling to survive pupil to an "A-B" honor roll student. We are so proud of her and best of all I get to spend lots of quality time with her. I know there are days that she misses friends but not the actual school and that she thinks Nana is the meanest teacher she's ever had. Over all though I believe this was the best decision we could have made and have no regrets. I thoroughly enjoy our school days and hope Alexis enjoys it as much as I do. She should since she is as much teacher as I am. I learn something new with her every day, both from books *and* life as a homeschooling Nana.

Deuteronomy 4:9 Only be careful, and watch yourselves closely so that you do not forget the things your eyes have seen or let them slip from your heart as long as you live. Teach them to your children and to their children after them.

All Aboard The Frankfurt Train!

I first met my old friend Darla while we were living in Germany. We both signed up to be Girl Scout Brownie leaders and got acquainted during the training sessions. Little did we know that this chance encounter would turn into a fast and lasting friendship where we would share many, many good times together. During our three years in Germany we shared lots of side-splitting laughs and barrels of tears; I still count her as one of my dearest friends though, much to our disappointment we haven't been able to see each other over the years due to living in different parts of the country.

Darla was always more adventurous than I and enjoyed introducing me to new experiences, one of which was riding the train to Frankfurt. She didn't drive in Germany so I would drive us to the train station in Hanau where we would hand over a few Marks (German money) for the short ride to the Frankfurt station. As I recall, it took us less than 30 minutes to get there but it was like traveling to another world. The Frankfurt train station was like a small underground city with lots of shops, restaurants and fruit stands. We loved taking all of our kids to visit! One day we decided to go an extra step in our adventure and planned to go outside the station since Darla had been there and knew her way around, at least more than I did.

Most of our excursions were unplanned so I had not kept our big van that day but instead drove our small German car, which was about the size of a Chevy Cavalier. Darla was watching some kids of a friend this particular day so we had a car full. Between us we had our own 6 kids and she had the 3 extra plus the 2 of us. The kids were always ready to go on the train so all were in high spirits. Her youngest daughter is a year older than Stacie so they would have been about 3 and 4 at the time. They were small so we improvised and since they would not all fit on the seats provided, we stuffed them in the front floorboard by Darla's feet with the rest of the kids crammed into the back on the seat and floor seat. It was tight but no one really complained because we were going on the train again! What a sight!

We had an uneventful and pleasant rail ride to Frankfurt where we shopped around for a bit before going up to street level. The kids were all excited but behaving beautifully so she and I relaxed and just enjoyed the day out. We had been walking and laughing as usual for a while when we suddenly realized that every one of the kids were quiet. Our jaws dropped to the sidewalk as we turned around to see what was up; we couldn't believe what we saw. We had been so engrossed in our conversation that we didn't notice the area into which we had wandered. The kids had though, and were standing and staring into a store that sold um..er, fancy lady stuff. Things like purple fur coats and various other items that the women who wore this stuff would use for the kind of business (legal in Germany) that required the wearing of this type of clothing. The bigger kids were standing looking into the window with their mouths open and not saying a word. Being the conscientious mothers we are, we gathered them all up (trying not to laugh in front of them) and herded them out of there post-haste. I don't know about Darla but I still laugh when I think about their faces.

We all had so much fun that day and my kids have never forgotten it, especially the end of our trip. Upon our return to the Hanau station, we stuffed, crammed and packed the kids back into our little car and drove to Darla's house on the economy. She was getting ready to move into military housing on the base so the rental agent would pop in at odd times to show the house. As it happened that day, the agent had just arrived at the house to show it to a married couple. They were all walking to the door as we drove up and parked. I doubt any will ever forget the look on the man's face as he stood and watched all eleven of us fall out of the car, laughing and whooping it up. Judging from his expression I'd venture to guess we looked like a bunch of clowns tumbling out of a circus car.

Where is a video camera when you really need one?

Proverbs 4: 11-12 I guide you in the way of wisdom and lead you along straight paths. When you walk, your steps will not be hampered; when you run, you will not stumble.

Alone In The Universe? I WISH!

As I've said on several occasions, I tend to forget that I'm not the last person alive in the universe which goes a long way in explaining how and why I manage to embarrass myself so often.

As many of you know I managed to totally humiliate myself and probably creeped out the mailman at the same time when I had to make the half naked dash past my open front door early this summer. My face still flames when I see the man which by the way, has been a while. I'm beginning to think he asked for a transfer since we've had a new guy for a few weeks. I should be relieved but recently walked to the mailbox just as he was pulling up and the smile on his face convinced me that he *knows* all about me.

Then too, shortly after what I now refer to as "the postal incident" I managed to mortify myself when one of the road crew working on the street in front of our house came to the door. You may recall that I mentioned I was working out with my Leslie Sansone walk at home video. I hadn't taken a shower yet and why bother brushing your hair when you're going to work out? I didn't bother to change into work out clothes and just walked in my shorts and T-shirt. The doorbell rang mere minutes before I was done so I was huffing and puffing hard when I answered it. I could have ignored it but had no doubt it was someone asking me to move my vehicle since they were ready to start tearing up the end of our driveway. I'll never forget the look on that guy's face when I answered the door. I'm almost positive that I saw a group of guys later talking to the mailman and I know they always looked at me funny whenever I left the house for the duration of the street work. Ernie told me afterwards that I should have explained that I was working out. Hind sight is 20-20, especially when it's someone else's.

Mistie, my oldest daughter was over one day near the end of the street resurfacing and long after they had finished on our end. She asked if I had noticed that they still spent a *lot* of time parked in front of our house even though they weren't working on our end any more. I too had noticed this but thought it might be my imagination. She thought it was because we had been very nice to them all, offering ice for their water, always speaking and waving, etc. I kind of liked that idea and agreed. Stacie my youngest daughter pointed out that they most likely park there because of the postal incident and the huffing and puffing answer at the door and are probably hoping for more shows.

Oh mamma, who needs enemies when I've got myself?

Not content to build my nutty reputation on my street alone, I then decided to put on a show for the entire teller contingent and lobby of customers at our credit union. Our CU opened a new location a few months ago with all drive through lanes. There is a window but it's sealed and that lane is ATM traffic only. All drive through transactions are now done via tube and all have little cameras that are positioned a mere six inches away from the drivers face with monitor screens mounted on the walls inside, visible for all to see. I had been feeling sick for several days recently but still had errands to run, including a trip to the CU. I asked Brooke if she wanted to go and looking back, wish I had asked her to drive. I sent my tube up and while waiting sort of zoned out while I listened to the kids chatter in the backseat. Have you ever been sick and afterwards your mouth feels all icky, gummy, dry, and nasty? Well mine did that day and as usual I forgot that I wasn't alone in some remote corner of the galaxy so started swiping my teeth and gums with my tongue, going at it really good then finally tried to clean my teeth with my finger. I stuffed my finger up under my lips and went to work. It wasn't long before Brooke brought me crashing back to planet earth with the comment, "Well that's attractive mom" I froze and looked directly into that obnoxious little camera, cringed then rolled my window up until they sent the tube back to me.

This latest incident though may be my worst yet. *When* will I learn? Ernie and I recently took advantage of someone being here to watch the kids for us so made a quick run into Big Lots. We went for specific items but whenever we shop there, we check everything since you never know what bargains you'll find. We were browsing up and down the aisles having a good time when I dropped into my solitary galaxy explorer role. Before I go on I need to say: I am *fairly* certain that I'm not the only female (or male for that matter) who's.......um.....mammilla protuberances get itchy. Really itchy, so bad that you can't ignore it itchy. So here we are strolling through the store when we come upon intersecting aisles. Ernie went on but I stopped and peripherally scanned left, right, in front and seeing no one around and unable to ignore the itch any longer, reach up to scratch/tweak/squeeze the offending body part. Too late I look UP and there across the aisle is a male store employee on a ladder, face frozen, with his arm stopped mid-way in the process of stocking a shelf, staring right at me and my scratching/squeezing/tweaking hand. In the blink of an eye I had just secured my reputation as a nut job. I hoped the floor would open and swallow me whole but since that didn't happen just coolly walked away and pretended nothing had happened. I made sure to avoid eye contact every time we passed him the rest of the time there but could see him watching me out of the corner of my eye. I told some ladies about this recently and one told me I should have shot him an icy look that screamed, "What?! You've never had an itchy nipple?!" Another friend reminded me about the crossed arm to conceal the scratch maneuver. Where was she when I needed her?!

As I see it, at this point I have two options. I can either (1) try mightily to remember that I'm not alone in this world while out in public or (2) get used to the stares and enjoy my newfound celebrity status as a nut case. With my increasingly lousy memory I think I'll go with option number two. It's a lot more fun.

1Timothy 3:7 He must also have a good reputation with outsiders, so that he will not fall into disgrace and into the devil's trap.

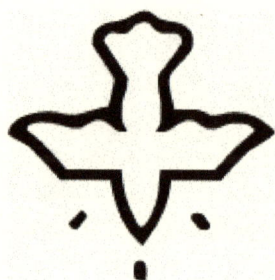

Another One Bites The Dust

Wooooooooo hoooooooooooo……..Oops! I mean woe is me. Tsk tsk, how sad. Anyone who has known me for any time knows just how much I despise vacuuming. I'd rather scrub toilets (gloves required) than vacuum. I think it's a hang-up from my childhood when my sisters and I had to clean house every Saturday morning and keep it clean in-between since my mom worked. We had a big house.

My current vacuum is a hateful beast in a long line of rotten beasts. We've had everything from cheapo Hoovers to a very expensive Kirby and an even more expensive Tri-Star. I've hated them all. I did try the 8 pound Oreck on a 30 day trial once and actually liked it. It was very lightweight and it had a handle that made sense. I didn't keep it though since I still had the ultra expensive Tri-Star. That ones in the attic now because I refuse to spend another dime on fixing the stupid thing. I think the head is broken and know nothing about how that happened. I even got to keep the cool cordless iron just for trying the Oreck. I'd really like to have one but knowing me I'd end up hating it too.

My Dirt Devil Feather Light (what they don't say is that it's about 15 pounds of feathers) has been acting up for some time. I've run over the stupidly short cord so many times that it's chewed up. Personally I'd like to meet the person who said, "Hey! Let's make a 15 pound vacuum, lie and call it a Feather Light then put an aggravatingly short cord on it!" What a marketing genius. He/she has assured that I'll never buy another Dirt Devil.

For some time now the power keeps going on and off, no doubt due to the chewed up cord. Then there's the noise level of this thing. It's so loud that you actually need hearing protection. We literally have to holler to be heard over it. The kids throw their hands over their ears and run from the room every time I crank it on. I swear it's like standing next to a runway as a jet lifts off. I told my brother, who worked as a vacuum repairman about it. As soon as I told him the brand and model he knew exactly what the problem is. However since he lives many states away and it still worked I just left it alone. This week the evil thing started snagging the Berber carpet in our family room. I figured this would finally be the end and we'd toss the thing out into the middle of our very busy street once and for all. It wasn't to be though. Ernie figured out the problem (he can be too handy at times) and I was back in business. Drats.

I'm elated, er I mean devastated to report that I think the creature is finally dead due to self-cannibalization. At least it sounds as if it's trying to eat itself alive. I was shoving the thing around the house when it suddenly seized up and made the most horrific, metal grinding metal sound. I don't think that I had run over anything but then again I had just finished vacuuming the kids bedroom. That's another scary story in itself. I quickly shut it off for fear that it would start shooting pieces around the room and maim someone. Jarod walked by it earlier and stepped on the power button, trying to be funny. The noise was so awful that it scared him and he shut it off quick and ran. I'm willing to bet that he doesn't try that again since he's already in a 3 ½ year old "there are monsters everywhere" mode.

Now I have to wait for Ernie to come home and officially pronounce it dead. In the meantime I am dancing and singing "Ding dong the beast is dead!" I know that I'll have to replace it but that's ok. With my track record of outlasting vacuums it will just be a matter of time before I can add another notch to my vacuum belt.   Another one bites the dust—literally.

Job 5:22 You will laugh at destruction and famine, and need not fear the beasts of the earth.

Anyone Need A Babysitting Job?

Irene and Nana have always had a knack for doing some silly (and downright dumb) things. Irene is now almost 8 years old (in 11 days!) and still keeps me in stitches, often because we've managed to get ourselves into a funny situation together. I've been her main care provider since she was born and when she was little said more than once that we both needed a baby-sitter. She often does things that will send me tripping down memory lane. This morning was one of those times as I flashed back to a day when she was almost 3 years old. I was in one of the bedrooms (where the computer was located at that time) and she was across the hall, playing in my bedroom. She wandered in to me with a pair of my old pantyhose from the trash can and asked me to hold the feet while she stretched them waaaaaaaay across the hall. Those babies looked like they were made for the Jolly Green Giant when we got done with them. Imagine my surprise when I discovered that these weren't old cast-off panty hose but actually brand new ones that I had lying on my bed.

Our day started off this morning with the usual frantic rush of trying to get Irene dressed and out the door to school. I was hurrying her as she sat on the floor and struggled to get one of her shoes on. She finally lifted her foot to me and said that it was tight and hard to get on. I twisted, shoved and forced until I got it on then tied it. I decided to loosen the ties on the other shoe and as I messed with it she mentioned again that the shoe was tight and felt weird. I glanced at her foot then at the shoe in my hand and started laughing so hard that I was choking—we had put the shoe on the wrong foot. A grown woman and almost eight-year old and we can't even get shoes on the correct feet. Some things never change—we still need a baby-sitter for the two of us. Interested? Call 1-800-We Laugh A lot.

Job 12:12 Is not wisdom found among the aged? Does not long life bring understanding?

At Least I Didn't Have A Jelly Fish Shoved Up My Rear End!

What follows is an accounting of my recent (as in 4 days past) hysterectomy. It will at times be a bit graphic and for this I apologize, but the story can't be told without these details. OK, maybe it could be told, but it wouldn't be nearly as much fun in the telling.

December 15th came screaming up on me, which is probably a good thing since, had I had time to think, I may have decided not to go ahead with surgery. After all, being the coward that I am, I had already refused to have the hysterectomy for the previous several years, against the medical advice of three well qualified doctors, and in spite of horrible health problems. I wasn't looking forward to the ordeal, in particular the anesthesia portion, but steadfastly held on while praying and asking for prayers of strength and faith. All prayers were appreciated and felt!

I was fairly stressed by the time we left for the hospital. My conversation with the Ambulatory Care Unit nurse the previous day over the spelling and pronunciation of my last name though hilarious and just like a scene straight out of an Abbott and Costello routine, did nothing to calm my fears and anxieties. The very last thing I wanted to hear on my way to the hospital was anything negative. Unfortunately for Ernie he didn't think about this and as we neared the hospital he mused: You know I've never heard anything positive about this hospital. My stress level finally peaked so I let him have it, informing him that the LAST thing I needed to hear was anything less than positive about the place that I was about to surrender myself to for slicing and dicing. He was sorry for thinking out loud and I was sorry for taking my stress out on him.

We arrived at the hospital 20 minutes before my appointed time of 9 AM. We were instructed by admissions to join the crowd already waiting across the hall in the waiting area. Oh boy, we get to sit with a bunch of sick people while I wait for them to process my paperwork for surgery. What giant among brilliant thinkers had come up with this admission process? I got more and more edgy as the clock moved towards 9. At a minute before 9 o'clock, they called me back across the hall to the window. The pleasant admissions clerk complained about her aching feet as she placed my wrist band on and had me sign paperwork before directing us to the ACU waiting area. I was called back within moments from there to be weighed. No I'm NOT sharing that information (way too graphic for even the strongest of hearts) but WILL share the fact that the low carb/fat diet I was on paid off and that I had lost six pounds over the previous couple of weeks! I was placed in room one and invited Ernie to join me as I disrobed and put on the hospital gown offered by the nurse. I insisted that Ernie tie me up the backside since I was not about to flash anyone as long as I was still un-anesthetized. I climbed up onto the *bed* and waited for the process that I knew would commence soon: IV, blood sugar finger stick, etc. A new twist was the leg pumps. These are sleeves that, once placed on the calves, are attached to a pump that inflates and massages the legs every few minutes. I have to say it was not an unpleasant experience having my legs massaged near constantly.

Around 10 AM, the anesthesiologist dropped by to chat. I called the day before to request Dr. Thomas, who had handled my anesthesia for the D&C in October. The nurse wasn't sure he was scheduled for that day but left a note just in case, assuring me that he would be happy to oblige if he were. Dr. Thomas was extremely efficient yet comforting, a combination not easy to achieve yet he did by being professional and still taking the time to place a pillow under my head when he decided that I looked uncomfortable on the table in OR. Unfortunately he wasn't scheduled, so another anesthesiologist was assigned. Oh boy—we were mere seconds into our conversation when it became obvious that this replacement was some kind of nut. He is obviously very intelligent and was attempting to educate me about my diabetes and risks, etc. Believe me the LAST thing I wanted to hear (after being told by my husband that he'd never heard anything positive about the place), was that though the risk is very slight, some patients lungs fill with too much oxygen and can't process it so it crosses over to the heart where it can cause a stroke or heart attack. The risk was slight but he felt that patients should be aware of this fact. Thanks a lot! The problem was he was kind of flippant about offering the information, so he sure wasn't building my confidence in him. I dared not look at Ernie since I could tell just by his body language that he was as disturbed as I. I was so shocked and horrified by it all that I missed much of what he said after this. Blessedly, before I knew it, it was time for them to roll me down to the OR. I had vowed not to go near it without Him so as they pushed off I reached out and literally grabbed the hand of my Jesus and squeezed hard all the way over. My doctor was already there when we pushed through the doors and I didn't let go, just held on for dear life and support. Dr. Heroux is a real treasure (truly) so I was reassured by her presence. I started to doubt her a bit though when she walked over to say hi. At one point she casually mentioned that I was going to like my anesthesiologist. I felt like asking her if she had ever heard Dr. Loony Toon's pre-surgery spiel but kept it to myself since I was afraid he might be in hearing distance and take revenge. You can imagine how pleasantly surprised I was when I looked up and saw a talking head that most definitely was NOT Dr. LT smiling at me, telling me that he was my anesthesiologist. (Ernie later told me that the scary guy had told me this but I guess I was so stunned that I missed the part where he explained that he wasn't actually handling my anesthesia but would be in the room to assist). I listened as he and the nurses worked around me. I have no idea when he administered anesthesia since he didn't say a word to me but the next thing I knew I was waking up in recovery. The very first thing I said was that I felt as if I needed to pee. Of course even in my fogged mind I KNEW I didn't since I knew they had catheterized me. I assumed it was pressure from the incision and hoped it would pass soon. The next thing I knew I was waking up once again as they moved me to the bed in my private room. From my short walk down the hall the next day I gathered that all of their rooms on the surgery floor are private. Sweet. This was definitely a nice surprise on top of the earlier less than nice moments.

The pain in my belly was exactly as bad as I had expected it to be. I have had two prior C-Sections so Dr. Heroux used that incision site to open me back up this time. I'll be forever grateful that I followed her advice and had the ovaries and tubes removed on this trip since I don't ever want to do abdominal surgery again. I was in for a pleasant surprise this time. I've heard about the medication buttons but had never been in a situation to use one. I can add them to the list of medical miracles for which to praise God. Those little buttons are fabulous! They pin it to your gown and instruct you to "just press it" whenever you need something for pain. I lost count of how many times I woke up long enough to eat a couple of spoons of ice chips then to press that marvelous little black button. To be honest I used it to escape back to sleep as much as for pain management. If I was sleeping I didn't feel pain.

My nursing assistant came in the next morning to get me up and walking. She left the distance and direction up to me so I turned right and headed up the hallway walking as fast as I could manage. I wasn't trying to set any records though—I just knew the faster I got it done, the faster I could get back to bed. I miss that bed. I got tired of spending so much time in it but at least I could adjust it so that my back didn't hurt. At all! I have arthritis in my lumbar spine and have trouble lying flat on it but had no aches or pains from that area for the duration. However one unfortunate side effect of spending so much time on my back was what we assume were bedsores. My back side was covered in blisters, big ones too. One was smack in the middle of my back. I found it when I was scratching and fortunately realized what it was right away. Unfortunately I didn't catch the one on my butt later that night until after I had scratched it open. Ouch. With three little kids in the house and constant phantom boo-boos, there are never any band-aids when you need one so I got to spend a few minutes painfully chafing before I could fall asleep.

I did manage to give myself a good scare the day after surgery. I was already in a *sitting position* so decided that it wasn't too far to bend over and pull my slipper back onto my right foot. Big mistake! Blood started gushing from my incision site. Still a little foggy headed, instead of calling for help I went back to bed. A couple of hours later, once again feeling the need to make another trip to the bathroom, I slowly got up from the bed but this time left a trail from bed to toilet. I hit my call button on the wall and told the unit clerk that I needed a nurse. An aide came quickly and just as quickly realized that we needed a *nurse*. She called the clerk and told her to send the nurse right away. We waited, then waited some more, so she hit the button again and again told her we needed a nurse. No response. She finally went down to the nurse's station and still we waited. I was calm but scared that I had really messed up with the innocent attempt to fix my slipper. The nurse finally came and helped me back to bed where she checked my incision and re-bandaged it. She checked back three more times before shift change and decided that it had most likely been blood that was trapped behind the incision and that no harm had been done. What a huge relief.

I had gone into the hospital with a sinus problem due to the southeast weather extremes. It didn't cause any real problems for me until my last morning in the hospital. I was restless and tired of lying in bed so got up to sit in the chair. I had not been there long when my sinuses decided to dump. I was sitting there choking and gagging; too far from the bed to call for help and naturally, my door was closed so no one could hear me. (One big reason I always prefer to have my door open but I had closed it myself so that I could wash up in privacy). I started having problems breathing due to the amount of drainage and anxiety. I finally calmed enough to say one of my most heartfelt prayers ever (and believe me I AM undeserving!): "Jesus help! As undeserving as I am I need you! I can't breathe. This coughing and gagging is hurting me and I'm scared. PLEASE go before our Father and ask Him to take this away. I can't deal with this on top of the surgery pain!" I then got up and moved to my bed where I called the nurses station and asked for some pain pills. Within seconds of calling I needed a box of tissues. My sinuses were clearing out so fast that I could barely keep up!! The next thing I knew, the nurse was there with my pills too. WOW that was fast! I popped them back, lay down and napped immediately. When I woke up less than an hour later I felt like an entirely new person! I spent the rest of the day telling anyone who would listen about the AWESOME thing that God had done for me. Not only did He answer my prayers but even went beyond them and moved the nurse to quick action and blessed me with a nap that removed the awful pain that I had been dealing with. He is truly amazing and I can't praise Him too much. Wooooo hoooooooooooo!!!!!!!!!!!

I do have one minor complaint about my stay. It's minor now but at the time it was important since I was convinced that they were sincerely trying to starve me to death. I last ate around 8 PM Tuesday evening when Ernie and I went to a nice restaurant in Emporia for his office Christmas party. As good as that food was, it wasn't intended to carry me for three days. The day after surgery, they brought me a bowl of beef bullion, Jell-O and a tiny glass of unsweetened tea with sugar packets and a cup of sugary cranberry juice for breakfast. I'm not a juice drinker anyway and I can tolerate unsweetened tea when necessary, but the bullion was tolerable for only 4 or 5 sips. There are few foods that I refuse to eat (obviously) and two of those are green and orange Jell-O. This meal had green, and judging from the sugar packets, was no where near sugar free. Lunch time arrived and it was more of the same, only this time it was chicken bullion and orange Jell-O with tea, sugar packets and apple juice. I told the woman who brought it to take it away since I could tolerate bullion of any flavor only so much, and that being diabetic I couldn't eat any of the rest. I KNOW that I informed everyone from admitting to the OR that I'm diabetic, but still her mouth dropped open and she said no one had told dietary! She went to the nurse's station and called downstairs to tell the dietician, then returned for my tray and said they would straighten it out. When dinner arrived I hoped to find SOMETHING palatable on my tray. I can't describe my disappointment when I discovered more of the same waiting, only the Jell-O color had changed. I was starting to get used to this not eating business.

Next morning breakfast time arrives and the hunger pains are kicking pretty good. I watched anxiously for the dietary cart to roll off of the elevators just a short distance from my room. My hope for a nutritious breakfast was soon dashed when I found…..yup more of the same! This time however they had included a cup of black coffee instead of iced tea and the requisite four packs of sugar. I spotted the dietary aide (a guy this time) out in the hallway and asked him to take it away once again explaining that I'm a DIABETIC. He just shrugged and told me to tell my aide who just happened to be passing by at that moment. She in turn told me that I would have to call dietary myself! She also offered the opinion "you know SOME diabetics DO eat Jell-O!" to which I responded "Yes we do—if it's SUGAR FREE". I dialed the number and informed the woman who answered that I was getting pretty hungry on this forced diet plan and explained yet again that as a diabetic I couldn't tolerate all of this sugar. She was shocked and said no one had told them that I was *diabetic* and that she would contact the nurse's station to straighten it out. At last—someone appeared to be listening. I knew I would be released later that day so when Ernie called to check on me I told him that if they didn't feed me something soon then to plan our first stop out of the parking lot to be for food. Lunch time rolled around all too slowly but I controlled my enthusiasm when I saw the carts roll off of the elevator. In fact, I sort of ignored the person who brought the tray until I glanced over and saw an actual plate with a cover on it. This could only mean FOOD and by golly there were Sweet n Low packs next to my iced tea! I'm not real sure since I literally inhaled the food but I recall that they had sent me a tiny salad (with dressing pack!) and a grilled chicken sandwich, breast on the small side but I wasn't complaining, with lettuce and thin tomato slice. They forgot salt but I ate so fast that I didn't have time to miss it for long. Oh and of course the required Jell-O which I ate in some confidence that it was sugar free. If I had it all to do over I think I would call my doctor's office and had it straightened after the second tray of sugar laden yet blah food though.

I'm SO thankful for many things! I'm thankful that Jesus held onto my hand even after I was out (I simply trust that fact), for the pain medicine, for the AWESOME way that my desperate prayers were answered, for my wonderful husband who was, is and always has been a fantastic partner, the prayers of so many who truly care about me, for FOOD, my family for taking good care of me since I've been home, my treasured Dr. Heroux and my friend Martha who referred me to her, the Tigger genes that allow me to bounce back so quickly that I inherited from my dad God bless him up there in heaven and also for my stuffed Santa which the nurses gave to me to use as my "coughing buddy". He was always close by while in the hospital in case a cough hit me. Once home, I showed him to the grandkids and explained what he is for. Every time I'd even look like I was going to cough they would take off in separate directions looking for "Nana's Santa!" As I heal and cough less often they realize that I need him less. In fact Jarod at 3 ½ has decided that Nana no longer needs Santa and wants to claim him as his own. Have I mentioned how thankful I am for my grandkids?

All in all it wasn't such a bad time. The awful female related problems will never be a concern again. I found a fabulous GYN; of course this happens just as I no longer really need one. The nursing care, though not stellar, wasn't as bad as many had tried to prepare me for (having worked in hospitals for so many years though long ago, helped me cope there). I can't say that it's a wonderful place but I can say that it's not as bad as some think. After all I survived and am thriving!

My friend Caron sent me the following story. Of course I had to wonder just what kind of friend would send such a hysterical story to someone three days post-op major abdominal surgery. It's such a funny story though that all is forgiven. And I'll try to recall this every time I get tired from my "job" as Stay-at-home Nana.

<u>LOVE MY JOB</u>

This is even funnier when you realize it's real! The next time you have a bad day at work... think of this guy. Rob is a commercial saturation diver for Global Divers in Louisiana. He performs underwater repairs on offshore drilling rigs. Below is an E-mail he sent to his sister. She then sent it to radio station 103.2 on the FM dial in Ft. Wayne, Indiana, who was sponsoring a worst job experience contest. Needless to say, she won.

Hi Sue:

Just another note from your bottom-dwelling brother. Last week I had a bad day at the office. I know you've been feeling down lately at work, so I thought I would share my dilemma with you to make you realize it's not so bad after all. Before I can tell you what happened to me, I first must bore you with a few technicalities of my job.

As you know, my office lies at the bottom of the sea. I wear a suit to the office. It's a wet suit. This time of year the water is quite cool.

So what we do to keep warm is this: We have a diesel powered industrial water heater. This $20,000 piece of equipment sucks the water out of the sea. It heats it to a delightful temperature. It then pumps it down to the diver through a garden hose, which is taped to the air hose.

Now this sounds like a darn good plan, and I've used it several times with no complaints. What I do, when I get to the bottom and start working, is take the hose and stuff it down the back of my wet suit. This floods my whole suit with warm water. It's like working in a Jacuzzi.
Everything was going well until all of a sudden, my butt started to itch.
So, of course, I scratched it. This only made things worse.

Within a few seconds my butt started to burn. I pulled the hose out from my back, but the damage was done. In agony I realized what had happened. The hot water machine had sucked up a jellyfish and pumped it into my suit. Now, since I don't have any hair on my back, the jellyfish couldn't stick to it. However, the crack of my butt was not as fortunate. When I scratched what I thought was an itch, I was actually grinding the jellyfish into the crack of my butt.

I informed the dive supervisor of my dilemma over the communicator. His instructions were unclear due to the fact that he, along with five other divers was all laughing hysterically.

Needless to say, I aborted the dive. I was instructed to make three agonizing in-water decompression stops totaling thirty-five minutes before I could reach the surface to begin my chamber dry decompression. When I arrived at the surface I was wearing nothing but my brass helmet.

As I climbed out of the water the medic, with tears of laughter running down his face, handed me a tube of cream and told me to rub it on my butt as soon as I got in the chamber. The cream put the fire out but I couldn't poop for two days because my butt was swollen shut.

So next time you're having a bad day at work think about how much worse it would be if you had a jellyfish shoved up your butt.
Now repeat to yourself, "I love my job, I love my job, I love my job

"**Psalm 4:1** Answer me when I call to you, O my righteous God. Give me relief from my distress; be merciful to me and hear my prayer.

A Tribute To My Dad

I have to admit this up front—I'm not too good at expressing myself with strong emotions involved without becoming pretty.......sappy. The feelings and thoughts expressed here are genuine though and I wanted to share just a little bit about my dad with you all.

His name was Charles James Laney but he was known as James or Jim to most everybody who knew him. A long time ago, a few even called him Charlie. To my siblings and me, he was Daddy until we got too old for such a term of endearment so was then known as Dad. Dad went to be with Jesus on June 28th, 2004. His family and friends will never be able to fill the hole that he left in this world but we still rejoice for him. Any sadness we feel at his passing is purely selfish, believe me.

I had just walked in the door from my first and only day as it turned out, of teaching Vacation Bible School at our church. The answering machine was flashing that it held eight messages so I knew something was up. A quick glance at the caller ID's while I hit the play button forewarned me that it wasn't going to be happy messages-all of the calls were from my brother and two sisters. Dad had been going downhill pretty fast after his foot was amputated a couple of months before due to diabetes complications. He had been in the hospital for several days and though back in ICU after a short time on a regular floor, we were hopeful that he would be home in a few days. He was to be fitted with his prosthetic foot a few days later. God had other plans for dad though, and called him home. The worst part for me upon hearing that he had died was that he was alone. No family had been there because he had turned bad so suddenly that there wasn't time to get anyone called. My mom, acting on intuition had called to check on him when she woke up that morning. The nurse was unusually candid and told her he wasn't doing well at all. Mom got my sister and brother-in-law rounded up and they were getting ready to make the drive to the hospital when they received the call that he was gone. This made me so sad until God gently reminded me-he was *not* alone because He had angels stationed in that ICU room ready to escort him home the moment his heart stopped beating. That thought comforts me like no words ever can.

Ernie and I flew out to Arkansas Wednesday morning. We weren't too sure that we wouldn't get off the plane to news that something had happened to Mom. She has told us for years that if dad ever went first, to expect her to go quickly behind him and she sincerely meant this. She has often told us of how a much loved Aunt and Uncle from her youth died within three hours of each other. They had been married for 50 years and had served as surrogate grandparents for my mom and her siblings. She adored them and was heart broken by their deaths. Mom and dad had celebrated their 57th wedding anniversary just a couple of weeks before dad died so we didn't know what to expect when we stepped off of the plane. So far, she is doing fairly well. Of course she has her moments and is very sad and lonely for dad but is in fair health. She is in the early stages of dementia so gets confused and is easily caught in loops, telling the same stories over and over but can be quickly led on to other topics so far. She is still living with my sister and brother-in-law and involved in neighborhood coming and goings so that will help occupy her.

The next couple of days after we arrived would bring many relatives and friends home. I saw cousins and an Uncle that I had not seen in over 30 years! It was a fantastic reunion and Dad would have enjoyed it so much. I got to visit with old friends, such as Charlie Arnce whom I hadn't seen in years. Dad had "adopted" Charlie many years ago when they worked together in Neosho, Missouri at Teledyne. We made sure that Charlie and his wife Ellen sat with family during the funeral. He was as devastated by the loss as the rest of us. We did have a good laugh though. I would have sworn I heard several years ago that one of Charlie's younger twin brothers had died and asked if it was Bob or Don. Imagine my embarrassment and delight when he informed me that neither had died! I'm so pleased for all of them.

During our visit, one of my nieces informed me that she always looked forward to my visits home because I'm fun. That's the nicest thing that anyone has said about or to me in a very long time and I was almost speechless which is a true wonder! I encouraged her to grab my sister next summer and make a Thelma and Louise trip out to North Carolina-but please skip the violence and the trip over a cliff!! I could just picture dad sitting and listening to our conversation and smiling.

We all went to the funeral home for the family viewing the afternoon before the funeral. Dad looked so peaceful and natural. It was very hard on all of us to be there but we tried to handle it gracefully, as he would have wanted. Dad was a great believer, so we had no reason to grieve for him, just ourselves.

Ernie, who was my tower of strength, and my brother-in-law Chuck, went back for the public viewing that evening. Ernie was struck by what a well respected man my dad was. He said nurses and a doctor from the dialysis clinic came for the viewing and all told him what a special man dad was. He was a popular patient with all of them because he was always happy and never complained in spite of the (at least) 4 hours he had spent every Monday, Wednesday and Friday being hooked up to machines. He never said a negative word to any of them and was always a wonderful witness. The husband of another patient also stopped by for the visitation and told Ernie that he was going to try and assure that some kind of memorial plaque is placed at the clinic in dad's honor. Ernie always knew that dad was a nice Christian man but was surprised and awed by the outpouring of love for him.

The funeral was Friday. We woke up to absolutely horrible weather. It was raining hard, thunder was booming and lightening was flashing. The cemetery is way out in the country and we knew it would be a huge mess if it went on for too long. Ernie and I stopped at Wal Mart on the way from our hotel out to my sister's to buy umbrellas since we hadn't brought any with us. Many of us, including Bob, dad's Christian home health nurse gathered at my sister's house and left for the church together. Before leaving, I asked a few others to join me in prayers that the nasty weather would take a break long enough for us to make that trip from the church. We arrived at the church to find many old friends attending. It was a hard jolt to see the hearse sitting in the driveway. I felt as if I had been moving in a fog for the past several days and would wake up to find it all a dream but this made it all real at last.

Their minister delivered a very hard hitting and bible based sermon for those of us in attendance, reminding all that they had a choice to make while there's still time. We all have to choose whether to serve God and spend eternity with Him or choose the world and be lost for all of eternity. He too had such respect for my dad, even though he had only known him since December. He told us that he had visited with dad on several occasions while in the hospital and even during his dialysis trips and that dad never failed to say "I love you Preacher" as he left. He left no doubt that dad had made his choice. What the preacher may not have known was that dad made that choice many, many years ago. My grandmother told me a story once of how dad, the oldest of seven kids, would stand on a stump and "preach" from the bible to his next oldest brother.

The thunder and rain continued throughout the sermon. We continued to pray for a break as the viewing began and as it continued. God is awesome and faithful and He never ceases to prove this. As the viewing ended, the rain, thunder and lightening *all* stopped at once! Not a drop fell from the sky as they wheeled the casket to the door for loading into the hearse. It was a moment that few failed to notice.

We had a sad drive to the cemetery, all realizing that this made it all final. Ernie had mentioned a day before that we should have arranged an honor guard for the funeral since he was a WWII vet, serving on the USS Tennessee but it was too late at that point to arrange. We were delighted to see just that when we arrived! There stood seven men in honor guard uniform, lining the drive. Dad already arranged it with his funeral arrangements. We're so thankful! The Honor Guards were all older soldiers. This meant so very much to us as they were from Dad's era. They saluted his casket as the Pall Bearers carried it to graveside. This almost undid me. I'm crying again as I recall that incredibly proud moment. One of the soldiers spoke briefly about dad being a hero from WWII, then told my mom to brace herself that the seven honor guards were going to shoot three times each, representing a 21-Gun Salute. I didn't know it was possible to feel any more proud of my dad than I already did but found that it was possible. They then presented mom with the folded flag and several spent shells.

We returned to the church following the cemetery for a fellowship period. They apparently have a committee that takes care of such meals and had a wonderful meal prepared with tables and places all set. It was a wonderful opportunity to visit some more with friends and relatives that we know we won't see again for a long time if ever. We'll be forever grateful to the ladies of the church for this service.

Ernie and I proudly carried the presented flag home with us on the plane, cradled by one of us all the way, so that he could make a display case for it. A lady on the plane was talking to someone else about how proud she is of her son who is serving in Afghanistan. She asked about the flag, wondering if we had family there too. I explained that my dad had died and that it had been presented by the color guard at the funeral. She wasn't sure what to say other than that she was sorry for our loss. I pray for her son's safe return.

We will always miss and love you dad! Even while we grieve, we rejoice that you are once again reunited with all of our grandparents, both of your sisters, Uncle Elwood and more friends and family than can be named here. If heaven is as we expect then we trust that you're busy visiting, helping others as you were always known to do and fishing with Granddaddy once again. We've no doubt that God was well pleased with your service on earth.

Dedicated to Charles James "Jim" Laney, born June 6, 1925 deceased June 28, 2004, an awesome Christian man who is now whole and well, living with our Holy Father for evermore

Deuteronomy 5:16 Honor your father and your mother, as the LORD your God has commanded you, so that you may live long and that it may go well with you in the land the LORD your God is giving you.

Baby

Baby is a stuffed cat who, once upon a long time ago meowed, purred and twitched her tail when her sides were gently pressed. Baby came into this family when Alexis was eighteen months old. She will be nine in July. I bought Baby for Alexis while out hitting yard sales with her, her mom and her Aunts. It was our last stop of the day and Baby took my last $1.50 to purchase. That is possibly the best money I have ever spent in my life. It was love at first sight for Alexis and there was no way I could refuse when she looked at me with her big eyes and asked me to buy it. The cat was promptly named Baby and she took her everywhere with her, including to bed at night. We figured Baby would be tossed aside eventually like so many other toys, but we were so wrong. Everyone in the family knows Baby and we all take part in any searches when she goes missing, which is rare since she keeps her so close.

Baby started out her life as a cream colored mechanical kitty but she's now a well-worn brown with a tail that needs stitching in place. She is such a part of the family that Bapa decided to give her a bath a couple of years ago when she was starting to look a bit grungy. He's a good Bapa.

There were a few times over the years when Alexis would forget baby at our house and cry for her at bedtime. I would reassure her over the phone that Baby was quite comfy though she missed her very much and looked forward to seeing her the next day. When Alexis started Kindergarten we explained that Baby couldn't go with her but that she would spend the days with Nana. I made a solemn promise to take care of Baby and make sure any of her needs were met during the day. It was actually quite fun for me to come up with new locations to place her in anticipation of Alexis coming home from school. Sometimes I would have her sunning on a windowsill, another time napping on the back of a chair or lying on one of the beds. Other times perched on the dryer in the laundry room by the side door, as if she were waiting to pounce on Alexis as she walked in the door. I think I had as much fun as Alexis did with this game. Her mom, Mistie was just like Alexis when she was little. My sister gave Mistie a stuffed dog that was hers from childhood. I had one just like it but mine had been gone for years. She promptly named the dog "Alpo" after my folk's beloved dachshund. She adored that stuffed dog, including the way he smelled and literally loved the stuffing to pieces. It separated from the middle and migrated to the head and rear but she still loved him. She would occasionally allow him to take a nap with Stacie, her baby sister. Unfortunately on one of these naptime occasions, Stacie woke up ill and got sick on him, so her grandmother bathed him. Mistie was kind of upset, saying her grandmother had washed his smell out. Still she cherished that dog and kept him until she finally lost him in a move several years later.

Baby has a broken tail now that needs to be sutured back in place and her meow mechanism quit working long ago but this doesn't make her any less loved. Alexis still gets upset when Baby goes missing as she did this past week. She finally found her last night at home. None of them felt well so they were sleeping together in Mistie's bed when Jarod got sick—all over poor Baby who got to ride over to Nana's house in a plastic bag this morning. I promised Alexis that I would bathe her and did just that. As I shampooed and scrubbed her fur, the memories washed over me and made me smile. Baby may be well worn and dirty beyond ever again seeing her original color, but she is still a very special member of the family. To this day I can still recall many details of our first meeting, right down to the house where we bought her.

I have an inkling that Baby is one of the few things in Alexis' life that she has always trusted would be with her and though she ages, will always be her best friend, never disappointing her. I doubt I will ever again spend money on anything as important as the love and devotion that that stuffed cat has brought to this family.

Addendum:

Sadly Baby was lost in November of 2004. Bapa and I took the kids to see an Air Show in Winston Salem, the first for all of us and Alexis took Baby. Somewhere along the way she was lost. We went back everywhere we had been and no one found her. I made many phone calls to follow-up, even a couple of months later but she is lost to us forever. We are all saddened by the loss. We just pray that someone found her and looked past the dirty, scruffy fur and realized that she is a much loved stuffed pet and gave her a good home.

Proverbs 17:17 A friend loves at all times, and a brother is born for adversity.

Bird Bowling

I hate sea gulls. We live two hours away from both the North Carolina and Virginia shores but still have more than our share of them locally, no doubt due to the two lakes and one river in our area. These birds tend to be full of poop so when we're headed into a store with sea gulls flying overhead I always tell the kids "Don't look up and if you do keep your mouths closed!" All day long they fly around squawking and foraging for food and when not annoying people with their raucous cries that remind me of fingernails on chalk boards and dropping poop bombs on unsuspecting shoppers, they're huddled in groups around parking lots sleeping.

I like to bowl or used to anyway. I didn't get to bowl often and when I did I wasn't very good at it. In fact I rarely scored higher than 90-110 but I still enjoyed the game. Unfortunately my knees start hating me after a couple of frames so I've been forced to give it up. I've found that it's not nearly as much fun sitting and watching.

Happily I recently invented a new form of bowling. It's not only fun but stress free on my knees. It's called *Bird Bowling* and this is how it works: First you have to find a parking lot, such as the small mall (I actually call it "The Small" since it only has about five stores left open) located a short drive from my house. Look for a large flock of sea gulls resting all helter skelter in a group taking up what would be valuable parking spaces if there were more stores, aim your car in their direction, hit the gas and watch them scramble. Well sort of. These dumb birds are really slow to respond. I'm not sure if they're suicidal or if maybe it's because they're so full of......well you know what.

I have to tell you this is a fun game! Especially when you have someone like my middle daughter Brooke in the car and you tell her to "watch this!" then take aim for the birds. I did this recently and she was laughing so hard that I thought she was going to have a breathing attack. I was actually worried that she'd pass out while she was gasping for air. In between howls she told me that I should at least honk my horn so they'd have a fighting chance. This from a woman who once sat in a parking lot and fed the same birds fried chicken! They loved it by the way. Her older sister was appalled and worried about mad sea gull disease but so far there have been no reports of sea gull attacks around town. The birds are so slow that Brooke was absolutely convinced we'd find one plastered to the front of my vehicle at our next stop. (We looked—there were none). It's just as much fun to bird bowl with the kids as it is Brooke. The girls start hollering while Jarod laughs hysterically and yells, "Do it again!"

So far my score is worse than real bowling. Jayne: 0, however I practice every chance I get. If you want to visit some time I'll give you free lessons then you can help spread the word about this great new game, no shoes or bowling lane fees required.

PS. This is what's called *tongue in cheek* so please don't call the ASPCA, Humane Society or the Audubon Society to report me. I really do hate sea gulls but wouldn't hurt one on purpose. I just like to add a little excitement to their otherwise boring days.

Bird bowling – the game starts to get messy

Several months after I wrote the first installment of bird bowling, all of the seagulls disappeared from town. We didn't see a single gull for ages. Finally one day last month we saw a lone seagull flying towards the Wal Mart parking lot and decided that he must be a scout bird because sure enough within a few days we were being inundated with flocks of poop machines once again. Oh boy oh boy, we could resume our favorite sport!

A couple of days before Christmas my oldest daughter Mistie, granddaughter Irene and I went on a last minute shopping trip ending with a stop at Big Lots which is located in a large parking lot. We saw a huge flock of gulls, so of course couldn't resist taking aim to slowly drive through them. We laughed hysterically as they squawked, flopped, flapped and took to awkward flight to get out of our way. With score remaining Jayne: 0, I found a parking spot on the end nearest the store and we were all still chuckling as we walked inside.

We finished up our quick shopping trip and walked out of the store. Another shopper was just ahead of us as we exited, still laughing and talking. We all came to a screeching halt though when we saw the dozens of shrieking seagulls flying around and dive bombing my new mini-van! They were all over this thing. (I realized too late that Mistie had her camera phone with her. How I'd love to have shared the sight with you all). As horrified as we were we had to laugh as we realized what was happening. The woman heard us giggling so turned to us and asked "Did you do this?!" What could we do but admit guilt? I urged them all to "RUN for the cars, DON'T look up and above all KEEP your mouths closed!" Fortunately we made it safely inside the vehicles without incident only to find that one of them had bombed my windshield with almost perfect aim. It missed dead center driver's side by only three inches. As funny as it all was this sort of behavior has never occurred before and it sort of creeped us out.

A few days later I had all three of my grandkids and two of their friends with me as we once again made a quick stop at Big Lots. As before we saw lots of gulls huddled in the parking lot and of course my grands asked me to demonstrate bird bowling to their friends. I'm slow at times but I do learn so told them we'd do it AFTER we got done shopping and were ready to leave the area. They ☐lipp and hollered all the way into the store about going bowling. Finally we finish shopping (never take five kids with money shopping by yourself) and headed out to the van while the kids all laughed in anticipation of going bowling through the flock still huddled across the parking lot. I was giving a friend who works at Big Lots a ride home and told her to watch as I backed from the parking space and took aim towards.....nothing. The birds were ALL gone. Every last one of them. We looked up in time to see the last one fly away over the building. At least they didn't drop any bombs this time.

This was very creepy. Consider yourself warned.

Bird brained warning

This warning may well give the term bird brain a whole new meaning.......Yesterday afternoon Irene and I ran a couple of errands after school ending with a stop at Wal Mart. When we got back out to the van I had a nasty surprise waiting—the birds had found us AGAIN and had once again bombed us! This time they hit us 3 or 4 times and it splattered but good. Several birds were still circling overhead so we hurried inside the van, mouths tightly closed. This is beyond creepy now. When told about it, Brooke found it all very funny. However she did say that she won't be bird bowling in her Jeep TJ anymore since she likes to take the top off on pretty days. Instead she said she'll use her dad's truck. There are lots of red trucks in town so maybe they won't recognize it while sitting in a parking lot. Or she could use one of her sister's cars, both white. White cars are even more common. I told her above all to be sure that none ever follows her home. We're a family of bird bowlers and if they ever figure out where we live, we're completely doomed.

Brooke had an interesting thought....do mini-vans that look like ours ever get bombed? I hope so because the thought that they're all that smart is realllllly scary.

PS: I did tell you that this is a warning and after reading this you may want to peek outside before leaving the house again. My friend Kathy, who lives sort of out in the country looked out after reading the last bird update and her house was being swarmed by a flock of bird brained seagulls.

Another friend who lives outside NY City had a similar experience. She said it's not uncommon to see seagulls but she's never seen them near her home. After reading an update on bird bowling she looked out and saw throngs of them around her home! Things may get even uglier now. I went to Curves this morning for my 30-minute workout and found a huge flock huddled in the parking lot near my parking spot. It was sort of scary funny— there was another van identical to my Honda Odyssey already parked there and it didn't have a single bomb splash. Of course as I drove away, in spite of al the attacks and warnings I simply couldn't resist; I had to do it. I laughed as they waddled into flight and said "this one's for the kids". Let the battles begin.

Genesis 1:22 God blessed them and said, "Be fruitful and increase in number and fill the water in the seas, and let the birds increase on the earth."

Blabbing Secrets

Eye'll be seeing you

This memory is dedicated to Mab, who upon learning that I had done so asked me the burning question, "WHY did you shave your eyelashes off?" Mab Graff Hoover passed away earlier this year and has left a huge hole in the Christian humor author community, but is no doubt now in heaven regaling the angels with her hilarious tales. She was my mentor and example.

My baby is now 21 years old and a senior at the University of North Carolina Chapel Hill (UNCCH) but I remember this as if it were yesterday. When Stacie was 9 months old, her dad's parents came to visit us. We were stationed at Ft. Hood, TX at the time so decided to make a day trip to Six Flags. While doing my hair and make-up (I was much younger and far more concerned with my looks then) I noticed that my eyebrows had grown out and looked rather scruffy. In my usual lack of wisdom and not having time to go have them waxed professionally, I grabbed my electric razor to have a go at them. I tried turning it every direction to get at the upper curve of the brow. Just as I was ready to give up, I heard a funny brrrzzzzztt sound. Thinking it was the battery quitting, I gave up and decided that the top of my glasses would hide the straggles. I finished up my make-up with eye shadow then grabbed my mascara. It was the weirdest thing.....I kept swiping at air. I thought "now that's strange" so leaned in to the mirror and saw I had shaved my eyelashes off, right down to my eyelid! I was so embarrassed I wanted to fall through the floor. I put my glasses on, said a prayer that no one would notice what my vanity had caused me to do and swore I would NEVER tell a soul. 15 minutes later, I was standing in my driveway telling two of my neighbors they'd never guess what I had just done............(Yes, they grew back and no, no one ever noticed they were missing).

I pull dumb stunts all the time and each time swear I'm never telling a living soul about it then within minutes I'm blabbing on myself....

BRAKE!!!

The first house that we rented in Alabama had a huge yard, so we bought a riding mower. I enjoyed mowing the front yard but hated doing the first half of the back yard. It was steeply sloped in parts and just plain scared me. I know if anyone ever saw me mow that section, they probably thought I was a nut case. I didn't care because I felt safer mowing it by driving up the hill then backing back down it. One day I was just getting started on the dreaded section and was daydreaming instead of concentrating on what I was doing. There is a swimming pool at the top of this section, surrounded by a chain link fence. I looked up just as the mower was getting ready to run into that fence. I panicked and forgot how to stop and had just enough time to think "I'm going to have some explaining to do to Ernie about how I ran the fence down". NOT! That darned mower kept going and drove UP that fence! I was screaming my silly head off when the next thing I knew, I was lying on the ground staring at sky with that huge riding mower lying on top of me. It only took seconds to crawl out from under it but in that time I thought..."Man! That hurt! I hope I didn't damage something. Oh wow! I wonder if anyone is around to help? Good grief, I hope no one IS around because I hope no one saw what just happened! (and) I am NEVER going to tell anyone about this one!" I crawled out, got the mower upright and noticed things were looking kind of distorted when I realized I had mangled my wire rim glasses in the "accident". Feeling very foolish, I walked into the house to calm down. Within moments of walking indoors I picked up the phone and started calling my kids. When they answered, I said, "You won't believe what I've just done....."

This story is one that was supposed to remain a shameful family secret forever. Unfortunately my husband sometimes likes to tell stories on me almost as much as I do.

Talking heads

My youngest daughter Stacie and I were doing a favor for our neighbors, Tom and Jo Ann, who had asked us to let their three poodles out to run and potty a few times, while they were gone for the day. We went over in the early afternoon to let the dogs out for a bit and stepping out on the patio shut the sliding door behind us. We heard it click which didn't make sense so we tried to open it only to find it was locked shut! I panicked as usual as we tried every door, window and fence gate. ALL were securely locked. The fence was 8 feet tall (once locked in, it looked more like 20 feet), so we couldn't safely climb it. We were trapped in that back yard. It was Sunday afternoon and NOT ONE person was outside, not even a kid on a bicycle. Any other time that street would have been buzzing with kids, cars and neighbors out in their back yards. Unfortunately we hadn't told my husband where we were going when we left. He was playing a game on the computer so we didn't disturb him; therefore he wasn't likely to miss us for hours. Tom and JoAnn were going to come home and find us trapped like the proverbial rat. I could just see their shocked faces when they got home and found us all sitting in their back yard, hot, sweaty and thirsty. The mere thought had me ready to dig a tunnel out bare handed. Instead, we drug a couple of chairs over to the fence where Stacie was ready to attempt climbing over. I was more afraid of broken bones than the total humiliation we were going to face when Tom and JoAnn came home to find us all stuck in their yard, so I quickly nixed that idea. We stood on the chairs and just barely clearing the top of the fence, started hollering in the general direction of our house across the street. Of course it was a warm day so it was closed up with the air on. We were wasting our breath. It appeared the humiliation was going to be complete when finally a pick-up truck stopped right in front of the house. The stranger inside had chosen to stop smack in front of this house to read a map. (I'm convinced it was our Guardian angel. I had never seen his truck in the neighborhood before and never did again.). He had his back sliding window open so we started to holler "Yoo hoo! Help!" for his attention. Try to imagine his look of surprise when he heard us yelling and looked over only to see a couple of talking heads staring out. Already mortified beyond belief I said, "Can you help us? We're trapped back here". We assured him it wasn't a joke then asked him to go across the street to my house and tell the man who would answer the door to bring the garage door opener over and let us out of the yard. God bless him, he didn't throw his truck in gear and drive off. We watched as he hesitantly got out and walked over, climbed the stairs and rang the doorbell, offering encouragement every step of the way by calling "Yes! That's the house! Thank you!" I can only imagine what Ernie thought when he answered the door to this stranger telling him that two females were claiming to be trapped in the neighbor's yard and wanted his help. (After years of being married to the queen of dumb stunts I don't think I wanted to know either) I didn't ask since he was kind of irritated with me, because in my total embarrassment, I felt he took too long getting over there and sort of yelled at him, which may explain why he told the neighbors what we'd done....even after I told him THIS time I am NEVER telling anyone about this.

The funny thing is, the door had never done that before or since. I am laughing just thinking about it again which is okay since we've never quite lived this most embarrassing incident down.

I firmly believe God blessed us with a sense of humor and that He has a tremendous sense of humor as well. I think He gets a lot of chuckles in as he watches our antics day to day. Personally I'd be bored if life were dull here. I've always said that if you can learn to laugh at yourself then you can be your own endless source of amusement.

Psalm 126:2 Our mouths were filled with laughter, our tongues with songs of joy. Then it was said among the nations, "The LORD has done great things for them."

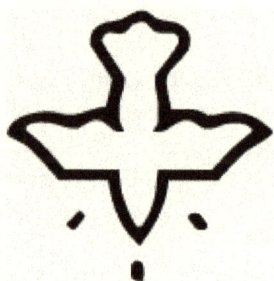

Bon Fires, Hayrides, Hugging Geese, And More!

Brooke, Irene and Alexis had such a busy weekend that they all needed to return to work/school just to get some rest. The little girls had so much fun though and won't forget this weekend for a long time. Brooke and Stacie started out Saturday taking them to a Holiday Festival at the Greensboro Coliseum. Brooke won 4 tickets for answering a question correctly on the radio, so off they went. They didn't get to spend much time at any display since the little ones were excited and curious (and bored with some) so wanted to keep moving. Moving until they got to the cooking demonstration where 4 year old Irene decided they needed to stop and watch. So stop they did and stuck they were. They were in the front so couldn't slip out without creating a ruckus. I gather this demo lasted a good 20 minutes or more and probably felt longer to the lady holding it since Irene peppered her with questions. Brooke said the woman was patient for most of them. I've been to some of those demonstrations so feel she should appreciate her interest since most people are only there for the samples, which of course Irene partook of with the rest of them. Later that evening Brooke took the little girls to a co-worker's annual Autumn Party where they got to roast wieners, go on hayrides, and just run wild for the evening. Irene enjoyed it so much that she even went on a second hayride without her mom. Alexis was too busy making Hannah another little girl there, jealous. Apparently Hannah (5) is used to being the center of attention and is quite smitten with a little boy named Dillon, who was also there. Dillon and Alexis, both 6 years old had a good time chasing each other and making Hannah see green. Poor Hannah, she doesn't realize a couple of things. First Alexis doesn't do this on purpose. She and Irene just have a way with the little men, which should make life quite interesting for the rest of us when they reach their teen years. Both are just natural little flirts and neither thinks a thing of flirting with another girl's man. Finally, Hanna need not worry because Dillon lives in Hasty, not High Point. Lucky girl, she might have problems if they lived closer. Alexis and Irene can't help it if they are just natural born beauties.

Sunday Brooke took the girls to the Renaissance Festival near Kannapolis, which is about 45 minutes from here. There they got to watch a jousting exhibition, hear and see wandering Minstrels, watched a man do a funny un-balancing act and got to see Mother Goose. A real live Mother Goose too—a goose in a dress and cape. I wish they'd taken a camera. The picture I truly wanted to see though was of them being hugged by an actual goose. Apparently he would wrap his neck around the hug-ee and rest his head on them. Of course both girls got and gave hugs, lucky goose. They came home with wooden swords, pretty new necklaces and cute toys. I wish I were a kid again so Brooke could take me for a fun weekend.

Boy Oh Boy, Nurses!

Brooke had the funniest conversation with Irene the other day. It seems Irene thinks all nurses are girls. When told that boys can be nurses too, she laughed so hard! Turns out she thought they would have to wear dresses and this was hysterically funny to her. It was quite funny hearing about it too.

Things To Be Thankful For

Irene frequently tells her mom she's the very best mommy in the world. There are lots of reasons for her to feel like this and one is when Brooke takes Irene to school she always parks and takes her to her classroom. Nana on the other hand drops her off in the drive through, always making sure she's in the capable hands of one of the teachers unloading the little kiddies each morning. I guess I miss out on a lot by not taking her but as I've said earlier, I'm not usually dressed for getting out of the vehicle. One day last week she took her and noticed little pictures for each child on the wall, with quotes of what they were thankful for in thought bubbles above their heads. Most were thankful for Mommy, home, pets, etc. As always our Irene had to be different and most entertaining. Hers said, "I'm thankful for Macaroni and Cheese every day!" This brought a big laugh and of course questions. The teachers told her they hadn't added the rest of her grateful thought which was, "And that's all!" Brooke had to explain that Mac & Cheese is her favorite food in the world, especially if it's from Winn Dixie's deli and that yes, she does eat it almost every day. We have boxes of the easy cheesy microwave stuff in the pantry for the days she doesn't get the deli kind. I'm just hoping she doesn't get tired of it before we run out.

Baby Jarod

Jarod recently turned 6 months old, is getting to be more delightful with each passing day, and has a smile that will bring you to your knees. He is now not only crawling but also is pulling himself to standing positions at the fireplace hearth and on anything he can reach to grab hold of. He finds drawer pulls that move fascinating as well as feet, toes in particular. He seems to have a fetish for toes and his Aunt Stacie says he's going to be a podiatrist. I'm going to paint my toe nails so they'll be really fun for him. Then again I may not. He was biting one of my toes recently (don't worry, they were clean) and he now has his FIRST tooth! It's sharp as a needle so I don't think I'll encourage the toe thing anymore. He's such fun and even communicates without words. When he's hungry he cries mmm…mmmm… until we figure out he wants FOOD. When he wants to go in his jump-up he starts bouncing in your arms. He even cries for Ba Ba (Bapa) when he can't make his mommy understand what he wants. He's a baby genius I tell you.

He's very curious so we have to keep an eye on him but I don't complain. I need the exercise.

Well, I just took a break and went to pick Alexis up at school. She was excited because they have a day off tomorrow for a teacher's work day and because she had mashed potatoes and chicken nuggets with ketchup for lunch. Proof once again it's the little things in life that are important.

Proverbs 31:30 Charm is deceptive, and beauty is fleeting; but a woman who fears the LORD is to be praised.

Boogey Man

It has been many years since someone tried to break into my bedroom window, but the fear is as real today as it was then. My stomach still clenches up when I think about that night.

We were living in Maryland and Ernie was gone. A lot. The last nine months we were stationed there he had gone on 57 trips! Some were short one or two day trips, some longer, the longest being the time he was in Saudi. The girls and I learned to cope and managed quite well in spite of missing him during the many absences. It helped immensely that one member of the family Lucy, happened to be large, 4 legged, and fiercely protective of us. She was always ready to answer the door with us and alerted anyone who knocked, that she was friendly as long as they didn't threaten her family.

I still remember the day I read about the weirdo who prowled around neighborhoods in our little town looking for unlocked doors and windows, allowing him easy access to the homes. Once inside he would find the master bedroom and either stand or lie on the floor next to the wife and fondle her until she woke up and realized it wasn't her husband. The "Phantom Fondler" as he was known would then run from the house without taking a thing or hurting anyone, unless you count their peace of mind. Oh how I wished I hadn't read that article about his latest fondling. Of course Ernie was gone so I don't think I slept a wink all night. I was convinced he was going to break in and that the girls would find me in the morning still in bed, dead from fright. I had several uneasy nights until I realized that not only were we outside of his normal area, but the odds of him choosing our house out of so many was almost nil. It still took many nights of my checking doors and window locks repeatedly before I could calm down and sleep well again.

Our house, situated on a corner lot was on a busy road that led to the Gunpowder River just a couple of minutes on down the road. There were no streetlights on this corner so the backyard was as dark as the inside of a deep well. For that reason alone in our almost four years living there, I never ventured out there after the sun went down. This particular night Ernie was in Panama. It was shortly after 10 PM on a Friday night and I had just gone to bed. The master bedroom was on the ground floor making it easy to hear the kids if they stayed up late in the living room. We had two windows across from the foot of our bed. One screen had a small hole in the corner that our cats used to enter and exit the house when no one was around, if we left the windows open. Stacie, in kindergarten at the time had gone to bed with me while Mistie and Brooke stayed up to watch a show on TV. Lucy, who slept in our room on her own bed (when she wasn't sleeping on our feet), chose to stay up with them. I had just started to drift off to sleep when I heard the screen on my open window being slowly ripped. I was groggy so assumed it was Midnight trying to get in through the hole and scolded her for tearing it. Even with the scolding, the tearing sound continued. About this time Lucy came tearing into the bedroom barking and snarling. I still didn't get concerned, convinced that it was Midnight having trouble fitting through the hole and told Lucy to calm down, that it was just the cat. Lucy ignored me and lunged at the window just as one of the kids swore they saw a hand come through the mini-blinds. Being in bed I wasn't wearing my glasses and not wanting to alarm them, I asked Brooke to just close the window and turn on the fan, all while Lucy continued to lunge at the window, snarling and snapping. In retrospect, I suspect Brooke was only inches from the pervert on the other side but being so dark we couldn't see him. I calmed everyone down and again assured them that I really thought it was just Midnight trying to get in. I was to discover in the morning how very wrong I was.

The next day was Saturday so the girls slept in, but as soon as Brooke woke up, she told me something that scared us all silly. She had gone to bed after calming down and found Midnight locked in her room, sound asleep on her bed. We went outside to investigate and found the window screen torn nearly out of the frame. I practically passed out from fear. We knew without a doubt that it wasn't the elusive fondler though. He never actually broke in since he always used an unlocked window or door and he NEVER brought attention to himself by making noise as loud as a tearing screen. No, somehow we had attracted a pervert all our own. To think I had lain there and would have let the guy crawl in had Lucy not gone into her "Someone is after my family—I'm going to rip and shred!" mode. I still shiver at the thought of such stupidity. I never slept with the windows open again after that unless Ernie was home. I also quit worrying so much about Ernie being gone. We had our fearsome and wonderful four-legged family member to protect us.

We all adored Lucy and still miss her terribly after all these years. I don't think any of us felt quite as safe for a long time after she died. Lucy was our angel on earth and I have no trouble imagining her running around heaven, playing happily while she waits on the rest of her family to join her.

And yes, they did finally catch the "Phantom Fondler". Turns out it was a guy who lived in the vicinity of his many victims, just as the police had long suspected since he was always so quick to elude them. I hope they all sleep a little better at night now. Personally I think I'd still sleep with all the lights on after repeatedly checking door and window locks.

Romans 13:10 Love does no harm to its neighbor. Therefore love is the fulfillment of the law.

Boooom!!!!!!!!

BOOM!!!!!!!!!!!!!!!! Just as I start to fall off into slumber land I hear a loud explosion. I jerk awake, heart pounding, and nearly jump from my bed, only to discover Ernie still soundly asleep beside me. There is no way that he could have slept through an explosion that loud so, realizing that I must have dreamt it, I snuggle back under the covers. I lie awake listening "just in case" and gradually drift into a sound sleep.

This has happened to me before so I asked my family if they heard any loud explosions the night before, but they all say no, nothing disturbed their slumbers. I KNOW that I heard this though, so *how* could anyone sleep through such a loud sound? Actually, lights should suddenly be turned on all over the neighborhood and sirens heard while police and fire units try to track down the source of this huge sonic level boom. But none of this ever happens. It's enough to make you doubt other people's sanity.

Then one day I read a letter in one of those "Dear Doctor" columns in the newspaper. A reader was describing the same thing—sometimes they hear an extremely loud explosion as they fall asleep that no one else hears. I'm not totally crazy! (Notice I said totally) As excited as I was to see this addressed by a fellow kaboom sufferer I was also afraid the doctor was going to advise them to seek psychiatric assistance. But no! It seems this is an actual disorder of sorts and it's called quite appropriately "Exploding Head Syndrome". If you're not a fellow exploding head victim then you may think I'm kidding. I'm not! I can prove it too—go to:

http://www.mayoclinic.com/health/exploding-head-syndrome/AN00929

You'll learn that while uncommon, sufferers describe terrorizing attacks of a painless explosion within their head. Attacks tend to occur at the onset of sleep. The etiology of attacks is unknown, although they are considered to be benign. Treatment with clomipramine has been suggested although most sufferers require only reassurance that the spells are benign in nature. You'll notice that no where does it say that sufferers are crazy.

I'm so thankful that it's benign and that this isn't a literal translation—imagine the mess that spouses and sleep partners would wake up to in the mornings. If it were literal everyone would have to go to bed with their heads wrapped in plastic bags leading to a whole new crop of problems.

Fellow nighttime "Exploding Head" sufferers, you can take solace in the fact that you're not nuts (at least as far as this goes) and can now relax as you fall asleep at night. When your head goes "BOOOOM!!!!, simply smile and go back to sleep as all's well and your head is still intact. However if your family and friends still insist you're a tad strange, well then I'm sorry, but you're on your own there.

Job 4:13 Amid disquieting dreams in the night, when deep sleep falls on men,

For more information just Google exploding head syndrome.

Brawling And Nibbling

Ernie and I look like we've been in a brawl. He has been working on the bathroom tile all weekend and the caustic tile cement has eaten away the tips of several of his fingers as well as the back of one hand. I'm sporting a bruised knee from banging it on the very sharp corner of the chest at the end of our bed. I've walked past that thing hundreds of times but just couldn't get around it this time. The next day I took a bag of trash out to the trashcan. It was getting windy and I was afraid the lid would blow open and scatter trash so grabbed the bungee cord that we attached to use for such situations. I pulled it down and just as I went to hook it, it got away from me and snapped back and hit me in the mouth. Oh boy did that hurt. I now have a fat/cut lip. I got tickled at dinner last night when I looked at Ernie's poor hands and felt of my lip. I told him it looked like he had hit me in the mouth and that I chewed his finger tips off. Needless to say I found this hysterical, at least until it made my mouth hurt.

Exodus 14:14 The LORD will fight for you; you need only to be still.

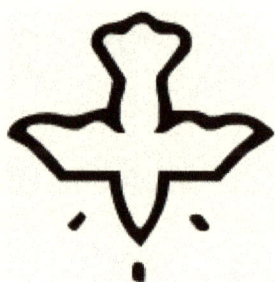

But Was It A Tyrannosaurus Rex Or A Brachiosaurus?

The grandkids have gotten me hooked on the computer game "Carnivores", a dinosaur hunting game. In a nutshell, your computer character (who is never seen until or unless a dinosaur jumps on you then you can imagine that scene) walks or runs around a jungle or woods hunting dinosaurs in modern days. Depending on your skill level, you have a choice of weapons including a huge sniper rifle, shotgun or crossbow. I can sit at the computer in a virtual world, tramping through woods with my heart in my throat while hitting the dinosaur call button for hours. The game is scary and addictive. The kids like to climb on my chair beside me and watch while offering pointers. I guess this technically makes it a family type game.

Though we are listed on the *do not call* registry, we still receive calls from non-profits and political organizations. These calls are every bit as irritating as telemarketing calls but thanks to caller ID we usually know when we're receiving one. As luck would have it we received one while I was busy chasing a dinosaur trophy so I handed the phone to (almost 4 year old) Jarod and asked him to handle it. The call on our end went something of like this: "Hi! What are you doing? No Nana can't talk! She's hunting dinosaurs! Ah oh, I think I hear one coming!" Hello? Hello?" Extremely disappointed he handed me the phone and said they had hung up. I'd have given an awful lot to have been on the extension that time. It may be that we're playing this game a bit too much. A few minutes ago while I was in the laundry room sorting clothes when one of Jarod's afternoon shows "Dora the Explorer" came on. He was standing in front of the TV watching and singing along. After her signature "Hola!" the very first thing Dora said was: What would you like to be when you grow up? Without even a moments hesitation Jarod yelled: A dinosaur! I'm still giggling and wiping tears.

Jeremiah 16:16 "But now I will send for many fishermen," declares the LORD, "and they will catch them. After that I will send for many hunters, and they will hunt them down on every mountain and hill and from the crevices of the rocks".

Cease Or Stop But Pleeease Don't Pause!

Pardon me while I get a little personal here but I am just a little confused. You see I'm peri-menopausal and no one told me it was going to be like this. I'm not complaining mind you—at least not about some aspects of it. I just wish that I had been warned that I was also going to lose my mind once I started into this scary world of matronly maturity.

I have become so emotional that it's embarrassing. I swear if I hear the song about the little boy trying to buy some gold shoes for his dying mother to wear when she meets Jesus one more time then I'm going to rip the radio out of my car dashboard. Do the DJ's not realize how difficult it is to drive while you're sobbing your heart out? And this is Christian radio! Ditto on ripping the radio out if I hear how Grandma got run over by a reindeer- it breaks my heart even when I'm hearing it for the umpteenth time of the season. I weep helplessly thinking about Grandpa being all alone now. The song doesn't say but I'll bet Grandma was on her way back home to get her hormone replacement therapy.

My memory is getting bad too. Scary bad. I was at the mall with Mistie yesterday and we talked about the poor shopping here compared to what we had back in High Point. When we got in line at J.C. Penney's checkout I glanced towards the front door and for a brief moment forgot where I was. I thought, "What the heck? Where am I? That street out there doesn't look familiar!" Fortunately I came back to my senses, but not quickly enough to stop myself from blurting out, "I just forgot where I am!" God bless the woman checking out as she turned to me and said she was sure glad she wasn't the only one who does that. I'll bet she's peri-menopausal too.

My mood swings are downright scary even for me. I don't even feel one coming on so can't warn everyone to get out of my path. If it gets much worse I'm afraid the entire family will want to divorce me. I work overtime trying to make up for the nasty moods so they will continue to tolerate me which they do. Then again they may all just be afraid of me.

The latest incident really makes me wonder about my personal safety though. I was just glad no one was around to witness it. Well Jarod was but he's a smart child so he knows better than to tell. Oh heck I'll tell. I was getting ready to go pick the little girls up at school and ran into the front hallway to put my shoes on. The hallway is very dim but I didn't take the time to turn the lights on, just slipped the shoes on and took off to go grab my car keys. I started walking back through the front room when I realized my shoes felt very strange on my feet. I stopped at the desk, turned the lamp on and looking down discovered that I had put my shoes on the wrong feet. My multiple personalities had a great little conversation over that one.

"Would you look at that?! You put your shoes on the wrong feet! Yeah I see. Dumb huh? Yeah you should feel dumb! If I were you I wouldn't tell anyone about this one!" Now I even have voices in my head mocking me!

None of the women in my family has ever gone through menopause. They all did the sensible thing and had a hysterectomy before they lost their minds. I thought I'd go against sound medical advice and be the brave one and blaze new family territory by facing the evil menopause monster. Unfortunately no one told me that it was going to turn ME into a monster. I've heard the horror stories about hot flashes and can honestly and thankfully say I don't have those-yet. I'll also have to say it's a good thing. I'm scared that I may have one during one of the horrific mood swings I'm having and that I'll turn into a fire-breathing monster. Talk about human combustion.

What a stupid name for this condition anyway. Why is it called menoPAUSE? It stops eventually, as in ceases. That would make more sense: menocease or menostop, not menopause. Good grief if I thought there was any possibility that I had to face this over and over I think I'd turn my fire breathing ability on myself.

So in the future, if you see a woman wandering around with her shoes on the wrong feet, muttering to herself and looking thoroughly lost you'll know she's almost certainly peri-menoceasal. In fact take a close look and if she looks like me would you be so kind as to help me get my shoes straight then point me towards home? Please? I'm quite sure I'll appreciate it.

Update:

I finally caved after the fourth doctor recommended a hysterectomy, and had a total job done in December of 2004. My ovaries were taken too, so I was plunged instantly into menocease. Who knew that menostop would be so much fun with peeing in your pants, short term (even 2 minutes later) memory loss and heat waves that make you want to strip naked and toss all my clothes to the floor regardless of what store you're in. So far I've resisted that urge but who knows what the future holds?

Isaiah 30:22 Then you will defile your idols overlaid with silver and your images covered with gold; you will throw them away like a menstrual cloth and say to them, "Away with you!"

Child Wonders And Wondrous Children

Irene and I were at a local Food Lion this week to pick up a few items. We parked next to a very nice, new convertible Camaro. As we were putting the groceries in the Jimmy, the driver of this car got in and put the top down. How many times have we seen this done? It's pretty routine for most of us but for Irene it was a wondrous thing! She was utterly astounded and said, "Nana, look at that car! How did she do that? I wish you could do that!" It was wonderful to watch her reaction.

After this morning, I am firmly convinced that 8 ½ month old **Jarod** is a baby genius. He takes after his sister, cousin, Mommy and Aunties. Irene has a real thing for pinching his chubby cheeks (not hard of course!). We frequently warn her that he will get revenge some day. This morning she and Jarod were standing next to Brooke who was seated waiting to help Irene put her shoes on for school. Irene, being her usual silly self, reached over and pinched Jarod's nose then she sat down on the floor in front of her mom. I laughed and again warned her that some day Jarod would get revenge. He was holding on to Brooke's leg walking to Irene so Brooke said it looks like he's going to now. When he reached Irene, he squatted down, reached out and PINCHED HER NOSE! We were laughing and saying, "Look at him!" Of course I had to call his mommy at work to tell her that her son is a genius. I need to set up a video camera and just keep it rolling at all times.

Both of the little girls have developed funny little obsessions. Every morning as I take **Alexis** to school, she looks at me and asks if her face is clean. It always is, but fortunately we keep wet wipes in the vehicle "just in case". I guess we run out the door every morning in such a hurry that she's afraid she doesn't look her best. Irene's obsession is her hair; every morning as we drive to school and even once there waiting in line to drop off she will ask, "Is my hair messy?" Since I rarely have a brush with me, I always tell her it's fine. Many days I say this as I'm smoothing it with my hand. She's going to catch some day on then I think I'll be in big trouble. Maybe I should make a note to myself to put a hairbrush in the car beside the wet wipes....

Psalm 45:11 The king is enthralled by your beauty; honor him, for he is your lord.

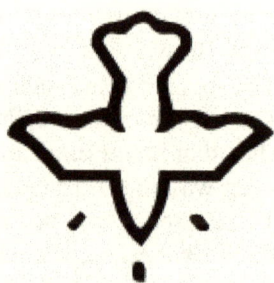

Chinese Food

One of my favorite authors wrote a piece that I felt compelled to answer. This is his story followed by my response.

Rich's Note: The Cat's Meow

I don't know about where you live, but around here the Chinese restaurants and take-outs are not very different from each other. The selections are pretty much the same, as are the prices and the tastes. There's a little variation, but not much. Beef and Broccoli and Chicken Lo Mein are pretty much the same. Granted, there are some places that don't use the freshest of ingredients and some that cause a concern for the neighborhood cats; but, by and large, Chinese restaurants tend to be alike. Based on the two places I ate at in Chinatown, San Francisco, other towns are the same.

I've always wondered why this was so, why some little place didn't go for a more unique slant on flavor. Not all Italian places are the same, even if they offer similar dishes. And look at pizza. Compare Pappa John's to Little Caesar.

P. F. Chang's opened a restaurant here not long ago and we tried it this weekend. I had the Mongolian Beef and Susan tried the Lemon Pepper Shrimp. We shared some Garlic Snow Peas and had the Lettuce Wraps as an appetizer. Eating their delicious food only reinforced my belief that variation is possible in Chinese food. It is most definitely possible to put a different spin on traditional dishes. I hope some places take the cue and try to be a bit more unique.

Rich can be reached at richrowand@erols.com.

Rich, sometimes Chinese restaurants do go for a different taste but trust me; this is not always a good thing. I went to New York City several years ago for training for my job with the Girl Scouts. What an experience! I was with other ladies who had either visited before or as with one, lived there until she was a young teen, so I had my own tour company. We crammed as much as humanly possible into a short weekend. One must-do stop was China Town. The sites were incredible and the smells were---awful. What a stinky place. However it was lunchtime and we were all ravenous from all of the tramping around NYC, so we decided to eat something in spite of the smell. The only problem was choosing which restaurant, there are so many! Just at that moment we spotted a man leaning out of a restaurant door waving at us to come inside. We all agreed this was a very friendly gesture so went in, thinking that this sure solved our problem of deciding. The restaurant was small but very clean. We also noticed we were the only non-Asians in the place but again in agreement, decided this would possibly be a very good thing. We were so wrong.

We placed our orders then sat back to wait, contemplating our choices from the wonderfully worded descriptions in the menu. There was a bank of fish tanks against one wall and we sat watching the fish swim as we waited, trying to identify the different species to pass the time. Ah! Our food arrived in fairly quick order and we were excited since as I mentioned, we were very hungry. The dishes looked delicious and smelled very good too. We all dug in and got one bite down when we realized this was the WORST food we had ever tasted, bar none. I'll never forget the looks on the other ladies faces as the realization hit home. I'm not a picky person and will eat most anything but I couldn't gag it down. None of us could. In fact I decided that the food tasted as if it had been prepared with the fish tank water. UGH! I can still remember how bad that food tasted all these years later. We decided it wouldn't be wise to say anything so we paid and left and made the short walk over to Little Italy (isn't NYC great?) where we had some Italian ice cream to clean our palettes.

My youngest daughter has a friend who was born and raised in NYC and when told this story laughed and said, "You should NEVER go into a Chinese restaurant in NYC where someone is waving you inside! There's a reason they need to wave customers in!" Gee thanks Colleen. Where were you when I visited?

Genesis 2:9 And the LORD God made all kinds of trees grow out of the ground—trees that were pleasing to the eye and good for food. In the middle of the garden were the tree of life and the tree of the knowledge of good and evil.

City Girl Or Country Coward?

I was fortunate while growing up to have loving grandparents throughout much of my childhood. My Poppy (my mother's father) died when I was two years old but I have heard many stories about him and love his memory. Grandma Alumbaugh, Grandma and Granddaddy Laney have all long since passed on as well, but the memories I have of them all will stay with me always and many make me laugh. Some still make me want to run and hide my face. I'm going to share a few of both.....

Grandma Alumbaugh lived in a fairly rural setting, but by no means in the country. She had neighbors all around, a nice sized yard and a screened in front porch. She also lived within walking distance of an old neighborhood country store and she would occasionally give my siblings and me change to walk there for candy.

Grandma was wonderful, very loving, patient, kind and not without a few odd notions. I remember spending a night once. I had a cold. She smeared Vicks Vapor Rub all over my then skinny chest then put waxed paper on it to protect my clothes. At the time I thought this was so weird but in looking back I realize my Grandma was being pretty smart. She didn't want extra laundry to do. I don't recall now what type of washing facility she had (my mom had a wringer washer for a few years of my childhood so I think Grandma may have too) but it wouldn't have been as easy as today to do a small load of laundry.

Grandma did one thing that I'll never understand though. She would offer us a cold 7-Up then promptly stir some sugar into it. We didn't want to hurt her feelings so Mom would always let us pour it down the sink as soon as she left the kitchen. I think this may be the reason why to this day I cannot stand 7-Up. She also kept a supply of Gingersnap cookies in the cabinet. I don't remember the brand but I do recall they came in a brown paper bag and were a nice size and very crispy with a real bite to them. I loved those cookies and still do. I buy some occasionally as a treat, always the kind in a brown bag though they aren't as good these days. But the first one from the bag never fails to take me back to my Grandma's warm and cheerful kitchen.

Grandma and Granddaddy Laney lived in the same town as Grandma A. but definitely in the country, at the end of a long, gravel, and often rough driveway. You always knew when company was coming because the dogs would raise a ruckus, giving you time to look out the living room window to see who was inching their way down that drive. That drive damaged more than one car with its potholes and gravelly surface.

I loved going to visit them—for a day. We went fairly frequently for Sunday gatherings after church and, having several cousins, we kids would spend happy afternoons playing together in their huge yard. They had a couple of sheep, a ram that was dangerously mean (I remember my dad and uncles looking at him and holding a bucket up. He ran at them and rammed that bucket so hard it's a wonder he didn't break the arm of the guy holding it), a huge sow and several stinky pigs. At one time they even raised cows and sold the milk. They would use some to make butter and they usually served fresh milk in the mornings. Being a city girl, born and raised on margarine, I HATED the taste of butter and despised the warm milk that Grandma served with breakfast. Today I love butter but still can't tolerate the thought of warm milk fresh from the cow.

I also remember playing softball with my favorite boy cousins in the huge backyard where my dad and Uncle Johnny (their dad) would go out and throw the ball for us. I once hit the ball so hard it went sailing out of the yard and into Grandma's huge vegetable garden. Uncle Johnny said I hit the ball as hard as any of the boys on my cousin Allan's little league team. I still swell with pride to this day just thinking about that moment. Luckily, I didn't get anywhere near Grandma's tomato plants with the ball. She once grew one plant so huge and prolific that it grew over 300 tomatoes on one plant! When one of my uncles went to work and told co-workers about the almost 300 tomatoes growing on it, they laughed and accused him of exaggerating. HA! With Grandma's approval, Uncle Elwood dug the plant up and took it to work where they counted the maters. The final count was something like 320 tomatoes on one plant! I wish I had inherited just the tip of Grandma's green thumb.

I still look back and laugh at the time my cousins, my twin Jayme, and I put black electrical tape on our faces for mustaches and beards then pretended that we were Mitch Miller. (Oh boy I am REALLY dating myself now!) Allan, Greg and Mike all got in trouble and Uncle Johnny made them sit on chairs under the shade tree in the yard. My sister and I didn't get in trouble but it sure took the fun out of the afternoon and we never did figure out why they got into trouble.

Both of my grandmothers were fabulous cooks and we always enjoyed great food when we visited. I look back fondly on memories of huge family gatherings at Grandma Laney's and eating till you couldn't hold any more. The best times were in the summer when we sat in the yard to eat. I enjoyed inside meals far less. The men always congregated in the dining room, the women in the kitchen and the kids all ate at tables set up in the living room. I always found this insulting and bided my time until I was big enough to join the women in the kitchen, which I finally did when in my teens. I was such a rebel.

One thing that no one, not even Grandma Alumbaugh could beat though were Grandma Laney's home canned pickles. To this day I would put her recipe up against ANYONE else's and I know hers would win. They were simply indescribably delicious. My brother would ask for a jar when we arrived and would sit and eat them one after another until he had a big pile of stems lying on the table in front of him. I experimented once and found this recipe works wonderfully for pickled vegetables too, so plan on making some this summer. No, the recipe isn't a closely guarded secret and I do share when asked. Everyone should have the opportunity to experience her wonderful pickles.

We spent many wonderful hours walking my grandparent's farm with my folks in search of poke greens, May apples and sassafras trees to dig up for their roots. I also have wonderful memories of wiener roasts over huge bon fires with my family, cousins and various Aunts and Uncles. I sometimes long for those simpler times, and wish that my own daughters and grandchildren could experience those undemanding times themselves.

Some memories aren't so precious though. My brother and sister, both older, always enjoyed going to visit my grandparents for overnight visits. I did too, if it was at Grandma Alumbaughs. Once, when we were about 7 years old, Jayme and I were sent to spend a few days with Grandma and Granddaddy. I'll never forget my Uncle David, who is my dad's baby brother, chasing Jayme and me onto the porch with the tractor shortly after we arrived. He was just having fun with us but it sure scared us! I felt better when Grandma scolded him though. We were so lost there. My cousins hadn't moved out to the country yet and though, in the same town were far enough away that they didn't visit often. This situation was tolerable enough as long as it was daylight out and I didn't need to pee. You see, being farm folks they didn't have indoor plumbing for much of my childhood even though these were the 60's and modern times. Yup, this means they had an outhouse. I hated that thing with a passion because of the smell and it always seemed to be infested with spiders. Apparently, spiders also don't have any sense of smell. I would "hold it" for as long as I painfully could before I would use that dark, smelly and scary thing. Nighttime was pure torture since this meant a trip outside in the dark, making some nights seemed endless. Those endless nights were only made worse by the distant howling of dogs on neighboring farms. I was convinced that they were coyotes just waiting for some desperate little girl to finally need a trip to the privy. I eventually reached the point where I just could not make myself go in there and face those miserable spiders so.......... I peed my pants. I just could not face it one more time. Grandma Laney was not only a wonderful cook but she was also very astute. She knew how miserable Jayme and I had been so she called Grandma Alumbaugh and together they decided to send my cousin Monroe out to pick us up and take us back to Grandma A's, not quite city, but far from country, home. I always loved Monroe, who was several years older and most importantly, old enough to drive. After this I adored him! We didn't need the dogs to alert us when he turned into the drive because we had been waiting anxiously for his arrival. I remember watching his car move carefully down the drive and realizing even then that this was the most excited I had been in days. It was so good to be back in the bosom of my loving and patient Grandma Alumbaugh. I loved Grandma Laney but preferred her in shorter daylight visits.

That all changed when I was twelve and my grandfather was killed in an accident while driving a truck for his employer. Grandma was suddenly alone in the country so my dad and some uncles got busy and put in indoor plumbing. Oh glory! I at last looked forward to going for visits. I missed Granddaddy something awful but the indoor facilities made the visits far more enjoyable.

Life changed for Grandma after that but she remained fiercely independent and stayed on the farm for many years after Granddaddy died. Her garden was still there but much smaller and she no longer raised cows. The pigs and sheep were gone long before Granddaddy. At one point, Grandma decided to supplement her income by raising 25,000 turkeys. Suddenly that treacherous drive down her driveway took on a funny side as those thousands of turkeys gobbled like crazy in response. If you've ever spent any time around turkeys then you know that they not only taste great but also just how dumb and easily alarmed they can be. Oh boy, sneaking up on them was fun, easy and entertaining. Moving them from one area to another was a real experience too. They just stand and gobble like fools while you try to herd them in the same general direction. What an exhausting but fun way to spend an afternoon on the farm.

I still miss my grandparents and always will. I'm so very thankful that I have such wonderful memories to carry with me and stories to pass on to my kids. I just hope we can build memories with our own grandkids that they can look fondly back on some day as well.

1 Timothy 5:4 But if a widow has children or grandchildren, these should learn first of all to put their religion into practice by caring for their own family and so repaying their parents and grandparents, for this is pleasing to God.

Classic Rock

Stacie and I took the little ones to Rocky Mount yesterday morning. It was a nice trip all told, and the kids were well behaved when normally they're bored with this frequent 30-minute trip.

I learned a couple of things on this drive. For one I still hate "moldy oldies" and that though I still prefer contemporary Christian music, I actually like Classic Rock which surprised me. Had I been asked before this, I would have said that I dislike all older music. Second, I learned that Stacie has pretty good taste in music, even if it is a bit eclectic. Some of her music is downright odd but she has a great classic rock collection that made driving that trip very pleasant; Songs that included Low Rider, Sweet Home Alabama and Hotel California.

She even had a copy of Inagaddadavida by Iron Butterfly. I'm totally shocked that this classic is still popular. I shouldn't be surprised though since it has, in my opinion, THE best drum solo ever played. Period. I can still remember the first time I ever heard this song. I was in the 9th grade at Memorial High school in Joplin, Missouri sitting in the balcony where all freshmen were relegated to sit for assemblies. I've long since forgotten the purpose of the assembly and the name of the upper classman who played out the skit of a caveman playing the song on a drum, but I have not forgotten how that song affected me. I sat transfixed as it beat its way into my heart and deep into my very core. I bought the album as soon as I could get to the store and in time introduced my kids to it at young ages which probably explains why they like it today. I'd pop the cassette that replaced the album into the player, crank up the speakers and let it rock. Apparently it burrowed down into their hearts and deep into their very cores where it will beat away until they can pass on the love of the greatest drum solo in the entire history of music to their own kids. In fact, some of the kids use the song for my ringer when I call their cell phones.

Inagaddadavida honey don't you know that I'll always love you?

Psalm 100:1 Make a joyful noise unto the LORD, all ye lands.

Clown House

It's almost ready to move in! Ernie and I love the house we are buying in Roanoke Rapids, even more so now that the rooms are "normal" colors. We are conservative people and as much as I say I'm tired of white walls, when it comes right down to it we pretty much stick to them. It's just so much easier to accessorize around a neutral white or cream, and you're far less likely to get tired of looking at those colors as you are say turquoise or periwinkle, and I don't intend to paint again for a long, long time.

An elderly woman (we aren't clear on this as the details are still sketchy) owned the house and she died a while back. She had been renting the house out and either didn't know what they were doing to it or may not have cared. The end result was the same; the house looked as if a family of circus clowns lived in it. We took digital before pictures because there really is no way to describe the colors adequately. You just had to see it to understand.

We have this wonderful ability (sometimes curse) to see the potential in things and not necessarily the reality in a situation. There was no electricity in the house when we looked at it, which we did twice. Even though it was daylight, some of the rooms were so dark we needed flashlights to see. We had the power turned on this week since we knew we would be working and painting and certainly wanted to see what we were doing. Our realtor met me at the house after I got into Roanoke Rapids Friday afternoon and handed me the keys so that we can come and go as we please. Excited, I went into "our house" and started choosing colors. What a sight! We knew the living room was turquoise but in the light it was VERY turquoise. The hallway was periwinkle (yes, you read that right) and one bedroom had royal blue and blue green trim, apparently going for an Aztec look judging from the curtain still hanging in the room. The color was scratched in places so we saw that it had been PURPLE at one time. Another bedroom had pink, blue, green and yellow wallpaper with an extremely bright baby blue trim. Underneath that had been lime green. Unfortunately these people had also painted all of the crown molding (we love the look of wood crown molding and may change it eventually), chair railing and baseboards. Finally, the master bedroom has a dark dusty blue color that we chose to stay with for now. The family room was an off white so we figured the renters moved before they could violate it.

We set to work and chose Moonlit Snow for the bedrooms with Snow Ballet as the trim color. The hallway is now April Dawn, an icy-almost-not-there blue/white. That stupid periwinkle, never a favorite color of mine, took an entire gallon of paint to cover and could stand another coat to look "right". I plan to do just that after we get all of the furniture moved in. Good grief we painted entire bedrooms with less! The wallpaper room had to have Kilz applied first. Ugh. The family room and the eat-in part of the kitchen got a coat of Olive Fog, a very nice off white color. The dining room isn't going to be painted yet but will be since it has gold figured wallpaper. Yikes! Finally our one non-conservative room is the living room. I wanted to pick up the colors in the couch so went for an Off Shore Mist (cream) on top and below the chair rail applied Victory Blue (navy). I started painting around the trim with the blue on Saturday and was nearly in tears. It was so BRIGHT against that turquoise that I thought I had made an awful mistake. I decided to see how it went though and once the top was painted (beautiful!) we finished the bottom and it turned out simply stunning. I am so proud of this room that I could pop my buttons. In fact I am proud of the whole house because we did it! I had no idea that two people could accomplish so much in one weekend but we did manage to paint all 3 bedrooms, the family room, eat-in area, living room and that hateful hallway. I can barely bend over today and can't remember when I last worked so hard but it feels good knowing the house looks so pretty now. Jack, our realtor, saw it only partially finished and was very impressed with the improvement. He should see it now. I firmly believe anyone who paints for a living deserves every penny they charge. I think we sweat off 5 pounds each then replaced it with the seeming gallons of water we drank.

We even managed to get some work done on the pool. As I said, the former owner died some while back (we think as much as two years before) and the pool was covered but unattended the entire time. Yuck, the cover collapsed into the water and the pool was positively black. Ernie has spent a lot of time, effort and shock-it getting it clean so it has gone from black to a funny turquoise color (what is it with that color and this house?) to a pond green color. We are just a couple of stages away from clear, clean water. Of course he may decide to dump it all and ask the fire department to fill it from the hydrant, something they do frequently around there. Though that water isn't clean it also isn't black, and can be filtered easily and much quicker. I am so impressed with his determination and hard work. This man could make the Energizer Bunny tired.

Since the house was unoccupied for so long, the spiders kind of took over. Yeeewwww I hate spiders. I found spider and cob webs in corners of the ceiling and fireplace and in window sills. I took a vacuum cleaner up with me so used it to suck up all of the ones I could reach then Ernie put the extensions from his shop vac on it so I was really able to get to them then. I spoiled the day for a few living spiders. Muahahahaha ask me how much I care. That vacuum quit on me later that afternoon just before I could finish cleaning the bedroom carpet. I thought it was because it was a cheap Eureka but now that I think about it, I'll bet spider guts poisoned it.

The best part of this house is the hardwood floors in the living room, front entryway and dining room. I have always loved and wanted hardwood floors. I grew up in a house with this type of floor and have always preferred them to carpet. Ernie likes them too so some day we plan to change out the carpet for wood tile. There won't be a strip of carpet in the house if I have a choice. Of course I went and almost ruined the floor in the living room. Well maybe not ruined it, but when I got a big blob of paint on the wood while carelessly moving a plastic sheet that I had been using to set the paint on, I was tempted to jump into that nasty pool outside and drown myself. Luckily (I really was repulsed by the thought) I was able to clean the spot.

Another fun part of the house is what I call The Cabana. The kitchen is small and has a breakfast bar area on two sides, with a base made of brick. The back side of the top cabinets have a shingle thing going, just like a Tahitian bar that makes you want to pull up a bar stool and sip cold sodas with little umbrellas stuck in them while listening to a Jimmy Buffet song.

The house still needs some TLC but we're up to the task, especially since the rooms no longer SCREAM at us as we walk in. We plan to have vinyl siding (it's mostly brick) and new windows installed and will put up or change some ceiling fans, change out some faucets and I still need to suck up about a jillion spider webs in the garage. I'll use the shop vac this time; maybe it can withstand the spider venom. One thing we took off of the list was removing the ancient looking intercom system. I was fiddling with it and found that the radio not only still works but that all of the rooms that have intercom have their own working volume control. We worked to background music all weekend making the job much more pleasant. We plan to leave it in place now which means Ernie won't have to patch the holes it would have left in the walls, freeing up time to work on the pool and other jobs on the honey-do list.

This is our 5th house so we know all too well that the list of chores is never done, however we look forward to settling in and getting started on this list. Fist thing on the to-do list: SUPO (Survive the Un-packing Ordeal.) Oh my already aching muscles.

Hmmm…the pool isn't THAT bad is it? Nah… I'm not that desperate YET.

Ernie moved into the house a week before I will, since he started his new job and I have to supervise the movers in our other house. He called home last night and in the course of conversation told me that the vacuum cleaner lives. This just proves my theory that it was spider intestines at fault.

I guess it just got ill and quit until they could be digested. What a pity since I hate vacuums almost as much as I hate spiders. This would have taken care of both hateful foes in one fell swoop. Oh well, the vacuum will be handy for sucking up any wayward webs. Besides I now know how to kill the beast if ever I reach my breaking point with vacuuming. Heeheeheeheeeeeeee

I live for the day someone invents a riding vacuum. Then again, maybe not since I can still remember my experiences on the riding lawn mower....

1 Chronicles 29:2 With all my resources I have provided for the temple of my God—gold for the gold work, silver for the silver, bronze for the bronze, iron for the iron and wood for the wood, as well as onyx for the settings, turquoise, stones of various colors, and all kinds of fine stone and marble—all of these in large quantities.

Cruising The Triangle For An EXCELLENT Time!

What can I say about our first cruise? It was awesome, perfect, fabulous, and incredible. Celebrity Cruise line uses the "X" symbol to signify Excellence and as far as my husband Ernie and I are concerned, they achieved nothing less on our trip. From beginning to end they attained their goal. I can't recommend Celebrity Cruise Line, Horizon specifically too much. The crew, represented by 50 nationalities, was exceptionally friendly and courteous and all spoke English!

Bermuda itself was a beautiful place, again English speaking. At times it was a surreal experience—almost as if we'd never left the states. Bermuda is rich in history, colorful (literally) and conservative while being courteous to their many tourists. It must get awfully tiring having tourists tramping around your tiny country but they handle it well. Bermuda is a mere 22.5 miles long and at its widest point approximately 2.5 miles across. Upon entering port you'll notice houses of just about every color imaginable. Interestingly, all buildings have white roofs. The cruise director explained that the roofs are made of lime stone which is a natural filter and that each is designed to collect run-off in cisterns for showers, etc. Surrounded by ocean and sprinkled with breathtaking beaches, ancient forts, and attractions for anyone, boredom was not a problem. Fatigue and tired legs yes! The island was formed from a volcanic eruption and (Steep!) hills abound. We managed to visit a very small portion but it was enough to assure that we'll return some day for another visit. Following is a sampling of our adventure both on board the Horizon and on Bermuda and our short journey away from reality.

One mystery solved

Two words we never heard mentioned by anyone on board ship were "Bermuda Triangle". We didn't even hear the passengers discussing it until the last day in port. I don't know about anyone else but I wasn't keen on talking about it. I didn't want to wake up somewhere other than earth to find we had solved the mystery. I wouldn't even buy an "I survived the Bermuda Triangle" keychain which was abundant in Hamilton. After all, we had only survived the trip in—we still had to get out and I didn't want to jinx us. As it was, I had a little mystery of my own right in the state room. We dressed for dinner each evening and most evenings I wore a skirt. On the second or third day at sea, I was getting ready for bed and tossed my slip on a chair since I knew I'd want it the next day. It was late (we rarely went to bed before midnight) and the door was locked, yet the next morning that slip had disappeared. We searched dirty laundry bag, drawers, even the suitcases though we knew they had been under the bed since unpacking. In other words, we tore that place apart but it was simply gone! We knew no one had been in the room with us so I finally just decided that it was a mystery and went without. The toilet system on the ship was amazingly functional and efficient, working on a vacuum system. When the knob was pulled up, the toilet made a roaring sound then SWOOSH everything was gone and it was refilled in an instant. That missing slip bugged us all day and at one point, Ernie laughingly asked if I had dropped it down the toilet somehow. I doubted it but said if I had, it was definitely a goner. The thought of that triangle business was never far from my mind for the rest of the day! Fast forward several hours to time to dress for dinner. We had been outside in the wind all day so I decided to take a shower. As I grabbed my waist band I felt an extra layer and realized that I had my slip on!! I had had it on all that time while tearing the cabin apart. I started giggling and didn't stop until I got out of the shower. I laughed every time I thought about it the rest of that evening. Ernie didn't catch on until bed time that night when I stepped out of my clothes and he saw my slip. Never knowing what to expect from me day to day he just said, "You had it on all the time didn't you?" I laughed and confessed to the deed while he just shook his head. So that's one mystery solved and it's now official—I've completely lost my mind.

The food! Oh my gosh the FOOD!

You simply will not believe the amounts and quality of food on board, but I have to try and describe it anyway. Food is available quite literally, 24 hours a day on board ship. From midnight buffets, to room service, to buffet lines, you'll find nearly anything that you could possibly want to eat. The dinner meal was a fantastic experience with menus complete with appetizer, soup, salad, main entrée and dessert. You could order any and all, and if so inclined could even order more than one of each item though I don't think anyone at our table did. We sure thought about it though. They even remember the diabetics and offer no sugar added desserts at every meal! We dined on everything from steaks to veal to lobster with shrimp cocktail and incredible appetizers that I could never hope to duplicate at home. One afternoon Ernie and I chose to order hamburgers for lunch at the outdoor grill on aft deck eleven. There was a huge buffet being offered inside but we were in the mood for burgers. Incredibly as we sat down we heard an older gentleman complaining about the buffet because it didn't offer anything he really liked, so he'd had to settle for "damned shepherd's pie"! With ALL of the food options on board he was complaining! He could have stayed in his state room and ordered room service for crying out loud and he had the nerve to complain. We frankly wished that he had taken that opportunity. I was one happy cruiser when we discovered that they offered a sushi bar every evening at 6:00. We thoroughly enjoyed our share almost every evening and felt this was all the more reason to be happy that we had chosen the late seating for dinner! I have no idea what other Celebrity ships offer but we were sure wowed by Horizon's food sculptor, who makes the most amazing ice and food monuments! We watched him carve a dolphin (of course! What else on a cruise ship? :o) in just minutes. I actually had to walk up to a display of a watermelon bowl holding a bouquet to confirm that it was food. The vegetable flowers were so delicate that they looked like real flowers! I must say though that the most amazing figure he made was when he carved the likeness of a passenger into a watermelon—again in mere minutes. Unfortunately I had injured my eye earlier in the evening and was sporting an eye patch while in intense pain so only got a few glimpses of the midnight buffet that displayed a lot of his work. We have yet to download the pictures that Ernie took that night so I hope they turned out clear.

Dining Partners and Wait Staff

Every little detail is covered when you arrange your tour, right down to what time you'd prefer to dine for your evening meal. We chose late seating (8:30PM) as opposed to the early seating of 6:00PM. I wish I knew who to thank for the incredible job they did when they placed us at table # 68! Not only were we privileged to be served by what we considered the best wait staff on board but had fabulous table mates as well. Mary, Pat, Lynn and Tom were all wonderful and so much fun to dine with! Pat, widowed and Mary, divorced work together (VP/Executives) at a bank in their Kentucky hometown and from what we saw and experienced, they must be a hoot to work with! Mary entertained us nightly with her delightful and brutally self-honest humor while Pat played "straight man". One evening while in port at Hamilton, Lynn and Tom decided to attend an island party instead of joining us for dinner. We had bonded so completely that we all worried about their absence. We were pleased to see them the next day and told them that they had chosen a bad evening to be gone. Mary thoroughly enjoyed teasing our waiter Paulo, who is from Portugal and Jose who is from Columbia and that particular evening she was in fine form. We laughed so much that night that my face ached by the time we were left the table. The wait staffs all had no more than 3 tables to attend so could devote a good deal of attention to each table and we required a lot since it was so much fun to watch them interact with Mary. The waiter at a table next was very talented at making various shapes out of napkins for one of the young ladies seated there so Mary asked Paulo why he never did things like that for our table. Paulo feigned insult and offered to let us move to another area which of course made us all laugh and beg for forgiveness. Pat then told Jose, who is a tiny little man who moves lightening quick, that she was smuggling him home in her suitcase and that she and Mary would alternate weeks at home with him working for them. Jose stopped, quickly looked from one to the other and said, "Do we get to be lovers?" then hurried away. The look on Pat's face was priceless and I would have given anything to have had a camera at that moment! We were all about to roll out of our seats laughing while we assured her that she had heard correctly.

More about Paulo and Jose (Oh and Steve!)

Every evening as we sat down to eat, Paulo or Jose would be immediately at our sides handing menus and placing the ladies napkins in their laps. I swear they did everything but chew our food for us! A little uncomfortable with such service at first, I quickly realized that a person could really get used to this kind of treatment. The entire kitchen and wait staff worked with such amazing skill and efficiency that we never waited more than a few minutes for any course. We were always awed by the huge trays of food that those poor waiters carried and joked that Jose had probably been taller at one time but had run several inches off. We were all more than delighted with the service and happily gave them both ratings of "Excellent" on our comment cards. This is the highest rating that can be given otherwise I would have marked phenomenal. Steve, the assistant Maitre d however, didn't rank very high with Mary. She just didn't trust the guy. He wore a name tag our first evening with his "real" name and the next night was sporting a name tag with "Steve" on it. This really nagged at Mary and she couldn't figure him out and didn't really care for him. One evening, she finally had to ask him about this name change. He was surprised by her observance and told some story about how his name is difficult to pronounce (I forget now where he's originally from. Bulgaria?) and that Steve is his third name. This didn't do much to restore her faith in him though and I suspect he knew this since he spent a lot of time stationed near our table. I just wasn't sure if he was trying to reassure or annoy her. I must say though, it was all very entertaining for the rest of us!

Ernie's 15 seconds of fame

Celebrity does a wonderful job of arranging entertainment for aboard ship and employs a very talented song and dance troupe that also serve as cruise staff. They are amazing! Rich the Cruise Director, is a very funny man who once worked as a stand up comedian and was great entertainment all alone but they didn't stop there! Horizon offered among others, musical reviews, an extremely talented young musician by the name of Samantha J and a comedian with a terrific talent for making up songs on the spot. We just happened to be sitting on the end of the second row, center stage during his show. I'm SO glad we were too! I'm awful with names so have since forgotten his name but "the comedian" was really funny. Rich, the cruise director, had mentioned that this guy was really good at impromptu songs so we were looking forward to hearing some examples—never expecting to become part of the show. As he walked down off stage for the first song, he zeroed right in on Ernie as if he was wearing a big flashing sign that said "Pick (on) ME!" I was as stunned as Ernie when Mr. Comedian rushed up, asked Ernie his name then stuck the microphone in his face. I was as equally stunned when my usually so calm cool and collected husband stammered out "Uh Ernie". The questions just got harder from there. Mr. Comedian (MC): Ernie, where do you work? E: uh.........in manufacturing. (I'm jabbing him in the ribs and reminding him that he works for Georgia Pacific). MC: And what do you MAKE in this manufacturing plant? E: uuuuuuh........(I'm poking and whispering OSB!) we make wood. By this point I'm so tickled that I can hardly think straight and Ernie just plain can't think straight. MC: So you make wood. What is your job there? E:..........................I...I'm the safety manager. (I'm still poking and jabbing his ribs reminding him that he's also HR but he missed that reminder). MC went back up to the stage and immediately made up a song that was absolutely perfect! It was as if he got inside Ernie's head, singing about safety and how you need to wear your yellow safety hat. What a hoot! I don't know which was funnier—MC or Ernie when he lost his cool. In 23 years of marriage I've never seen him lose his composure like that and I have to tell you, it was GREAT! I still laugh when I think about his face and how he couldn't even remember his job title.

Jayne dances the Conga and is recognized by a celebrity!

We didn't get to hear nearly enough of the fabulous Carribean band called Phase Five (or was it 5?) that played on board several times. They were awesome and sounded just like UB40 which happens to be one of my all-time favorite bands. One night at dinner Mary and Pat told us that they were going to the party on deck eleven and urged us all to go. So we did just that. Enrie and I intended to stay just a little bit but got caught up in the music, dancing and contests. One woman named Nancy worked on all of our nerves with her constant silly behavior which was intended to get attention and it did but hey, she was on vacation and having a good time at least. I however don't much care for being in the spotlight since I'm fairly conservative. We had front row "seats" on the wall around the spa so got to see everything up close. The music got louder and everyone got caught up in the fun so when the band invited everyone to join "the world's longest conga line on board a ship" lots of people jumped up to join in, including our own Mary, Pat, Lynn and Tom. I was *really* surprised and very hesitant when Ernie jumped up and told me to come join it with him. *Me*?! Dance in a CONGA LINE???!..... wellll....OK! So I jumped in, grabbed hold of Tom's shoulders and started conga-ing. It's a wonder that poor Tom could walk the next day since I conga-ed all over the backs of his feet the entire way. I felt like a complete idiot out there, dancing and shaking as we snaked along the deck, up the stairs and back down the next back to our starting point where we then had to LIMBO. *LIMBO*?!! *ME*??!.......Welllllll....OK! And I had a ball. I never cease to amaze myself. I threw all caution to the wind and had a great time even while I felt silly doing it. I just figured lots of other people were dancing too and I'd never see most of them again after we got back home. I was so caught up in the fun that I didn't realiz that the band was apparently paying as much attention to us as we were them. How do I know? Well the very next afternoon as Ernie and I were walking down the sidewalk in Hamilton, just outside the ship, we passed two very cute (and young) men who'm I recognized as Phase Five (5?) band members. One of them looked at me, grinned real big and said "Hey! How're you doing?!" I was kind of flattered that he recognized ME then it hit me—he'd probably seen me doing the Conga the night before. Ooooh dear, my conservative soul shuddered as I remembered how silly I must have looked shaking, dancing and foot stomping my way around that deck. Guess what though. I didn't care! I had so much fun that it just didn't matter. I do still feel bad about poor Tom's feet though.

Drama on the high seas

We only pre-planned one outing for our time in port and that was helmet diving. We looked on-line and we both agreed that it sounded like fun. I know a few people who were shocked by this since I tend to be not only conservative but a little cowardly as well. I'm just not a thrill seeker. I get scared just *hearing* about my kids antics when they go camping in the mountains and on white water trips with their cousins. Still there was something exciting about the thought of going down into the water and swimming with the fish. We were even going to play with a moray eel! The morning of the dive arrived and I was still fairly calm about the idea though truth be known, I was starting to get a little quivery inside. We were surprised at the number of people going and for some reason that was comforting. In all twenty four people were making the dive and yahooie, one lady was bigger than me! THAT was very comforting. We got underway and while the lone crew member drove the boat, Hartley the dive director/tour operator gave us a speech about what to expect and offered to take Polaroid pictures of everyone for a mere $7/picture. While everyone but us dug for their wallets (We felt kind of cheap but it worked out) Hartley made up the dive list. We were in the second group out of four going down. This too was comforting. I didn't want to be first and being someone who isn't very patient at waiting, didn't want to go last. *Then* Hartley dropped his bombshell; the water is less than 75 degrees so we'd all have to wear wetsuits! *What?!* I've never even seen one in person much less worn one! That's when I started getting lots more quivery on the inside. I was convinced that I'd never fit into one and even if they had one big enough the description of "it's just like putting panty hose on—on your whole body" just didn't sound like my kind of fun, especially in front of a large group of people. I sat and watched as the first group struggled into their suits. The larger lady was in the group going last so I couldn't watch to see if she found one to fit, darn it. I don't know if you've ever been in one so let me tell you they *aren't* the most flattering outfit. This realization upped my anxiety level just a bit more. While we waited for the first group to go down, I wandered over (not far on this small boat either) to check out a book that was lying on a counter. It turned out to be the Bible! I was tickled and flipped it open to look for some words of encouragement. Unfortunately I couldn't find anything that directly dealt with my anxiety over how awful I'd look in a wetsuit but I *did* feel better and relaxed a lot. That lasted until Ernie walked up with two suits, fully expecting me to put one on. He is probably the world's most patient man, (that's just one of the many reasons why I adore him) and he good-naturedly started helping me into the suit. I think I heard someone say it was like trying to Unpeel a banana and had to laugh in agreement. I was surprised at how easily the suit went on though so relaxed and sat back, contining to watch as we waited for our turn. I was still feeling good about finding the bible on board and decided that this dive business didn't look so scary. Hartley and his assistant helped one person at a time step onto a ladder on the back of the boat, had them step down a couple of rungs then plopped a huge, very heavy bell shaped lead helmet with air running into it on to their heads. They then stepped down some more, dropped into the water and out of sight. Piece of cake. When the first group came back up after their alotted thirty minutes all were laughing and talking about how awesome an experience it was. Now it was our groups turn. Hartley called me and Ernie to the front where I told Hartley I wanted Ernie to go first so that he'd "be down there waiting on me". Down he went and Hartely came back up for me. I told him that I'd seen the bible and thanked him for having it there as they got me ready to take on the helmet. Things were happening so fast that I really didn't have time to think much. Before I knew it the helmet was on my head and I was going down the ladder. The instant my head went under water I started to hyperventilate. (my chest is getting tight and I'm starting to breathe a little heavy as I write this!) I could hear the air coming into the tube and just as importantly could hear it but I could *not* breathe. I flew back up the ladder in a blind panic and started motioning for the deck hand to *get that helmet OFF*. Hartley came up beside me as I was telling them thanks but NO thanks, I couldn't do it. He started telling me that yes, in fact I COULD and WOULD do it. I'm still not sure how he did it but he convinced me to try it again. Afterwards, in looking back I realized that I had been "talking it but not walking it" when I thanked him for having the bible on board. In other words, I gave God lip service but quite simply forgot to take Him down with me. The second attempt I said a quick prayer as they changed my helmet (a psychological trick I'm sure) and went back down again to a bewildered Ernie. He had seen me go up and had no idea what had happened. Unable to hear anyone but yourself in those helmets I could only smile and wave.

Hartley had us hang onto a guide while he went back top to get the rest of our group and was gone a while. I was very calm but still thankful that I could see the boat and light above while we waited since this process took a while. It turned out that a woman in our group had also panicked. I felt bad, thinking that I had scared her but her brother reassured me that she's scared of everything. I don't know how she felt afterwards but I was *so* thankful that Hartley had not taken no for an answer!

What an amazing experience to be under water with the sunlight filtering down through that gorgeous blue water, those beautiful fish, the incredible coral and best of all the moray eel! I knew that we might well see the eel but was still surprised when he came swimming out. I was so excited that I was babbling and hollering "Look! This is SO cool!" even though no one could hear me. We got to "pet" him as Hartley guided him through our hands then watched as he was fed a treat. In all of the years that he's been doing these tours the eel has never bitten anyone. He swims with his mouth open and looks for all the world as if he's smiling, no doubt in anticipation of the treat that awaits him after his handling. All too quickly our thirty minutes was up and we were headed back topside. The trip up was reversed so I was next to last and Ernie was last. As you come up the ladder, there is a T-shaped bar that you're supposed to grab as you haul yourself on board. Hartley's assistant had only been with him for four days (I'm sure glad I didn't know this going down since he was the one running the air into the helmets!) and distracted by other passengers as I came up, was standing next to the bar. As I made a grab for the bar he jumped back—and straight overboard. It happened so quickly that no one really knew what happened *except* that (1) he blamed me and (2) he can't swim! I was horrified by both facts and ever so thankful that Hartley was in the water as he swam over to help him to the boat. Once we all got back on board I filled Ernie in on what had happened since he'd once again been in the water while all of the drama was taking place. He was so pleased that I finally agreed to go back down since he used to scuba dive in waters even more gorgeous than those in Bermuda and knew what a treat it would be for me. I'll never forget the experience and we'll both always wonder----why in the world a man who can't swim chooses to work as a boat hand on a deep sea diving tour....

(Oh! And about those $7 Polaroids? The camera got wet when the "water proof" case it was in leaked. Everyone but the first group who got their pictures done before it leaked, got a refund of their money. We had taken our own water proof disposable so Hartley used it to take our pictures. Sometimes it pays to be frugal).

As The Sand Turns

Ernie and I rode the bus out to one of the several gorgeous beaches on Bermuda one afternoon so that he could snorkel while I splashed in the water. I had a very scary experience while swimming in Panama City Beach, Florida several years ago and have hated swimming in the ocean since, so I didn't actually do much splashing and never ventured more than waist deep but I still had a good time. I'm an avid people watcher so was delighted that the little cove we were in offered plenty of people watching prospects, one of which though short is one of my funnier memories of our time in Bermuda. Ernie was happily gawking at fish and comparing notes with fellow snorkelers while I wandered around in the water and watched the shore. A couple of good-looking young guys walked out to the water and from their conversation I gathered that they were from Bahston. Easy enough to deduce from their accents and their comparison of the beautiful blue water that we were standing in to the waters of Bahston Hahbor. They soon grew bored so decided to explore the sea and wave worn craggy rocks around the cove. I worried about them since these are some huge and rough looking rocks but they climbed like agile monkeys and were soon gone. Alone once again, I had to find new entertainment so looked to shore where the two cute young things who had come with them were sun bathing. Little did I know that a mini-soap opera was about to unfold.

Another attractive young man walked up to the girls and from their gestures I could tell that he was being told that his friends were "out on the rocks". He walked out to the waters edge to look for them and when he didn't see them walked back to the bathing beauties. As he walked up to them, two of the biggest muscle bound life guard type males that I've ever seen walked up from the opposite direction. I immediately nicknamed them Buff and Puff. He greeted them as if happy to see them but I could tell that he was a little uncomfortable by their appearance. Buff and Puff stood and talked to the girls while flexing their muscles, with third wheel friend sort of prancing around on the periphery of the group. Suddenly the sweet young things both nodded jumped up and tossed their towels in their bags and made ready to leave with the Buff and Puff! Poor third wheel had no idea what to do—should he go with them, ask them to stay or wait for his friends? He actually tried all three options. I could tell that he was asking them to wait for the two rock climbers but the girls ignored him so he ran down to the water and tried calling to his friends who were too far out to hear him over the crashing of the waves on the rocks. What to do?! He ran back to the group who was by this time ready to leave. And so they did, without as much as a backwards glance. At this point as amused as I was by this unfolding drama, I felt sorry for the kid too. He literally ran back towards the water, stopped and ran back to where the girls had been sitting grabbed his stuff then ran to try and catch up with the group. He ran around the hill and I never saw any of them again so have no idea if he caught them and if so, what they did with him. I did see the guys come back from their rock climbing expedition just as we were leaving so I at least know that they didn't fall off of the rocks into the ocean. I just wish I knew what their reactions were when they realized that they had been abandoned. As with any soap opera, there is no ending. How unfortunate for us all.

OUCH! That *REALLY* Hurt!

As I mentioned earlier, Ernie and I enjoyed the sushi bar almost every evening. We looked forward to trying a little of everything on it and I think I could have eaten my weight in rice and raw fish. The only thing that stopped me was the thought of being too full for the fabulous sit down dinners that we always knew would be waiting for us at 8:30. One evening we started out to the back of deck eleven as usual and spotted Lynn and Tom already sitting at a table. We headed over to join them and as I walked out something flew into my eye. It *really* hurt too. We sat outside chatting while we ate our sushi (nothing, including pain was going to come between me and my sushi!) and I rubbed at my eye trying to remove it. I even tried pulling my eyelid down over the bottom one but nothing helped. We went back down to our stateroom around 7 to start getting ready for dinner and I decided to try plunging my open eye into a basin of cold water and as a last resort, tried washing it out with the shower. I probably made things worse doing that but I was getting a bit desperate with the pain. When we joined our group at the dinner table, it was obvious to all that something was wrong since my eye was red and swollen. By the time we finished dinner around 10, it was also starting to run enough that I kept having to dab at it with my napkin. It was also starting to hurt even worse. I couldn't imagine what I had gotten in it that would hurt so bad and suspected that I had scratched my cornea. I've never done that before (and hope I never do again) but had heard how painful that is. I was alarming everyone with the obvious pain so they encouraged me to see the ship's doctor. Ernie and I returned to our state room and called down only to be told that since it was after hours (they closed at 9) it would be an automatic $100 charge. I was in so much pain by that point that I didn't care so we walked down to the hospital. I was so stressed that my blood pressure was a shocking 176/100 too! The nurse put some eye drops in that completely blinded me and scared me a little since they hadn't warned me that this would happen. I imagine my blood pressure shot up a few more points while I tried to remain calm. The doctor diagnosed a scratched cornea and the nurse put some numbing agent on my eye, bringing blessed relief. She then irrigated my eye which returned my vision, but also washed the numbing agent out so I was in pain again. She put ointment in my eye, placed a bandage over it and handed us a bill for $152. I sure was glad that they had at least been extremely pleasant. I was instructed to return the following evening for a re-check and dressing change. We made a pass through the midnight buffet, which looked gorgeous from what I could see, but I was in too much pain to really care, so we left after Ernie took a few pictures.

The following evening we were back on deck eleven enjoying our sushi (I *told* you nothing came between me and my sushi!) and were once again sitting with Tom and Lynn. As we all got up to move inside Lynn grabbed her arm and said it felt as if she had been stung. We looked closely at her arm and realized that she had actually been burned. Thinking someone was on the deck above smoking, we looked up and realized that the smoke stacks were directly overhead. Hmmmmm We went back down to the hospital for my follow-up where my blood pressure was better. Unfortunately my blood sugar was elevated. I know it was because I had just eaten that darned sushi. We mentioned the incident with Lynn's arm and asked if this could have been from the stacks and wondered as well if my eye could have been burned. Ernie mentioned that he thought my eye looked blistered. They did another one of those blidning eye exams (I was prepared this time) and sure enough, it was a burn! This meant that I had to use an extra ointment as well as take an oral antibiotic. My eye was feeling a bit better by then (the nurse had once again put numbing agent in then promptly washed it out) so I was starting to worry about the mounting bill. It turned out that I had apparently been seeing an assistant doctor who explained the situation to the head doctor who happened to drop in while we were there. When he heard about the stacks and the fact that Lynn had been burned at the same time of day, same deck, he voided all charges! We hadn't been asking for this but sure didn't argue. This was just more proof for us that Celebrity Cruise Line is a class act. I'm also convinced that God had a hand in the outcome. Why? Well, we had tried to go down to the hospital earlier than our scheduled time so that we'd have it out of the way. However they had a closed sign up when we got there so we decided to go have our sushi and go back at the appointed time. Lynn got burned and as bad as I felt about that, it made us realize that I had possibly been burned as well. Then, when we went back down at the correct time, the closed sign was still up so we tried the door. They were open all along! Had we gone in when we tried the first time we wouldn't have known to ask about a burn and my bill would not have been voided. See? Prayer does work even when the prayer is simply for relief!

PS. Yes my eye is fine now. I found out that the eye is the quickest healing part of our body and though the pain was so intense it felt as if I'd never be normal again, I actually only had to wear the eye patch for 3 days. That was a lot of fun too. I figured that I may as well have some fun with them so asked Brooke (who is very artisitic) to draw an eye on my patch. She did just that—a really BIG blue eye (I have brown eyes), complete with eye lashes and eye brow. What fun that was! Every time the kids looked at me they freaked out. When I took a nap in my recliner, they felt as if I was still staring at them even with my one eye closed. I just told them to remember that I had my eye on them.

A side bar on Panama City Beach

I have been asked about my very scary experience in Panama City Beach, so thought I'd share with you in case anyone else happens to be burning with curiosity. We lived in Alabama at that time and would occasionally drive to the Panama City/Destin area to swim. We had a pool even then, but everyone else in the family liked going, so I would tag along. I didn't especially like going, even before I had 20 years scared off of my life span, because I hate sand. It had this annoying way of getting up inside my swimsuit and I always felt like ground beef by the time we made the 2 hour trip home.

This particular trip, Ernie, Brooke, Stacie and I had been in the water for a couple of hours. We read in the newspaper that undertows were a real problem and had pulled a couple of swimmers out to their deaths recently. I'm not a strong swimmer (not a swimmer at all really) so was extra careful about staying close to shore while we swam. Ernie had wandered off away from us and called for us to join him. I was about half way to him when he said, "Oh by the way, I'm not touching bottom here". I instantly panicked and at that exact same moment I felt an undertow grab me. I know what it means to go blind with panic now because that's just what I did. I started swimming harder and faster than I ever thought possible and yet was getting absolutely no where. Ernie saw my panic and asked what I was doing and called that I was swimming parallel to the shore. All I knew was that my life was flashing before my eyes and I just knew that I was going to die. Everything was happening so fast that I didn't even think to pray, I just swam for all I was worth. After what felt like hours I finally broke free of the undertow and made my way to shore where I plopped down on the sand, shaking with terror and exhaustion. I refused to as much as stick a toe back in for the rest of the time there and swore I'd never go near the ocean again.

I later found out that I had actually done exactly what you're supposed to do when caught in an undertow. Well sort of. You're not supposed to fight it but you should attempt to swim parallel to shore. Was it instinct that took over? I don't know. Personally I felt as if there was a presence with me and am convinced that my guardian angel was there, giving me the strength and ability to swim as never before nor since. I've only been to visit a beach twice since. The first time was a few years later when we took my twin sister, who had came to visit us. She had never seen the ocean so in a moment of weakness I agreed to go. It was worth it too just to watch her have fun. The last time was in Bermuda and that will last me a lifetime. I figure why tempt fate? My guardian angel may be busy next time.

History in the making

I have told Ernie that we could be rich if I could only package and sell him. I may be the first person in history to go on a cruise, eat like a pig and still lose 2.5 pounds. Most people gain so much that they have to diet afterwards and no wonder with the fabulous foods served. Ernie however, has a sure fire plan to assure you don't gain and it's really quite simple; Walk till you're ready to drop. We walked on board ship taking the stairs every chance he got. Our stateroom was on deck eight and the ship had twelve decks so there were lots of stairs. I hate elevators so usually agreed to take the stairs if there was no one else waiting on the elevator. I have this weird little hang-up. I figure if there are others on it then it won't get stuck between floors. Then again, we frequently had the opposite problem. Some people would try to cram themselves into an already nearly full car to the point that you couldn't have paid me to get on. I was afraid it would plummet to the bottom of the ship. It was truly amazing to see. There were at least two elevator banks on each deck, but people acted as if this would be their one chance to get on and many were only going one deck. I spent a lot of time huffing and puffing up and down the stairs but felt proud of myself too. Our first stop in port was at St. George and we were anxious to tour. We learned that St. George isn't a town like Hamilton but is more of a colony and at one time was protected by Fort St. Katherine. There is also an old church I that we wanted to see. St. George was to be the capital of Bermuda but those plans changed and the church was abandoned, with a new one built in the new capital.

We (I) struggled up a long hill to get to it and once there, figured we would turn around and head back to the shopping district. I figured wrong. Ernie wanted to keep walking since we knew that the Fort was "near by". I didn't want to appear to be a whiny baby so agreed though I was definitely whining on the inside. Who knew that an island would have so many hills? Bermuda was formed by a volcano eruption long, long ago and apparently it cooled before it could develop a lot of flat ground. We rounded a corner at one point to see a beautiful beach called "Tobacco Bay". What a welcome sight too since I was really thirsty. We had heard that some places liked to take advantage of tourists but this stand wasn't gouging on the price, not that I would have complained at that point. It wasn't long before I was complaining though. I had worn a brand new, never worn before pair of tennis shoes and my feet were not happy with me. We left the beach with every intention of going back to swim later (not on my list of must do's though, trust me). On we trudged around the up a hill and around a bend and there before us was the highest hill I'd ever contemplated walking up. On top sat Fort St. Katherine and Ernie had every intention of walking up to it! I was silently asking God for mercy and endurance. I hate feeling like an old party pooper (and just plain old) so onward I marched. A tour bus passed us as we neared the top and I shot looks of pure green eyed envy at them as they drove by. We had made it though and I was proud of that fact. I wasn't sure I'd survive the trip back down but I had reached the top! We then tramped all over the fort, up and down dark corridors and out to the sea walls where we looked down at the parrot fish feeding in the rocks below us. I had hoped that it being built of rocks that the fort would be cool inside but that was merely a dream. It was hot inside! We took a few minutes break to watch an interesting video on the history of the fort. I wouldn't have cared if it was brain numbing boring since it meant we got to sit for a few minutes. Finally, after about an hour of history lessons we headed back down the hill. My poor feet were really starting to kick up a fuss by this point and still had to carry me back to the ship. We walked and we walked then we walked some more. By the time we made it part way up the last big hill I was beginning to wonder if I would survive. When I spotted the benches around a golf course I suddenly had hope that I could hang on and so I did. I pushed on until we got to the tree where I collapsed. Two older couples who were sitting there resting as well laughed at me. Had I had enough breath in me I would have told them that they should be impressed, that I had just survived a forced march to the top of God Have Mercy Hill. Ernie was starting to get a little concerned by this point but I bravely told him that I could make it while secretly doubting that I would.

Make it we did though (obviously) and when we looked at the map, figured out that we had just walked 4.5 miles round trip. That's the most that I've walked in many, many years. We used to go on Volks Marches in Germany but I was a much younger person then. How I miss my youth. We never did make it back to that beach. Though it was only half the distance, I simply couldn't face the thought of that trip again. After lunch and a change of shoes we did go shopping in town. My feet continued to complain even after the shoe swap but I can ignore them for something as important as shopping.

Man the lifeboats!

One last memory that I must share before it's completely forgotten occurred just minutes after we boarded ship. We were shown to our cabin as we boarded at 4PM. Within minutes an announcement was made that all passengers were to grab their life vests (which were stowed in our closets) and head to one of the lounges for a life boat drill at 4:30 PM. We were instructed to wear the vests to the drill and that further instructions would be provided at that time. I'm not all that crazy about water outside my shower or back yard pool and was slightly nervous about being set adrift on a ship in the middle of a vast ocean so was pretty anxious at the thought of a life boat drill. They sure didn't show those on Love Boat! Since it was too late to back out on going I decided to follow instructions and donned the vest. I got that silly thing on and told Ernie that if the boat sank I didn't have a lot of faith in the vest keeping me above water and in fact I was concerned that it would help drown me. Talk about uncomfortable and awkward! As we walked into the lounge a staff member coughed slightly and smiling at me said, "Uh miss, you have your vest on backwards". He then proceeded to help me put it on correctly. It's a good thing I was distracted by my nervousness or I might have jumped overboard and started swimming for shore right then and there out of sheer embarrassment. Of course I'd have allowed him to correct my vest first. Shortly after he got me settled into my vest properly, we were all herded according to our deck level to our assigned life boat decks where we spent all of two minutes being instructed in what to do in the event of an emergency. We were then released to enjoy the rest of our cruise. I'm so pleased to report that we were not required to have another drill for the duration of the cruise and best of all, never had to climb into a life boat. In fact, I ignored them every time we walked anywhere near them. Yes I tend to live my life in a state of denial. Not surprisingly the ostrich is one of my favorite animals.

In closing I want to urge you one last time to go on at least one cruise in your life time. Being treated like royalty is something that must be experienced since there are simply no words to describe it accurately.

Bon voyage'!

2 Chronicles 9:21 The king had a fleet of trading ships manned by Hiram's men. Once every three years it returned, carrying gold, silver and ivory, and apes and baboons.

Curly, Moe, And Larry

Most people know from my story about 911 to *not* ask me for assistance in an emergency. Now you can add "don't ask Jayne for advice on where to get a haircut" to the list. Why you ask? It's a sad story but I'll try to get myself together long enough to explain.

Ernie wass going to Atlanta for a training conference in a couple of days and he needed to get a haircut before going since his hair was getting very shaggy. Normally he gets his haircut at Ft. Lee, Virginia when we go up every 4 to 6 weeks but we just didn't feel like making the hour long trip this weekend. Where to go? Hmmmmmm "We need to go to Wal Mart for coffee and creamer anyway" say's I, "Why don't you go to the hair salon there?" "OK" he trustingly responds, "Let's just do that."

BIG mistake.

We walk in and the very sleepy girl at the counter checks him in by asking "Do you want clippers or scissors?" We should have run away then. He jokingly tells her that she's the expert, that's her decision. He then explains that he gets a military style cut with tapered sides, short on top and off the ears. We missed our final opportunity to *run as fast as we could in the opposite direction* when she asked, "What does tapered mean?"

I had an exchange to take care of so told him I'd return after that. I stood in line for several minutes and expected him to be about done by the time I returned.

Oh my sweet Lord......

The girl has (and I kid you not) shaved the back side of his hair and has a fantastic bowl cut going. My mouth dropped open and when I looked at him I saw murder in his eyes. I just sat down and started giggling. The further she went with it the harder time I had not falling in the floor laughing. Ernie starts to make subtle faces at me and when I see him make a shooing gesture aimed at me with his hand in his lap I had to get up and leave. I just know he would have gone for my throat had he seen me come apart, so I ran out. I called Stacie nearly in tears from laughing at this point and told her if her dad comes home without me, then he's killed me and she needs to make sure the police ask him where he's dumped my body. I start to worry that she may help him hide it when instead of laughing with me says "I can't BELIEVE that you took him to a Wal Mart hair salon! Don't you remember me telling you about (her friend) Srav's layered haircut where they cut one layer all the way around her head?!" (Laughing so hard now I'm crying) Hey, I didn't FORCE him to go.

I prayed hard between gasps of laughter that she would somehow make it come out OK and she did...well... sort of. He no longer has a bowl cut when all is said and done but does have a bad and very choppy look to the sides, and I'm going to carry the image of my very conservative, handsome, hunky, bearded husband in a bowl cut for the rest of my life.

As he walked out he said "I'm never asking you for advice again and from now on I only get my hair cut at Ft. Lee." Then he mumbled something about her asking "What does tapering mean?" and that he should have gotten up and left right then.

Pardon me now—I've laughed so hard that I'm exhausted. I need a nap.

Follow-up....

It occurred to me that my story of Ernie's haircut may have sounded as if I did this on purpose. NO WAY! I adore my husband of over 24 years as much (more) the day we married. I love the way he looks with a great haircut or shaggy. I just wasn't thinking when I suggested the discount haircutters. However this doesn't stop me from having some fun with it. I still can't look at him without giggling. Apparently he hasn't looked in a mirror because he'll look puzzled and ask "What??" when he catches me.

Mistie stopped by with the kids on their way to the Rocky Mount Children's Museum that same afternoon and Jarod was proudly telling me that he had "new hair". (His mom had spiked it) I told him he'd better not tell his Bapa or he'd be jealous.

Sincerely I didn't do this to him on purpose but I will forever enjoy the memory of my dear husband looking just like a bearded version of Moe ooooooooooooooooeehohohoh..ahahahahahahahahahaha

Jayne (just call me Curly)

Matthew 10: 30-31 And even the very hairs of your head are all numbered. 31So don't be afraid; you are worth more than many sparrows.

Damn Dam!!

We are all familiar with the term "ignorance is bliss" and I'm here to tell you it is, or was. Middle daughter Brooke has stolen my bliss. Sometimes it just doesn't pay to have family who works in the public sector.

Brooke, oldest daughter Mistie and I were out driving around town looking at houses after lunch at Pizza Inn a while back, having a blissful time when Brooke oh-so-casually mentioned something that she learned at work; that we (Roanoke Rapids) are smack in the middle of two dams and that if one of them ever broke we'd be under water within five minutes. What?! We live not only near one but TWO dams? Dam! I'm a nervous wreck now and my stomach has been tied in knots ever since she oh-so-casually mentioned this little fact to us. She even thinks my reaction is funny. I've told her if I wake up in a cold sweat at night that I'm dragging her out of bed to sit up with me. Of course I'll first have to make sure it isn't cold water lapping at my bed that woke me.

Since we were in the general vicinity of one of these dam dams when she informed me of this terrifying fact, she asked if I wanted to see it. At first I was afraid to go. After all I want to be as far away as possible when—if it breaks so that I can get a head start running. Then I decided it may make me feel better seeing it up close. It didn't. That dam looks so flimsy! It's not very impressive and sort of small. It scares me to think that this short, somewhat narrow wall is all that's keeping us dry. I've already decided that if we enter a heavy rain period I'm heading north away from the dams. I won't take I-95 though. They have those tunnels in Baltimore that run under the water. I used to despise going through those things when we lived up there. I was always sure the walls would crack and water would rush in to wash us away just as we got to the middle. The tunnels are kind of dark so it's difficult to watch for trickles of water but trust me; it's not impossible.

Brooke is very relaxed about the idea of being caught between two dams and soon tried to change subjects on us by asking if I know what she wants for Christmas. (This is assuming a dam doesn't break and wash us away before then.) I said, "Yes, a swim vest!"

Our real estate agent told us all about the two lakes and one river around here. He also told us all about the canal walking trails around the river and a little history of the area. He did not however, mention the two dams or that this entire area could one day be one giant swimming hole. I wonder if I can go back and sue him for misrepresenting the area?

There are some beautiful houses that are built right on the lake. As we drove around the area I found myself tsk tsking those foolish folks working around their yards in obvious blissful ignorance. I'll bet if I sent Brooke to have an oh-so-casual chat with them that you could pick up some lakefront property really cheap shortly after.

Mistie thinks I'm an alarmist but I think I've come up with a perfect solution to my problem. I want to buy a boat. We can save money though since we won't need a boat trailer. We can just set the boat in the front yard and jump in at the first sign of rising waters. We could even make it a houseboat since if this place goes under, we're going to need a place to live.

I miss my bliss.

Genesis 7:7 And Noah and his sons and his wife and his sons' wives entered the ark to escape the waters of the flood.

Do You Hear That Sound?

While still in the process of unpacking from our move to our home in Roanoke Rapids recently, Ernie and I took the grandkids and made the trip to Ft. Lee, Virginia to restock the larder and buy household supplies. As it turned out we had no need of radio due to the cacophonous chorus in the backseat. Ernie and I were (and are) thankful this is only an hour's drive.

Alexis (with a slight whine) "How much further do we have to go?" Irene (with a lilting whine) "I'm coooold, I want a blaaaaanket!" I can't be certain since it has been many years since I spoke baby wah myself but I feel confident that Jarod was saying "I can't believe you people woke me up early to poke a few spoons of cereal at my face, dressed me and stuck me in this stupid car seat! You KNOW how much I hate this car seat! Oh and by the way did either of you supposed grown-ups think to bring some COOKIES with you?!"

No, we didn't think about cookies but thankfully some were found in a baggy in a seat pocket. I did fortunately however, remember the drinks.

As for the rest of the day I spent it emptying a seemingly endless supply of moving boxes. I started to suspect someone was going behind me and refilling them. That's the only rational way to explain why there were so many left. Have I mentioned before that we just have TOO MUCH STUFF?

Calgon take me awaaaaaay!!!!!!!!!!!!

Isaiah 13:4 Listen, a noise on the mountains, like that of a great multitude! Listen, an uproar among the kingdoms, like nations massing together!

Doi!!! (Or How To Have Fun With A Telemarketer)

As you surely know by now, it's a rare day that our house is dull. Just look at Friday evening when the Jimmy blew a head gasket. At least we hope that's all it is and not a cracked cylinder head......Then Saturday morning our 41/2 year old 51 inch TV finally quit. It has been going in and out for months, in spite of spending quite a bit of money for repairs. We were told after the last one that if it goes again, just dump it. Coincidentally we decided to go ahead and take the plunge and replace it that same morning. We didn't realize when we placed the order on-line that it was pretty much gone so we're glad we ordered the new one. The new TV should be here in about a week. Personally? I think the Jimmy and the TV are somehow communicating but that's a whole different story.

So is it any wonder that when an opportunity for some fun presents itself, I jump on it like a duck on a June bug? You may recall that I've had fun with telemarketers in the past when I allowed Jarod to handle the call while playing a game on the computer and he informed them "Nana can't talk right now, she's hunting dinosaurs! Ah oh I hear one coming!" He was so disappointed when they quickly hung up. Since then he's lost interest in "those calls" because they all hang up pretty quick when they hear his cute little voice. Anyway back to my story. Mistie was here this afternoon talking to me while I was working on my freebie newsletter when the phone rang. Caller ID showed "Unknown Caller" so I ignored it. We signed up with the National Do-Not-Call Registry but still receive several political and not-for-profit solicitation calls (which are immune to the DNC registry rules). Within minutes the phone rings again and ID shows "Unknown Caller" once again so I picked the phone up and just laid it on the desk. I could hear the caller saying, "Hello? Helloooo" followed by whistling before they finally hang up. I went back to my newsletter when the phone rings AGAIN! Man this person is persistent. So I pick the phone up and though I'm holding it away from my ear, hear the guy talking to someone there with him and he say's "I can hear the line pick up but they seem to be talking on another line." I am irritated but this tickles me so of course laugh. I hear him again say "Hello?" before I hang up on him. AGAIN the phone rings within minutes! I hear him whistling into the phone then he blows into the mouthpiece. I tell Mistie that this is getting old so I blow BACK into the phone, laugh at him and hang up. Back to my newsletter, grumbling and grouching I go. Mistie makes the excellent suggestion that if he calls again to say something such as "411, what city please?" to really mess with him. I like that suggestion and almost hope he calls back.

Five minutes later he does. Fighting hard to contain myself I answer, "411, what city please?" Thunk—HE hangs up on ME! I am really laughing now and tell Mistie that was so much fun that I hope he calls back again. She tells me if he does that I should answer "911, what's the address of your emergency?" Ooooooh I really like that but tell her she'd have to handle that call since I'd surely mess that one up. Gee I hope he calls back!

Three minutes later he does just that. Oh boy, oh boy! I hand the phone to Mistie who in her best 911 telecommunicator voice say's "911, what's the address of your emergency?" Of course the effect is ruined since Jarod has decided that he wants in on the fun and stands in front of her hollering while Alexis loudly tries to drag him away. I am laughing so hard that I'm nearly in tears when I hear her say......."you're calling about a TV that who ordered?" Say WHAT???!!!! He's calling about the TV???????!!!! Oh now I'm laughing so hard I can hardly talk as she hands me the phone.......

Yes as it turns out it was a young man with the TV people, wanting to confirm our order before they shipped it. I can barely stay straight as he reads the information to me. I have to get his number to call him back since I need to confirm something with Ernie then I take the plunge and apologize. I explained that all of his calls showed up as "Unknown Caller" and that though we're on the do-not-call list, we still get lots of unsolicited calls, and we tend to ignore those but he was just so persistent. He just laughs and say's he understands perfectly, not to worry about it. I promise to call back after speaking with Ernie and hang up. I confirmed everything with Ernie then called him back. I was still laughing when he answered and I asked him if he was going to send us a "build it yourself kit" TV and if he was going to personally deliver it, if so then I wasn't going to be here. He told me that he'd been told he was funny looking many times but never funny and that I had made his day! Oh and UPS will be delivering.

Brooke called while all of this was going on and when told what happened said, "You should be embarrassed to even tell anyone." Who ME???? No way!!!!!!!! She should know me better than that by now. If you can't laugh at yourself then you have no right to laugh at others. HAHAHAHAHAHAHAHAHAHAHAHAHAHAHAHAHAHAHA

Deuteronomy 2:19 When you come to the Ammonites, do not harass them or provoke them to war, for I will not give you possession of any land belonging to the Ammonites. I have given it as a possession to the descendants of Lot."

Driver's License And Registration Please Ma'am

I've told you in the past about the usually hysterical things that our little blonde pulls. She keeps us entertained but sometimes the things she does aren't funny until *after* the fact.

Irene and Alexis each have pretty, pink Barbie Jeeps that they enjoy driving all over our large yard. Many times, one will drive while the other rides shotgun or even on the hood waving like some beauty queen in a parade. Alexis is an excellent driver though she recently has problems staying out of the street. I've warned her that I'm going to yank her battery if she strays again. Irene on the other hand drives like, well like a blonde. We have stood and watched her drive straight into a tree! Fortunately for her and the tree, she can't go terribly fast in this Jeep so both survived the collision.

Earlier this week, we had some beautiful afternoon weather so the girls went outside to play. I had recently charged their car batteries so they jumped in and started to chase each other around the yard. Jarod caught site of them in the yard and insisted by way of baby language on going outside too. He was fascinated with Irene and her Jeep so I strapped him in and told her to take it slow and easy. Irene giggled non-stop and Jarod seemed to enjoy it too, though he wouldn't take his eyes off of Nana. A neighbor up the street was out taking a stroll and chatted about all the fun taking place in the yard as she went by. It was such a pretty afternoon but the fun part was about to change. Alexis eventually decided she wanted to ride with Irene too so I took Jarod out and set him in the driveway where he stood watching. Alexis was getting ready to climb in when Irene, for reasons known only to her, slammed the gear into reverse and hit the "gas" pedal. I heard Jarod scream and disappear in one fell swoop. I jumped up from the chair where I had been sitting and reading and ran over to the accident scene. It was pure pandemonium from there. Irene was screaming and crying, "It wasn't my fault! I didn't know!" I was screaming back saying things such as "Yes it is your fault, you should have looked! Where's Jarod??!! Get in the house! WHERE is Jarod?!" He had completely disappeared so I picked the back of the Jeep up and there he lay, with the Jeep pinning him down. I grabbed him up while Irene sobbed and wailed on. My neighbor had walked up the road out of sight just before the vehicle/pedestrian accident occurred and must have thought we had suddenly lost our minds. I really need to call and explain what happened and assure her that mind loss is a frequent event in our house.

Thankfully Jarod is unhurt and only has a small mark on a cheek. Irene has recovered and in retrospect, it's quite funny. It was so bizarre the way he disappeared; standing there one second and gone from site the next.

Thankfully too, being a baby Jarod has a short memory and won't remember being run over by his cousin in the pretty, pink Jeep. Just to be sure he's safe with her from now on though, I may put pillows on the bumpers and the underside.

Psalm 32:7 You are my hiding place; you will protect me from trouble and surround me with songs of deliverance. Selah

My husband and I tried to be good parents. We tried to prepare them to face difficulties and always strove to be honest with them. Like all parents though we failed miserably at times. At times it was due to human frailty and other times just due to sheer exuberance and enthusiasm....

Eeeeeeeeeeeeeeeeeeee!!!

Our "baby" Stacie turned 21 years old this past week. It boggles the mind to think about her and all of her friends being this old. It seems like yesterday that they all used to travel together between home and ASMS in Mobile, a boarding school for genius types that they attended during their junior and senior high school years. Of course they were all very mature for their ages, even then. Those two years are still so fresh in my memory that it feels like we should still be there.

Stacie hosted a birthday party this last weekend and many of those same friends went to Atlanta to celebrate with her. Tina and Audrey, two of her best friends, stayed for a couple of extra days so that they could all go to Six Flags over Georgia for a "girls' day out" today. Stacie bought a season pass at the beginning of summer and has gone a couple of other times already so the pass has paid for itself. They are all excited and looking forward to going which is saying a lot for Stacie, for you see she has some bad memories of amusement parks and roller coasters.

We were stationed in Maryland for 4 years, having moved there when Stacie was 5 years old. Ernie went to attend military school in Kansas just two weeks after we arrived and was gone for months. He eventually moved closer to home and was attending school at Ft. Lee, Virginia just four hours away, so he was able to come home every weekend but two—once when he went on a "field trip" with his class to Civil War sites and the other time was when he asked us to go to him. King's Dominion is just a short drive from Ft. Lee so we traveled to him so that he could treat us to a day of amusement. I loaded up the kids and a friend of Mistie's on a Friday afternoon and off we went in high spirits. Little did I know that before the weekend was over, Stacie would have reason to bitterly resent us for many years to come all while providing me with years of giggles from the memory.

When we arrived Mistie and her friend took off, arranging to meet up with us later. Ernie and I took Brooke and Stacie and started looking for rides. I sincerely don't enjoy being scared enough to nearly pee my pants so I stayed on the ground with Stacie for many while Ernie and Brooke looked for the wilder rides. The scarier the better is their motto. We did manage to take Stacie on some milder rides. At one point Brooke stayed with her while Ernie and I went for a spin on a roller Coaster named "The Rebel Yell". This was totally out of character for me since as I said I don't enjoy walking around in wet underwear. Caught up in the excitement I agreed to ride.

I LOVED it! It was sort of like flirting with death as we crested that hill and started zooming about a million miles an hour over the rails. I was terrified and having the time of my life at the same time. We got to the end and I said, "Let's do that again!" The line was short so that's exactly what we did and once again I was thrilled to the core. When the ride was over we found Brooke and Stacie waiting on us so I said, "Let's go again!" In our excitement to go we forgot to warn Stacie that the ride would be a little wilder than she was accustomed to-that she may in fact be cheating death in mere moments. Brooke climbed into the lead car with me and Stacie got in behind us with her dad.

After what seemed like a wait of years, the cars finally started moving forward with a lurch. Brooke and I were having a ball as we laughed and put our arms in the air. With excruciating anticipation we slowly approached the top of the hill—then we started to scream as we crested and started down.   Screaming from behind us was suddenly drowning our screams out. We managed to turn and see Stacie; eyes bugging and mouth wide open screaming her lungs out. Being the rotten mother I am (My kids tell me I would win Worst Mother of the Year award if there ever was one) I started laughing and laughed all the way to the end of the ride and in fact for the rest of the day. I was laughing hysterically and would have been in danger of falling out had we not had a safety bar holding us in. ALL we could see was huge eyes, a wide "O" for a mouth, teeth and a uvula. (You know, that dangly thing in the back of your throat) She was furious with us when we finally reached the end. After that we couldn't even coax her onto the tamer kiddy rides. Huh uh—no way, she didn't trust us any more, not even for a carrousel ride.

I went back to work that following Monday still laughing and snorting as I told the story and to this day I *still* have fits of giggles thinking about it. She has yet to forgive us and probably never will.

Oh my precious memories, how they linger. I hope you had a marvelous time at 6 Flags today Stacie!!! (Giggle, snort)

Ephesians 6:4 Fathers, do not exasperate your children; instead, bring them up in the training and instruction of the Lord.

Falling Stars

It is not even 5:30 in the morning and here I sit writing. Sigh...This morning was supposed to host the spectacular meteor shower that newspaper and local meteorologists spoke of for days. We aren't supposed to see another like it until 2099! I was so excited that I called my sister in Arkansas and told her and her kids to "set your alarms so you won't miss this spectacular show!" Ernie set our alarm for 4:45 (that's AM). When it went off I leaped out of bed, grabbed my warm robe and woke Irene up so she could (in her words), "Count the stars and watch them fall". I wrapped her in a blanket and outside we went to catch this stellar performance. Our local meteorologist said we could expect hundreds every 15 minutes so we stared up in bleary eyed but wondrous anticipation........and we waited. Then we waited some more. Finally we saw one that was so fast we almost missed it. Ernie joined us at this point, just in time to see another one zipping past. Shortly we saw one that was so bright it was like a photoflash, and left a trail for several seconds. These were followed by a few more, some so fast we almost wondered if it was an illusion.

It didn't take long before Irene got bored and wanted to go back inside, until I reminded her that she wanted to count the stars. She perked up, started counting and finally announced, "There are too many to count". She catches on quickly. However we certainly did not see hundreds or even dozens in the fifteen minutes we stood in our yard with our heads turned heavenward. Still it was worth getting up just to see the few we did. It reminded me of the very first falling star I saw as a child while standing in my front yard and the feeling of pure wonder that has never left me.

Chilled, we went back inside a little after 5:00. Miss Irene declared she was going to watch cartoons, a notion I quickly vetoed when I told her we were going back to bed. She reluctantly went with us and crawled into bed with us, where she never quit moving or making noise. Finally after about 10 minutes of this she rolled over on her side and I thought she was finally going to settle down and go back to sleep for an hour or so. Instead she leaned on one hand and tapped me on the shoulder proclaiming, "The sun is up!" and then so was I along with her. And here I sit writing about our falling stars while Irene watches her cartoons............

Genesis 15:5 He took him outside and said, "Look up at the heavens and count the stars—if indeed you can count them."

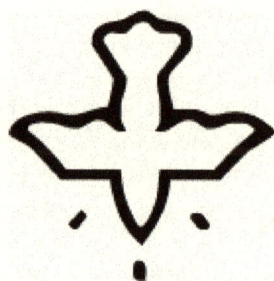

Fishy Foster Family

We suddenly found ourselves being fishy foster parents at the end of Stacie's last freshmen semester at Wake Forest. Colleen, one of her dorm friends was flying home to New York and couldn't take the fish with her. So Uti and Spleen (Colleen named them, NOT us!) came to live with us for the summer. Unfortunately, Spleen has gone on to fish heaven. It's a tragic story that I will share in a moment. Uti, a gorgeous Beta, is here to stay permanently. If Colleen wants custody again she will have to take us to family court first. We are mad about this silly fish and will never ever give him up.

Spleen was a Danio and according to the nature of this breed, was very hyper. He would speed swim all over the bowl and jump up in the air. Brooke took pity on them because they lived in a plastic fish bowl. And invested in a tank with filter and bubbler bar. They were so much happier! I decided to be nice one day and clean the tank since the water was a little cloudy so moved both fish into a large bowl, while I cleaned their home. Unfortunately Spleen engaged in some of his fishy acrobatics and jumped out of the bowl, landing in my dining room floor. Even more unfortunate, he wasn't found until he was dead and dry. Worst of all, *Irene* found him. She came running hysterically calling, "Nana! There's a fish in the floor!" It was obvious mouth to mouth wasn't going to bring him back even if I had been inclined to try it, so I grabbed a napkin and tossed him in the trash can. Irene, who has always talked too much, told everyone who would listen about finding the dead fish and that "Nana threw him away!"

Brooke decided Uti looked lonely so she visited the fish store and bought some new fish. We now have a large Danio by the name of Big Old Bully Boy and two zebra Danios, whom he bullies, hence the name. She also bought some cute little neons, one of whom is named Leon (we just call the rest Leon's freonds) and an algae eater. Irene named her Ms. Fish Nagy. I don't know what is in the food she buys, but these fish are all getting huge! Ms. Fish is scary big. Fortunately for the rest of the fish though, she only sucks on algae.

Uti is hands down our favorite fish. We had no idea fish could have personalities! All are fun and do funny things but he is one hysterical fish to watch. He loves to play in the bubbles from the bubbler bar, scooting down behind it, relaxing then allowing the bubbles to carry him to the top. He does this repeatedly, much to our endless delight. He also hides in the neon pink cave that Brooke added, swimming out to chase Big Old Bully Boy. He isn't aggressive; he's just having fun. The absolutely funniest thing he does though sends me into fits of laughing. He will be swimming along, stop dead in his path, lean on the cave or the wall of the tank, and just lie there. It looks for all the world as if he's gone into a dead faint. I asked Brooke if she thinks he could be narcoleptic.

Brooke is totally enthralled with these fish, and read that a water lily is a good thing to have in a fish tank, so she bought one and set it in the corner. Uti has decided this is his very best friend in the world. He LOVES this plant. He swims into the roots, tangles himself all up, and just lies there. When she takes it out, as she did recently, he is almost despondent. She took pity on him tonight and put it back in and we watched to see what he would do. I swear he had a huge smile on his face when he spotted it. Last time we looked he was swimming in and out of the roots, caressing and being caressed. I find it nearly impossible to eat fish now and may never go fishing again.

This story was written some while before our wonderfully entertaining Uti was found dead in the aquarium. That was a seriously sad day in the Nagy household and we all still miss our little friend.

1 Kings 4:33 He described plant life, from the cedar of Lebanon to the hyssop that grows out of walls. He also taught about animals and birds, reptiles and fish.

Flight Of A Chicken

Ask any chicken—flying is unnatural. God didn't design us to fly. After all, we're *chickens*.

My dad passed away last week and we had to get home quickly. My husband decided the best route for us to get there for the funeral was by air and though I hated the idea, had to agree. We would fly out of Raleigh, choosing to go through Atlanta rather than Memphis, and he quickly made the arrangements before I could turn cowardly and insist we drive.

We got a late start out of Raleigh (our plane was coming from San Francisco and diverted to Las Vegas for a medical emergency) which didn't hurt my feelings in the least. The longer I could put it off, the longer I could breathe without nearly hyperventilating. The nervousness wasn't helped by the fact that good old Delta, who had been informed when we made the reservations that this was a bereavement flight, had assigned us different seat rows. It was an easily fixed snafu but did nothing to build my confidence in them.

Shortly before take-off the flight attendants started their pre-flight instructions into terror. I hate those oh-so-calm lectures on how to place an oxygen mask and how your seat is a flotation device in the event of the need to land in water. This time they didn't even do it personally—it was all done via overhead drop down video screens every few seats. I wasn't sure whether to view this as confident arrogance or plain indifference.

All too soon we were taxiing down the runway so I grabbed Ernie's hand (normally I'd grab his nearest knee but he was working a crossword puzzle in the newspaper he'd bought in the airport so his knee was blocked) and started chanting "Oh Jesus! Oh Jesus! Oh Jesus!" over and over and over, unable to stop the tears that gathered in the corners of my eyes. I was very glad to see him so relaxed because had he been nervous they wouldn't have been able to drag me on board with a team of horses.

Taking off is the WORST part of flying for me. I absolutely hate it. I try to keep my eyes closed and pray like crazy. Just as I started to relax and ease up, the plane would shake. How anyone can enjoy flying will remain one of life's biggest mysteries for me. I finally felt Ernie wriggling his fingers and realized that I'd been squeezing awfully hard. He was still flexing them when we landed in Atlanta fifty three minutes later.

It finally occurred to me to picture Jesus in the cockpit. Before we ever got on this plane, I had envisioned every passenger in a "Jesus Bubble" and wrapped the crew and entire plane in one as we boarded and imagined angels all around the wings. So, it was natural to visualize Jesus in the cockpit—one hand on the pilot's shoulder and the other on the cockpit panel. He stooped ever so slightly to see out the cockpit window. As I chanted, He turned to look at me with a smile, motioned for me to pipe down then turned back to the window. I had started to calm down when we hit a small turbulence pocket. He turned to me once again, still with a smile and once again motioned for me to remain calm. I saw Him turn back to the view outside the window and note that *He* at least was having a ball flying.

Thank you Jesus—we arrived in Atlanta safe and sound. One flight down and only three more to go. As we waited for our connecting flight to Arkansas, angels and Jesus Bubbles abounded as I continued to pray for the safe travels of those around me.

The only fun part of the trip was the train ride from Concourse A to C in the Atlanta airport. I always feel as if I'm going to fall flat and in fact wondered out loud just how many people do manage to fall in a day as that thing takes off at a break neck speed and slams to a fast stop. I think the drivers of those things may well be required to have sadistic streaks. If they can hear the comments and sounds as they take off and stop, then they must surely also get more than a few chuckles a day.

We prepared to board in Atlanta only to find that reliable Delta had done it again—assigned us separate seating in rows 1A and 2A. This was a much smaller jet in a much smaller terminal area, and the desk attendant had no way to change it for us so we had to wait until we were aboard to arrange the seating. Thankfully it wasn't long before the man who was due to sit by me arrived and graciously agreed to switch with Ernie. I'm very thankful; I'd really have hated being responsible for maiming the hand of a total stranger during take-off.

This placed us in the very first seats of the plane where I was able to see straight into the cockpit, and listen in as the stewardess and pilots chatted and joked. I wanted to tell them that this flying is serious business so please act like it but decided that would be rude. Instead, I told Jesus that this is a very full flight and remind Him to stay close by the pilots and He, always faithful, did just that.

As mentioned, this is a very small jet so we had only one stewardess. I glanced at her nametag and saw her name is Arlene. I thought this is a very old fashioned name for such a young (inexperienced?!) and pretty girl. She has piercing, light blue eyes and a calm demeanor. I watched her as she worked, not two feet away from me. I knew she had seen how nervous I was since she kept stealing looks over her shoulder at me. I wanted to reassure her that I wouldn't be trouble since I was pretty much paralyzed by fear, but we started to roll and she seated herself in a fold down chair, facing me. Every time we rolled and stopped, I closed my eyes and silently prayed a little prayer. After several minutes of this she got up, took a couple of pills from her purse and tossed them back with a quick drink, all while glancing back over her shoulder at me and shaking her head. I would have laughed if I weren't so darned scared.

It's finally our turn for take off and once again I was squeezing hard enough to crush bones. Fortunately for Ernie this time I was able to grab his knee so couldn't get a grip strong enough to break it. The passenger who traded seats was now behind us and he sneezed. It's then I realized that I've seen too many movies because it flashed through my fear fogged brain that this is how scary-stuck-in-the-air-refused-landing-due-to-mutant-disease-airplane movies start.

This thought was soon sidetracked by the pilot's announcement of our 28,000 foot cruising elevation. You know, I WISH they didn't all feel compelled to share this information. This is simply not need to know info! Truly, if they really feel they must communicate then they should offer some sort of warning in advance so that us chickens on board can fluffle our ear feathers to cover our ears or stick our chicken fingers (and you thought they were man made foods) in our ear holes. I resisted the urge to loudly sing "lalalalalalalalalala!!" as he made his announcement. I had already attracted enough attention and though it would mean no more flying, I really didn't want two guys with a funny white jacket waiting on me when we landed.

Ditto all of the strange noises. Someone could make a fortune if they would invent sound proofing that blocks the weird noises that all airplanes seem to make while zipping along at hundreds of miles per hour, thousands of feet in the air. I was ever so thankful that Ernie is a seasoned traveler and can offer reassurances that it's nothing more than the landing gear going down, even if he's making it up. I've always read to keep an eye on the flight crew—you'll know it's time to panic if/when you see them panic which probably explains the pained smile that I always seem to observe pasted on the faces of every flight attendant that I've ever flown with. Imagine all those chickens on board watching your every move.

I had taken a very good book with me so tried to concentrate on reading in between scary announcements and noises. However, the flight seemed to go on forever. I was starting to worry just a bit that the pilots were lost or, just like out of some airplane horror movie, had decided to fly until we run out of fuel when they *finally* announced our approach into Northwest Arkansas Regional and we started our descent. I actually almost enjoy landing and smiled as the wheels touched down. I was safely on the ground for the next two full days. I was happy to be there, even if it was under sad circumstances.

Two flights down, two to go and I fully intended to not think about it at all in the interim......All too soon it was time to board another plane for the first leg of our trip home. Once again it was a small jet as we left Arkansas for our flight back to Atlanta and as before, we have only one stewardess. I glanced at her name tag (It helps to know the name of the person you're watching like a hawk for signs of panic) and think how odd it was to see yet another attendant with the name of Arlene. I wondered what the odds are. Then I realized the tag said not Arlene but AIRLINE employee. I thought this was too funny and laughed at myself, which helped to relax me a bit. Unfortunately this feeling didn't last long as the now nameless attendant (I forgot to take notice of her actual name) announced that they would be holding a few of the smaller checked bags up for owners to identify as the weight distribution was too heavy for the underside so they needed to place three bags up top. Too HEAVY???!! And they're simply going to redistribute to the inside of the plane??!! I seriously wanted to jump up and run from the plane but due to the bags and owners blocking the aisle, I was stuck. Thank you God—we made it to Atlanta just fine in spite of people who insisted on packing fat bags. I did notice that you decided to have some fun and shook me up just a little with some quite unnecessary turbulence. Gee thanks.

At last, three planes down and one to go as we boarded the plane bound for Raleigh. Literally we were at the back of the bus—the next to the last row of seats. In fact one of the engines was right outside of Ernie's window. I'm not crazy about the view from the air but this is ridiculous. Ugh Ugh Ugh. At least Delta finally got it right and gave us seats together—albeit in the nursery section. We were stuck in the back with three families, each with three kids. I expected a very noisy and even aggravating flight, but was pleasantly surprised that all nine children were very well behaved. One family had a little girl who appeared to be about two years old and though well behaved in the terminal, had me worried that she would fuss during take-off. Bless fully, she fell asleep before we even started to taxi and slept until landing.

This jet was so big that we had a couple of flight attendants just for our section and one of them resembled Sandra Bullock, one of my favorite Hollywood stars. I didn't catch her name but suspect the odds are that it's not Arlene. (Nor for that matter Sandra)

We arrive in Raleigh a few minutes late due to being so far back in the line for take-off from Atlanta but otherwise the flight went smoothly. I started to feel like a pro at this. I still grabbed Ernie's knee, but without squeezing. We had changed sides so that he could have the window, so in the event I did squeeze, any bruises would at least be evenly distributed.

It was impossible to see much outside his window due to the huge engine blocking the view but I didn't notice any real weather when I worked up courage to look out the windows on the other side of the aisle so it was something of a surprise when it started to rain just moments after we landed. Judging from the reactions of others around us, I think it was a surprise to most. I believe that it was just one more example of God taking care of us on this trip.

I truly did try to have faith that we would be fine and did trust most of the time regardless of the whining, chanting and death grips. That doesn't mean however that I enjoyed even one second of my time in the air. After all chickens weren't designed to fly so this big chicken is home to roost—and hopefully for a very long time.

Psalm 55:6 I said, "Oh, that I had the wings of a dove! I would fly away and be at rest-

Forgiveness Twenty Seven Years Late

Twenty-seven years ago this past September, I drove Brooke from Arkansas to San Antonio, Texas for heart surgery. I hate flying (am actually petrified) so drove her by myself. I was kind of nervous never having driven further than the six hours to Oklahoma for her frequent check-ups prior to surgery, and those trips with company every time. To make matters worse she woke up with a fever the morning we left. Since there was no way to reschedule, I just dosed her up with Children's Tylenol and hit the road.

My dad and brother-in-law had mapped my route for me, using an atlas. Being somewhat apprehensive about the trip, I went over it again the evening before leaving, when I noticed that the road just kind of stopped in Dallas where the route appeared to drop off. I showed the map-spot to my dad but he said, "You'll figure it out when you get there". Mind you, he knew I wasn't exactly an experienced traveler, but I trusted him. As it turns out, I should have made him sit down and re-map me but hindsight, as the saying goes, is 20-20 and my sight was crystal clear afterwards.

The trip was uneventful in spite of Brooke not feeling well. This actually worked in my favor because it meant that she slept a good deal of the ride. The only major problem I had was the air conditioning freezing up so that I would have to turn it off and drive with the windows open. Fortunately it quit doing this as the day cooled off.

Thinking about that spot on the map as we got closer to Dallas made me more and more tense. I pulled in to town and just as the map showed, was dropped off but, unlike my dad's prediction, I had no idea where to go from there. None. I panicked and tried to get on the emergency channel of the CB radio that I had borrowed, but some rude person kept talking over me and he didn't even have an emergency. I sincerely hope that guy never has a problem where he needs assistance. Finally giving up, I pulled into the first hotel parking lot I saw which was a Holiday Inn high-rise. I explained to the guy on the front desk (in a swanky looking lobby, at least to this country bumpkin) that I was lost, behind schedule and needed a room on the ground floor since I'm also afraid of elevators. I think he took one look at my scared expression and the sick little girl holding my hand, then decided we were on the lam because he gave me directions to the interstate. It was after 9 PM at this point, and being too exhausted emotionally and physically to make any sense of his directions, got back in the car and drove up the street to a much more hospitable Days Inn where we took a room, which they promptly had to change because the phone didn't work in the first one. This was long before cell phones and several years before Al Gore invented the Internet and Mapquest.com so my dad and brother-in-law had calculated I would pull into

Dallas around 6 PM. You can imagine how frantic my mother was when I finally called. I told her about being lost and how I didn't have a clue where I was or how I was going to get out the next day. Remember, I was not experienced at driving long distances and the truth is, I don't think I had ever read a map before this trip. Pathetic I now realize, but this was the sad case. Mom being a good mom, and not one to tell me that I'd "figure it out" gave me the phone number for my cousin who lived in the Dallas area. I called Wendell, whom I had not seen since I was a child, and explained my predicament then threw myself on his mercy and begged him to tell me HOW get out of town the next morning. Wendell did better than tell me and offered to meet me at the hotel at 8 AM. God bless him, I relaxed knowing I was now in good hands so took Brooke next door to Wendy's where she only wanted tomato slices for dinner. I slept an exhausted but restful sleep that night, secure in the knowledge that Wendell would rescue me. Good to his word he was there when I went to check out the next morning. Brooke even woke up feeling like her old self again. Cousin Wendell offered to show me some sights on the way out of town, but I told him to "just get me out of here!" I found out later that he had to drive 50 miles one way to come to my rescue but he didn't utter a word of complaint. When I saw him at a family reunion a few years ago, I told him I still consider him my hero.

The rest of the trip went smoothly, unless you count the pervert who followed me for some distance between Waco and the turn off for Killeen. He kept waggling his fingers at me in little waves, would motion for me to follow him off at each exit and changed lanes when I did. I had survived Dallas so ignored him in confidence, until he finally lost interest and took the exit to Killeen.

I stayed with friends of another cousin in San Antonio and the husband mapped me a much better route back home that didn't drop me off at any point in Dallas, or anywhere else for that matter. Just to be sure though, I flew my twin sister Jay (who isn't afraid of flying and actually enjoys it) to San Antonio and had her ride home with me.

I was so traumatized by that trip, that for the next many years I made sure I took few trips alone. I didn't have much choice four years ago when I needed to drive up to Roanoke Rapids from our soon to be former home in High Point, to help Ernie paint rooms in the soon to be new home. I was terrified of getting lost but Ernie and the girls all assured me it was an easy trip. I was still nervous, as I recalled being navigator for Ernie once years before, causing him to drive 10 miles the wrong direction in Maryland, all while staring at the map in front of me. I think my brain lacks some necessary section required for map reading. I'm pleased to say though that they were correct, it was a successful and mostly easy trip.

I think I can now let go and forgive my dad and brother-in-law for their transgression committed twenty seven years ago this past September.

Numbers 17:12 The Israelites said to Moses, "We will die! We are lost, we are Lost"

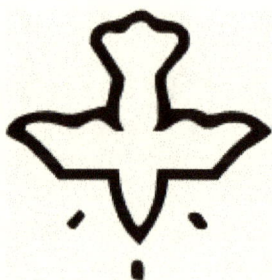

Fun And Games

Incredibly, our little Jarod is 11 months old today! I can't believe how fast time has gone. I do admit though that there was the period from about 2 ½ to 41/2 months that I thought one or both of us was not going to survive. He was bored and wanted to be held every moment he was awake. Survive we did though, and this child is a delight. He keeps us busy plucking him off the stairs, and grabbing him as he jumps from the fireplace hearth to a chair. He is *all* boy. He even invented a couple of new games this weekend. Friday evening Alexis was lying in her mom's lap when Jarod ran up, bit her on her leg, grinned at Mistie and took off running. He was going to make another run at her but his mom headed him off. Alexis was quite indignant but we all thought it was funny, which only added to her indignation. Alexis wanted to bite him back quite naturally, but Mistie explained to her that he's just a baby and wanted to play with her and that he must learn that biting hurts. Later in the weekend he was playing when he spotted his pacifier lying in the floor nipple side up. He walked up to it, bent over at the waist and picked it up with his lips. This was so much fun that he took the game a little further by placing M&M's on the coffee table and picking them up with his teeth. He's not a year old yet and already showing signs of genius. He is such a happy little guy who finds much to laugh at throughout his day, offering us opportunities for our own laughs in the process. We hear him chuckling frequently about things that we normally wouldn't see the humor in ourselves. Not only is he a genius, he's also very therapeutic for our souls.

Irene continues to add many hee-haws to our days as well. Ernie has been playing a computer game that involves fighting some sort of dinosaur, which is all well and good. The problem is Irene decided that he needed her assistance playing the game. She has gotten into the habit of standing next to him and saying things such as, "Run! Run away Bapa! Run this way!" And as the computer voice screams in the agonizing throes of death she will sadly announce "Oh noooo Bapa died!" At least she did this until Bapa got tired of it and told her he really didn't require her help. She now listens while perched in her mom's or my lap while watching TV. When she hears the screams she'll nonchalantly announce that "Bapa has died again!"

Aren't kid's fun?

1 Corinthians 9:25 Everyone who competes in the games goes into strict training. They do it to get a crown that will not last; but we do it to get a crown that will last forever.

Fun In The Kitchen With The Kiddies

As much as I enjoy my grandkids and always did my own kids (though they may tell you differently) I don't enjoy time together in the kitchen. This is probably because I don't particularly enjoy baking and cooking. I can bake certainly, but it's not a chore that I want to spend hours performing, and having kids help just makes it harder to get done. That said have you ever found yourself baking sugar free cookies with more help from the kids than you need or want and find the chore anything but amusing? Then try this recipe out for some fun baking with the kids...

Put flour in mixing bowl then tell 7 year old granddaughter that she can turn the powerful Kitchen Aid mixer to 4. Watch and laugh as flour flies and kids run away shrieking. Did they come back for more?

OK then, ask 7 year old to pour a cup of unsweetened Carob Chips into dough and sighing, finally give into their multiple requests for some of the "chocolate chips". Watch the precious little faces of the 7 year and 20 months old as they say Mmmmmm and pop the chips into their eager little mouths. Start laughing wildly as you watch their faces change from looks of rapture to looks of horror. Gasp for air as you clean up the mess that the 20-month-old grandson makes spitting the chips out onto the counter as 7 year old quickly runs for the trash can while dribbling chocolate colored drool.

Collapse completely, then wipe tears of laughter as you gain hold of yourself, re-reading the brown sugar replacement box and realize you used waaaaay too much— just as they take their first bite of the hot from the oven cookies.

After resting and gathering your wits about you once again, take ingredients out of cabinet and ask 5 year old granddaughter, who just woke up from a nap if she would like to have some fun making cookies with Nana.

1 Chronicles 23:29 They were in charge of the bread set out on the table, the flour for the grain offerings, the unleavened wafers, the baking and the mixing, and all measurements of quantity and size.

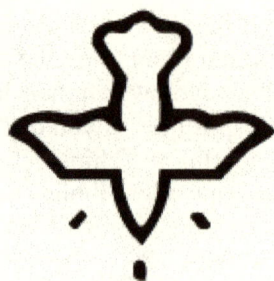

Fun With Kids And Grandkids

As you may know I am known as Nana to my grandkids. Alexis was the first grandbaby and she named me as well as dubbing Ernie "Bapa". I love being called Nana. I waited for a long time to hear it and when I finally did, got a big kick out of hearing, "Nana can I have a banana?" It's the little things make me happy.

Yesterday afternoon, Jarod was enjoying one of what turned out to be one of many bananas. (He stole an entire bunch from the counter and ultimately ate them all-somehow leaving the peels intact.) I walked up as he was eating it and he excitedly showed me his treat. I could literally see the light bulb go on when he realized that he was showing his banana to Nana. He stopped, looked at me then his banana and started chattering so fast I couldn't understand, but I just know it was something funny about Nana and banana.

Yes kids are a lot of fun. Mostly. There is one story involving my youngest daughter Stacie though, that I don't think is very funny almost 16 years, later. She on the other hand when told this story recently thought it was hysterical. I had had it buried in my memory for a long time when something triggered it recently. I don't know what did this, but wish it had stayed buried.

This nightmarish occurrence took place just a short time before we returned stateside from Germany. Mistie and Brooke had already returned to the states to their grandparents in Georgia, to start school since we were returning well into the fall. Ernie was on an extended field trip, and my best friend had just returned to the states as well. Stacie was 5 years old and in Kindergarten. Our neighbors across the hall from us had three boys. The oldest was Mistie's age making him a very young teen. We had all been stationed at Ft. Hood, Texas together so I knew this family fairly well.

Ohhhh I still want to crawl under the desk as I type this.

With it being just me and Stacie at home for long periods, I got to be very casual and obviously careless. The front door of our small quarters opened into the living room, which led straight to the hallway so when the door was open you were looking back towards the bedrooms. One day, after taking a shower I just grabbed a towel (which sadly wasn't large enough to cover me) and made a dash for my bedroom, which was caddy cornered at the opposite end of the hallway from the bathroom. Unfortunately for all involved I hadn't heard the doorbell. As I ran out of the bathroom, Stacie opened the front door—wide open. There I was dripping, naked and smack in the middle of the hallway. I whirled around to see the neighbor's teenage son standing there, mouth open as wide as the door. Ooooh mama I was hoping the floor would just open and swallow me. I sort of suspect the neighbor kid was hoping for the same to happen to him. I can easily imagine that he's still in therapy to this day.

Now that this horrific memory has re-surfaced, next time Stacie complains that my weirdness has rubbed off on her I'll just smile and tell her it's a mother's revenge.

Genesis 3:10 He answered, I heard you in the garden, and I was afraid because I was naked; so I hid.

Funny Kids And Nana Puddles

I write a lot about the things that our wonderful little blonde Irene, says and does. Now that Jarod is getting a little older, he has been providing me with lots of funny stories as well. Alexis doesn't tend to get as much written about her because she is our serious one. This doesn't mean that she isn't special at all, as you will see. Jarod and Irene are the special, *silly* ones and all three of them have recently been conspiring to entertain us as well as melt me into one big Nana puddle.

We've been spending a lot of time outside lately landscaping the yard. I had planted some new flowers yesterday afternoon and was sitting on the porch taking a break, and watching Ernie do some brick work along the sidewalk. Alexis was standing between my knees, leaning back against me while I gently rocked her. I told her I needed to get up and she responded, "But Nana I feel like I just want to stay like this forever!" You know of course that I stayed right where I was until other, more fun activity in the yard caught her attention. I was just a big old puddle of melted Nana by that point, and forgot why I had wanted to get up in the first place.

Jarod is quite a little character who has been on a roll this week. A few evenings ago he was dragging one of Ernie's gardening tools around and smacked himself in the leg with it, which caused him to raise a ruckus for a few seconds. I was busy so when told he was fine, went on with what I was doing. I wandered out to the garage to talk to Ernie a few minutes later where Jarod was happily playing and chattering. He looked at me, grinned then remembering his "injury" said, "Oh!" then grabbed his calf and walked bent over saying "Oh! Oh! Oh!" all the way to the stairs where he continued to hold his leg and cry "Oh!" all the way up to me while I nearly fell off the landing, laughing. I patted his leg and made sympathetic noises and he chattered at me and went back downstairs to play by his Bapa again. I think this child may have a future on the stage some day.

Later that same evening Brooke was bent down putting something in the refrigerator door. She was starting to get ill with the flu and was feeling weak. (That's her excuse anyway). Jarod walked up behind her and put his hand under her shirt to pat her back where he discovered her bra strap. Oh boy! He was delighted by this discovery so gave it a yank and promptly pulled his Aunt Brooke down until she flopped down on the floor, flat on her butt. What a sight and what a great laugh we all had at her expense.

We finished up the yard work for the day so Ernie, Jarod and I headed indoors to start dinner. Ernie grabbed Jarod to carry him in, but he was determined not to go and yelled all the way up the stairs and across the porch. When Ernie started in the door with him, Jarod grabbed the edge of the open screen door then after Bapa peeled him loose, grabbed the door frame. He was determined but his stronger Bapa finally won that argument. As strong as this child is, we may be in for some tougher battles down the road.

Liz Curtis Higgs tells us we should look for the funny in every day. I say we should listen for it as well. Sometimes we can even create the fun ourselves. This morning all three kids were sitting at the breakfast bar playing, when our more serious Alexis held out a Barbie doll and asked me to feel the dolls head. I did and felt a short, sharp object sticking out. Being the not-quite-average Nana that I am I said, "Hmm must be a brain tumor" Alexis gave me a pained look and told me she didn't think Barbie had a brain to have a tumor. Irene piped up, "She does NOT have a brain—she's a DOLL." As I left the room chuckling, the two little girls were talking and agreeing that dolls can't have brains. I went back in a few minutes later in time to hear Irene yell that Jarod had popped one of her doll's heads off. I guess he wanted to find out for himself whether dolls have brains......

Isaiah 60:21 Then will all your people be righteous and they will possess the land forever. They are the shoot I have planted, the work of my hands, for the display of my splendor.

Future Nurses?

I have been thoroughly "nursed" tonight. While I was sitting at the desk, Alexis and Irene decided that I was "very, very sick" and proceeded to treat me. I had my hair brushed back, and checked for bugs (I do *not* have bugs in my hair!) then they brushed the "bugs" into a bag. I had cotton balls stuck between my toes to keep them warm and had a baby doll tucked in on my lap. The topper was the pencil stuck in my mouth to take my "tenchamer". When Irene finally pulled it out she pronounced "She's getting older and older!" I was hoping she'd give me a pill to reverse that. I had an orange clipboard held in front of me and told to repeat the letters that Irene said first. I guess it was some sort of eye/hearing test, and I'm so pleased to say that I passed.

They've gone on to play something else now, so I'm hoping this means that I'm all better or at least no longer rapidly aging. I'm just happy that I didn't mention my aching back. It scares me to think what treatment that would have required.

1Samuel 25:6 Say to him: 'Long life to you! Good health to you and your household! And good health to all that is yours!

Good Bye Old Friend!

I'm one of those weird people who enjoy doing laundry. I hate putting away but find washing and drying laundry to be very therapeutic, especially when able to hang them outside to dry. This portion of your day assures no one will bother you, out of fear they'll be pressed into helping.

Sadly my beloved 15-year-old GE washer has finally given up. She has tried to warn me for some time now, with lots of funny groaning noises and occasionally stopping for a while but she always started back up again so I ignored the signs, hoping she would get over whatever was ailing her. This is such a sad day for me.

I love my washer. It has been like a member of the family since January 1989 when we brought her and the dryer home while living in Maryland. They have moved from there to Colorado, then to Alabama (2 locations there) then to North Carolina, again two locations. She has stood the test of moving and run her heart out for me. She has been therapy for me on the days when I, stressed and tired, wanted nothing more than the solitude that comes while washing and hanging clothes to dry. Or on cold days toss them into the dryer and watch the steam rise outside the window. Who needs a therapist when there's a washing machine in the house?

We went to our local Sears appliance store to look but they only have two or three in stock and none of those are on display. I refuse to buy a washing machine on impulse or under pressure. I hope that the replacement will be a member of the family for a very long time too so want to choose wisely. Soooooo we will go to Lowes after church tomorrow. In the meantime at least the cycle was on rinse so I can wring by hand then dry the items in the dryer.

Oh dear, speaking of dryer, he has been acting kind of tired lately, not drying as quickly and not heating up properly. I hope he doesn't grieve too hard, and gives up too soon.

I suppose I'd better go start wringing clothes out, and saying my fond good-byes now. It feels criminal to just set her out on the street for trash pick-up so I won't mention that part to her.......

Sadly the dryer quit about a year later. We now have a Maytag set that I like very much. I still think fondly on my basic GE washer though. She was a true work horse among washing machines.

Exodus 19:10 And the LORD said to Moses, "Go to the people and consecrate them today and tomorrow. Have them wash their clothes.

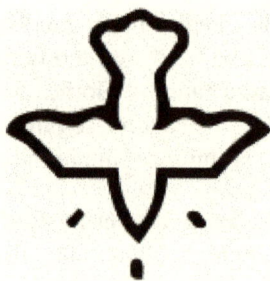

Grandkids, You Gotta Love Them!

Jarod, who turned 8 months on Christmas day, loves his Bapa as much as Bapa loves Jarod. Ernie went to Georgia Christmas day (afternoon) so that he could go hunting with his dad and brother Bill. (It was a very fruitful trip. He got two deer and could have gotten more) He came home Friday evening so he wasn't gone long, but these grandkids all missed him. Alexis and Irene asked where he was and when he was coming home again, at least twice a day. In the interim, they decided they love and missed him so much, that both of them want to marry him when they grow up. I told them they can't because I'm already married to him and I don't share.

Jarod is normally an incredibly happy baby, especially since he began to crawl and maneuver on his own. However we could detect restlessness in him while his Bapa was away. If we needed proof we got it once Bapa returned. That boy was delighted to see him and lit up like a light bulb when he saw him. He was eating dinner when Bapa came in and as soon as he finished went straight to him. It wasn't long before the baby got sleepy and wanted his bottle so we jumped to it while he wailed and made his wishes known in no uncertain terms. As soon as the bottle was ready he snuggled in to Bapa's arms and went out with a contented sigh. The only sign of his unhappiness was a single, large tear running down his cheek.

Mistie came over to pick Irene up to spend the night the next evening and set Jarod in the floor. He spotted his Bapa and made a beeline straight for him, grinning the whole way. Bapa scooped him up, and they did some major male bonding for a while.

Joe came for a visit and arrived on Christmas Eve, meeting us all at a favorite Chinese restaurant for lunch in Winston-Salem. He hadn't seen the kids for several months so Jarod didn't recognize this strange man that Alexis was calling Daddy. Ernie carried him into the restaurant, and turned him over to Joe immediately. We sat at the opposite end of the table, leaving the baby and Alexis on Joe's end. It wasn't long before Jarod started looking around for a familiar face. His Aunt Brooke was sitting next to the chair his Mommy would take as soon as she arrived, and he was ok with that until he kept looking and spotted us at the other end of the long table. He started clouding up and the tears started flowing. He kept looking at us with a panicked look of "I want my Bapa and Nana!" Poor little guy, it didn't help that we laughed as we reassured him that he was fine. I felt bad for Joe, but even worse for the little guy since he didn't understand why we wouldn't rescue him.

Jarod is going to be a major heart breaker for sure. He is so cute that even when dressed in blue, people ask if he's a boy or a girl. He has a devastating smile that just confuses the issue. When he starts messing with something he shouldn't, such as the phone on my side table, he'll just stop, look at us and give us a smile that would melt the hardest heart ,then go on his way.

Brooke got Jarod a walk behind toy that converts to a riding toy for Christmas. He hasn't mastered the riding part, but loves that push walker and scoots all over the house with it. Watching that little guy go is the cutest thing I've seen since the granddaughters were learning to walk. It won't be long until he's walking on his own since he stands for long periods all by himself, and will almost forget and take a step alone. We expect him to do just that any day.

Brooke and I got a good laugh over a "secret" stunt I pulled on Irene recently. First allow me to explain. I have been famous all my life for hating peanut butter. My kids know I hated it, Ernie knows it and anyone around when a jar was opened knows I hate it. Until recently. After I was diagnosed diabetic in March of this year, I struggled mightily to find something that I could eat for breakfast that wasn't loaded with sugar or carbohydrates. Up until then I was a pre-sweetened cereal addict, most likely because as a kid we got very little other than Cheerios, Rice Krispies and Corn Flakes. Growing up, my kids joked that their mother was the only adult they knew who bought sweet cereal for themselves, and not the kids. Breakfast choices became a real chore upon the diabetes diagnosis. I had to eat since diabetics must eat regular meals but the choices were much slimmer. I was desperate to find something I liked that wouldn't raise my sugar level or raise my nicely low cholesterol. Finally one morning, in desperation, I spread some peanut butter on toast and have been hooked since. I will only eat Peter Pan Reduced Fat CRUNCHY though and if I get low, will make a trip to the store just for that. I worked too hard to find something I like. My kids still watch me in awe and wonder, and can't believe their mother is not only eating but actually enjoying peanut butter.

As I said, I will only eat Peter Pan Reduced Fat CRUNCHY and Irene will only eat creamy. While shopping recently, the store we were in had NO Peter Pan Reduced Fat Crunchy so I bought Skippy Reduced Fat for both of us in the preferred style. Irene was still working on a jar of open PP so I stored the Skippy in the pantry. She has heard me profess my loyalty to the one kind of peanut butter so many times that recently she told me that she isn't going to eat "that peanut butter in the blue jar", that she'll "only eat the peanut butter in the red jar!" I understand her dilemma but refuse to waste the jar of Skippy so I recently took care of this little problem. While she was busy elsewhere, I transferred the Skippy to her nearly empty PP jar. She has been happily eating it since though I do notice a little less enthusiasm for it.

We all laugh when we see the commercials for Jif saying choosy moms choose Jif. This may be, but we also know that "Picky moms, Nana and Irene pick Peter Pan".

Psalm 103:17 But from everlasting to everlasting the LORD's love is with those who fear him, and his righteousness with their children's children-

Grandma's Porch

I woke up from a short nap yesterday with my grandmother's porch on my mind and yet, I hadn't dreamed about it during the brief nap. I've always trusted that God inspires most of what I write about, so believe it now as well.

My country grandmother's porches weren't very impressive, yet I hold many good memories of them. The front porch was smallish, supported by a foundation of concrete blocks. We didn't use that door often because her very long driveway ended at the side porch. I do remember running around her huge yard with my cousins one day, and as we passed that porch something caught our attention. We got within a couple of feet before we realized it was a huge black snake curled up on the blocks! Screaming for help at the tops of our lungs, we ran away from the porch as fast as we could. My cousins were country kids, so most likely responded with screams because their silly city cousins were yelling in unnecessary terror; after all it was only a black snake. YIKES, what am I saying? A snake is a snake in my thinking.

Grandma's side porch wasn't very large either, at least at first. This is where the wild kittens, that always seemed to populate the property hung out with their poor, worn out old mom. My mother had given the mama cat to Grandma years before, telling her she thought it was a Tom. Old mom-tom turned out to be a baby making machine and produced litters several times a year, right up until she died. Try as we might and we tried often, we kids couldn't ever catch even one of her kittens, who always dove under the porch for cover.

In later years my grandmother had her side porch expanded and screened in, and she used it for storing lots of items, including her house plants. Many years ago, my older sister Kandy was given a Begonia from Grandma, that at the time she received it was over twenty years old. Last time I was home she still had that plant too! Grandma had a marvelous green thumb and showed off with gorgeous flower beds of zinnias, daisies and chrysanthemums planted along the driveway and a huge vegetable garden in the side yard. She could grow some awesome vegetables too. One year she grew a tomato plant with over 300 tomatoes growing on it.

My grandma lived on 40 acres so there was always a lot to observe from her porches. After my grandfather was killed in a traffic accident she raised turkeys, 20,000 plus to be more exact. For a long time all you could see was a sea of turkeys. It was all you heard too since those delicious creatures were easy to scare, and would gobble up a fuss whenever a car came down the drive. They were better than any guard dog. I'll never forget the really hard rain we had one year. It washed turkey poop from the 20,000 plus turkeys into her side yard, contaminating her well water. She couldn't drink from her well for several weeks. Thankfully it wasn't something that was visible from the porch.

Another view from the side porch was the dreaded outhouse. How I hated that thing and how happy I was when she finally got indoor plumbing! It wasn't a nice view and the recollection still conjures up memories such as the constant colony of spiders and "the smell" that I'd rather forget.

My city grandmother had a glider on her screened in front porch. All of us kids liked to sit out there and glide while the adults talked. We had a nice view of her neighbor's yard across the street. Being a very small community, almost country itself the properties were large so we had lots of room to roam so no one felt invaded. My city grandmother also had a substantial vegetable garden and in the mornings we could sit in her kitchen and watch the birds try to feast on her produce.

We kids used to enjoy walking around the city grandmother's neighborhood. I found one house particularly fascinating, where each spike of the iron fence was topped by a penny. I was convinced that the owners must have been very wealthy to have pennies adorn their fence. The people across the street from that house had stone lions at their driveway entrance. Those didn't impress me much, but they did sort of scare me. Neither house was visible from my grandmother's porch but when I think about her home my mind tends to wander off the porch to the surrounding homes as well as the little store where we'd walk after Grandma gave us change to go buy penny candy. Every trip, whether to the store or a walk around the neighborhood required stepping off of that front porch that holds so many precious memories.

Years later grandmother moved further into town onto a busier street. I loved to sit on her front porch and watch the people go by. This may be where my people watching tendencies took root. Her back porch was the portal and a path to the neighbor behind us. That neighbor was a long time family friend, and in fact all of my siblings and I called her Grandma. We loved to go visit with her, and felt truly blessed to have another grandmother just a few steps from our true grandmother's back porch.

So how about you? Do you have treasured recollections of your own cherished porch that you'd like to share? Send them on; I'd love to read about your memories.

Job 28:24 for he views the ends of the earth and sees everything under the heavens.

Green Riding Mowers And Pink Jeeps

Ernie mowed the yard this afternoon, using the riding mower we bought him for Father's Day. After he finished he took the little girls for a spin, allowing each a turn riding and "steering" it in the street right in front of our house, and on around the corner. Yes, we live on a very quiet street. Alexis drove first, having a ball of course. When Irene got on, Alexis jumped into her pink Barbie Jeep and drove behind them. I hollered to Brooke to come watch this, and just as we got to the door we saw another man on a green riding mower driving the opposite direction on the other side of the street! The two men waved and kept going. What a sight, Ernie and Irene driving the mower, Alexis chasing them in the pink jeep and another riding mower driving the other direction. I really need to start carrying a video camera everywhere I go. And I always thought this was a quietly, normal neighborhood.

Luke 1:65 The neighbors were all filled with awe, and throughout the hill country of Judea people were talking about all these things.

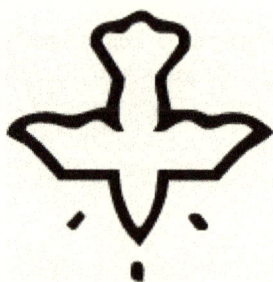

Guilt And Pleasures

Monday is typically my laundry day, and you all know how seriously I enjoy doing laundry. I know it's weird but it's true. Part of this past weekend was wet and chilly, but today dawned beautiful and clear so I had the extreme pleasure of hanging heavier items outside on the clothes line.

I waited until Jarod went down for his morning nap around 9:30, then went out under brilliant blue skies to stand at the line and enjoy the ritual of bending and hanging in the quiet of the back yard. Hanging clothes is a mindless task, so my mind can safely wander to just think or have little chats with God. This morning was no different, and I was taking pleasure in being outside when my thoughts were suddenly interrupted by the shrill screeching and squawks of some birds in the trees. From the sounds of it, I guessed a predator bird made the mistake of trying to raid a bird nest. Mom and dad must have been close by and caught the thief in the act, running him off in short order. I applauded their good parenting skills and quick reaction in saving their babies.

Several hours later, after the little girls got home from school I went back outside to reverse the process and take the clothes down, folding them as I did so. The wind had picked up during the day and was still pleasantly warm.

I love the smell of fresh line dried clothes, so took time to breathe deep from each towel as I folded it. Ernie brought Jarod outside to play with the girls, and as I folded and sniffed I could hear the whine of one of their Barbie jeeps in the background as they gave Jarod a ride around the yard. I realized this is one of those sweet moments in time that you wish you could just freeze and preserve forever, making me feel guilty for ever asking for more than this.

Psalm 16:11 You have made known to me the path of life; you will fill me with joy in your presence, with eternal pleasures at your right hand.

Hairy Spiders And Wacky Sisters

Not everyone who knows me realizes that I have a fraternal twin sister; I am the baby by twenty-three minutes. While I am a veteran military wife, she chose to settle in Arkansas around the rest of my family. Jay and I are as different as day and night. She's blonde, I'm a brunette. She's shy and quiet and I'm well, not. She tends to be restrained with most people who are not family or close friends, I hardly know a stranger. Jayme will let her wild side show on occasion though, and when she does watch out.

One memory I'll never treasure is a visit the kids and I made to visit my family in Arkansas a few years ago. My folks recently sold their home and moved into a senior housing complex, but prior to this they lived over 25 years in the house they built themselves on Beaver Lake in Rogers, Arkansas. The house is a beautiful split-level, situated a short miles drive from the water. Since it isn't on the waterfront, they had lots of trees and foliage all around. The slithery type wild life soon figured out that they needed to re-locate once construction started. Unfortunately, the multi-legged critters were more than delighted with their new digs, settling in and setting up neighborhoods and spidery interstates. One particular guy, a brown recluse, set up house in a suitcase and got to take an unplanned trip to Chicago with my dad on a business trip for his job. Apparently he was less than thrilled to wake up in a strange place and bit my dad on a calf when he put on a pair of pants that the fiddle back hid in. If you know anything about the evil little things then you know how poisonous a bite can be. His diabetes complicated dad's bite and he came very close to losing his leg. To this day, dad has a very deep hole in his calf where the nasty creature bit him. There is justice though, as my dad was able to kill it before it got away to hide in the room and assault some other unsuspecting hotel guest. Anyway back to my scary story and scarier sister.

The visit with my kids took place in summer, so the vile little creatures were very active. I recall a couple of nights in bed when a spider, running across my forehead, woke me up. It would seem that my pillow was smack in the middle of their hairy legged speedway. Ugh. One was so big that he hit the wall with a thud when I panicked and slapped him off. I slept with the lights on every night after that. This is a very big reason I was more than thrilled to stay in a hotel when we all went back last summer. No trees, no foliage, no spiders in sight.

A few days before we left for our return trip home, one of the kids reported seeing a very large black spider sneaking around my suitcase. I don't know why they didn't kill it, but personally gave serious thought to storing my suitcase in my folk's chest type freezer for the duration. As distasteful as the chore was, I decided I had to inspect the suitcase because I didn't relish the idea of taking that thing home in the car with us. I took every piece of clothing out, shook it thoroughly then stomped on it just to be sure. I checked every baggie of jewelry and perfume, then carefully poked around in the pockets and corners of the suitcase. You have *no* idea how scary this was since I was looking for a black spider in a black suitcase interior.

Eeewwwww....Thankfully no spider was found. However I couldn't face the thought of crawling into that bed again until I checked it. Enter my depraved twin sister---She went downstairs to the bedroom with me and helped me strip the bed down to the mattress. We shook and checked every square inch of bedding and pummeled the pillows. Finally the comforter was the only thing left to inspect. We each grabbed two corners and shook it hard. I was just starting to feel safe again when Jay yelled, "There it is!!" then she threw that darned blanket on my head. I started screaming, flailing, and fighting it off as fast and furiously as I could. After an eternity, I tossed it to the floor only to find her and my kids standing there laughing like loons at the "funny" joke. My family may be nice but they are *all* warped.

I gather word got around about the flying trip that the monstrously large spider made into the wall and they re-routed their roadway because I didn't have any more incidents of spider stalking for the rest of the visit. We never did find that sneaky spider either. Do I harbor bitter feelings towards my sis? Nah! In fact I'm almost ashamed to admit that I hoped the creepy thing hitchhiked home on the back of her sneaker that night. Almost.

Exodus 2:4 His sister stood at a distance to see what would happen to him.

Have You Ever Wondered........?

I'm a sleepy head in the car and have trouble keeping my eyes open on the thirty minute trip to Rocky Mount. At night I'll occasionally have trouble sleeping, tossing and turning while chasing some zzzz's. Maybe I should visualize myself lying in bed suffering with insomnia next time I travel, and when lying awake in bed can imagine myself riding in the car. I have figured out one way to stay awake in the car though, and that is to watch the world passing by our windows as we zip down the road. It always gets me to wondering about things. Possibly you've been in this situation; scooting on down the road and before you know it, you find yourself wondering......

One car caught my attention a while back as we traveled down I-95. I was driving so assure you that I didn't allow my attention to wander for long, but this didn't stop me from wondering about the North Carolina license plate which read: 4ENSICS. I noticed that the driver appeared to be a 40 something blonde and got excited about the possibility that this may have been "the" Kathy Reichs, author of several fabulous books featuring fictional character Temperance Brennan as a forensic anthropologist. I describe her books as CSI in book form, and have read all that she's written so far. Tempie may be fictional but the character is based on Ms. Reichs' actual career in North Carolina and Canada. What a crazy yet thrilling thought— that I may have actually passed the famous and fabulous Ms. Reichs as we passed like the proverbial two ships in the night, or day in this case. I believe that Kathy does live in North Carolina so it's certainly within the realm of possibility that it was her traveling south on I-95 on that morning this past March. I can dream, right? I'll no doubt always wonder anyway.

As my mind wanders from Ms. Reichs I find myself wondering about the people we outrace in our journey down the interstate. I see couples in cars and wonder....where are they going, why are they traveling? What kinds of lives do they lead? Are they newly weds? Oldie weds? Old newly weds? Criminals on the run from the law? That's not a nice thought but a possibility at least, however slim. Are the people sad, possibly going to a funeral for a loved one? Or maybe they're contemplating divorce or infidelity or financial difficulties. Are they headed to a long anticipated vacation or family reunion? The possibilities are endless and though I'll never know the answers, it doesn't keep me from wondering.

As we pass truckers pulling into an open weigh station I find myself wondering....do they enjoy being a trucker? Is this a job that they love or one that they hate? Even if they love it does it hurt their family life? If they hate it, do they drive because they have no other options? Do they ever just get so sleepy that they fear they can't keep going, but feel they need to keep going to stay on schedule? I wonder if a truck driver's life isn't just a little bit lonely.

Have you ever wondered about the mostly unsightly and downright ugly advertising blitzes, commonly referred to as billboards? South Carolina along the I-95 corridor is like the billboard capitol of the south. It seems they have a billboard every 50 feet, touting everything from linens, bible and cigarette outlets to every hotel chain and restaurant known to man. I'll admit that some are amusing, from the cheesy South of the Border signs (I'm experiencing a mental block and can't think of a single one at the moment) to J.R's Outlet sign where they admit to being "The World's Largest Tourist Trap". My favorite was seen recently on our trip to Georgia. It simple held the words: "Hey watch this!" and had the name of a hospital ER off to the one side. Some of the billboards have long been abandoned and I can't help but wonder to whom they belong, and why they allow them to fall into such a sad state of disrepair. After all, judging from the sheer number of the things they must be a goldmine of revenue.

Looking down from the advertising monstrosities I see—fence. Actually miles and miles and miles of fencing. I have to wonder....who erected these fences? When did they do it? WHY did they do it? Many are obscured by trees, and some separate farms, businesses or homes from Interstate yet are unbroken from the fencing before and after the farms, homes and businesses, so they must be one continuous run which makes me wonder, where do the fences start and where do they end? I even see one short and random fence standing at the road edge of a field, constructed of various kinds of rocks. It appears to serve no purpose other than to make a person wonder *why*.

Speaking of homes, some are built very close to the Interstate. I wonder why? Some are old and may have been there before the road was built, but some are obviously new and deliberately built close. Maybe they got a great deal on the land, but I wonder if they ever get used to the traffic noise or if they ever really feel safe. Those miles and miles of fences are just wire after all, and not much deterrent from criminals who may be traveling the Interstate or drivers who may get sleepy. That thought would bother me more than the noise I think.

I wonder how many cars a day travel the interstate from border to border, getting on and off along the way. I detest I-95 and I-20 and often feel as if half the population of the south is traveling along with us. I imagine my mini-van as a horse on a track as I spur it on while the other drivers and I jockey for lead position.

South Carolina has signs posted that announce a $1,000 fine and prison (as opposed to mere jail time) for littering. I can believe that they'd fine someone but have to wonder if they really send people to prison. I think if a candy wrapper flew out my window in South Carolina that I'd stop and hunt the thing down. Then there are the signs that make no sense whatsoever. We passed a sign that said "1/2" then a short while later a "1". Where was the "0"? I'm no math whiz, but believe you can't have a whole without two halves. Right? And what in the world does the sign touting CSM421 road test mean? How will we know if the road passes the test?

Who decides what to plant along the roadside? Is this done by committee or individual? Maybe it's the same faceless person or people who decided to erect the miles and miles of fencing. I really like the wild flower projects along the Interstates and wish "they" would decide to plant miles and miles and miles of wild flowers. There's even a palm tree oasis along I-20. It's a little out of place but pleasantly unexpected and a nice touch—I like that.

I see women traveling alone, many from out of state and wonder about them. Where are they going and why are they going alone? I'm not a person who enjoys solitary travel. I get easily flustered and very nervous if I even suspect that I'm lost while driving alone. Thinking about it, I realize that I don't believe I've ever driven to Rocky Mount alone and I know that trip well. I admire women who can travel alone yet feel a bit sad for them and hope they don't get lost.

Finally there are sooo many motor homes and travel trailers on the road. I wonder about them….where are they headed? Where have they been? What's their next stop? Is it possible for passengers to relax enough to sleep in one as the driver trundles on down the road? My biggest question though is how they can afford to keep driving those monsters in these crazed with greed days of rip-off gas prices…….

Judges 19:17 When he looked and saw the traveler in the city square, the old man asked, "Where are you going? Where did you come from?"

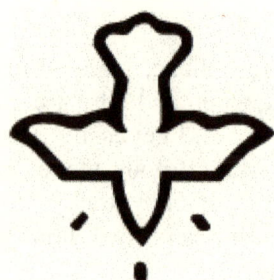

Help! Emergency!! Someone Call 911!! (But Please, Don't Call Jayne)

I have a dear long time friend who is a nurse. There was a time that she wanted me to go to nursing school too, thinking that I would make a good nurse. Poor dear, she was the victim of misguided thinking of the worst kind. Had she known these little family secrets, she would never have suggested it

Few outside my family know this, but in emergencies you can count on me to react one of several ways; I'll either panic on a major scale, I'll laugh at you or I'll pretend nothing is wrong. Sometimes I do all, and none of these is very helpful when you're in the middle of a crisis.

I'll never forget the day I was standing at my kitchen sink when I heard Tom, our neighbor straight across the street start yelling. I looked out and saw Ernie running across the street so I took off too. When we got there, we found Tom pinned to the ground by his massive motor home! He had been lying in front of it, working on it when something slipped allowing it to run forward, pinching his leg and thoroughly trapping him. This motor home was so long it filled their driveway. Ernie started trying to figure out a way to get him out while I ran back home to place a hysterical call to 911. As I recall, it went something like: "911, what's your emergency?" HELLLLLLLLP!!! Myneighboriscaughtunderhismotorhome!!!!!!!!" "Ma'am, calm down please and repeat what you said." I managed to convey the urgency of the situation then threw the phone down to run back across the street to "assist". There I was, trying to PUSH this block long motor home forward......all by myself. A woman driving by stopped and asked if I needed help. I don't recall what I said, but she drove off with a slightly frightened look on her face. Fortunately we lived just a few blocks from the fire department so they were roaring up, lights on and sirens blaring within minutes. They extracted our neighbor with little fanfare and were still there when his wife drove up. She got out of the car and calmly asked what was happening. (She's my hero). It seems this wasn't the first or even second time she had come home to find the street filled with flashing red and blue lights. I am in awe of her composure and even humor in this emergency. As for myself, I hadn't run in years so the next day I could barely stand much less walk. Tom spent a few days on crutches while I felt like I needed some myself.

I suppose the motor home incident was some sort of payback for my sending him running to our house a couple of years before this. It was the Monday after Thanksgiving, and I had dropped a toaster pastry into the toaster while I sat at the computer to work on a letter. I lost track of time and some time later heard a crackling noise. When I turned around, I saw flames shooting from the toaster. I started screaming and running around in circles yelling "FIRE!" I called 911 and shrieked something about a fire while Mistie grabbed Alexis who was 4 months old at the time, and hit the front door running. I ran out behind them, saw Tom and screamed something incoherent (I was hysterical and don't remember for sure what I said) and he came running. I continued to run in circles while he assessed the situation. Finally he yanked the cord from the wall, quickly filed a bowl with water, and then threw the water on the toaster. By the time the fire truck got there it was all over except for the smoke and my embarrassment. We did have some fairly heavy damage to the cabinets and counter tops. Our toaster, electric can opener and coffee maker were total losses as well. Losing that coffee maker hurt the worst, and in fact all of the appliances were replaced that very day.

I still cringe in embarrassment when I think about the day that I locked the kids and myself in our apartment in Germany. It was November 1984 and we had just arrived and were living in temporary quarters on the 4th floor of one of the stairwells on a housing kasern. I got into the habit of leaving the key to the laundry room, which was located in the basement, hanging on the hinge of the only door in and out of the apartment. I shut the door a little too hard one day, and the key swung over wedging itself between the door and the jam. When I tried to open the door it was jammed tight. I know because I tried pulling and tugging it open with all of my strength. Ernie wasn't due home for hours, and we didn't have a phone since we were only there for a month while we waited on our economy apartment to be completed. I panicked big time. I was immediately convinced the building was going to burst into flames and that we would perish. The windows were tiny, not to mention four floors up. I started beating on the metal door and screaming for help. It wasn't long before I heard a woman neighbor's timid voice asking "Is everything ok in there?" I responded that NO the door was jammed and we were stuck inside. While I pulled she shoved and we got it to open. Much to my horror and seemingly never ending embarrassment there stood ALL of my neighbors and most of the kids in the stairwell. Have you ever wished a floor would just open up and swallow you?

When Irene was seven weeks old she got very sick and almost died of Whooping Cough. Her Bapa had to perform CPR twice before the military finally sent her to a civilian doctor, who immediately had her admitted to the local civilian hospital. Brooke had to stay around the clock with her in the hospital and I would go relieve her during the day so she could go home to take a shower. I knew the procedure if the alarms went off but lived in terror of them anyway. It was so frightening to know that my tiny grandchild's life depended on quick and CALM reaction. One time the alarms started squealing and I wasn't able to get her to breathe, so I tore out into the hallway, frantically looking for a nurse. There was none in sight so I just opened up and started yelling at the top of my lungs. I had lots of nurses then. They quickly got her breathing and reviewed the procedures with me while I apologized. Was I embarrassed? Not this time. This was a baby who was going to die if I didn't get help fast. Today this child is a healthy and incredibly bright and funny nine-year-old.

When Stacie had an accident on her scooter and broke (mangled) her wrist, I took off with her in the Jimmy. That we arrived at the emergency room as intact as we were is a miracle, as I took off with flashers going, horn honking and eyes bugging. A driver out there to this day, is in peril of his life. He actually refused to get out of my way in spite of all this and even slowed down deliberately. His face, which I saw it in his side mirror and his vehicle are burned into my brain forever. I took the final turn into the ER parking lot on two wheels. This is one time the Army hospital ER staff didn't take their time, though the radiology tech almost got taken down for making a personal phone call before he did her x-rays. Everyone else kept a healthy respect for this wild-eyed mother bear with the injured baby cub.

Then there are the times that all I can do is laugh. Alexis was four and Irene would have been almost three years old. They were both at our house and I had left them with their Bapa while I ran some errands. When I came in I heard both little girls crying, and obviously in pain. I ran to investigate and found all three of them in the laundry room. The little girls were white faced and Bapa had a very contrite look on his own face. Apparently he had lost track of them long enough for them to get into, and play in my bucket of powdered laundry detergent. They somehow got it all over their faces and in their eyes. Bapa was trying to clean them with a wet cloth, and all I could do was stand and laugh helplessly. It's a memory that still makes me laugh. What a sight!

The summer after we returned from Germany, we loaded the kids and dog in the van to go visit my family. We were stationed in Maryland at the time and my folks live in Arkansas so we spent one entire day traveling before stopping at a hotel in Tennessee for the night. We unloaded the van then swam for about an hour before going to dinner at a nearby Bonanza. I tried to warn the kids not to eat too much since Mistie and Brooke had a very real problem with car sickness. They didn't listen and ate dessert after stuffing themselves full of dinner. We stopped for gas on the way back to the hotel, where Mistie announced that she was going to be sick. I ordered her out to the grassy area "just in case". After a few minutes I asked Brooke, who still harbors bitter memories of this night, to go check on her while I remained with Stacie. By the time she got over to her, Mistie was on her knees throwing up. Brooke took one look and started throwing up too. I could do nothing but sit and laugh so hard I couldn't speak and could barely breathe. Ernie was pumping the gas when he heard all the commotion and walked around to my side of the van to ask what the heck was going on. I could only point and laugh so hard I thought I was going to join the girls!! I still howl with laughter when I think about it. The girls have never forgiven me and would nominate me for the Worst Mother of all Times Hall of Fame if one existed. This just makes me laugh harder.

Speaking of Germany we lived in a beautiful new townhouse for the first eighteen months of our three year tour, before moving into quarters when the dollar to Mark ratio fell. This townhouse had gorgeous, stone tile floors in the entry hall and a magnificent wooden, spiraling staircase leading to the bedrooms upstairs and one to the open basement below. I got it into my head one time to wax the floors and stairs using a paste wax. (And I did this on my knees!) The floor looked nice and being stone wasn't slick. The stairs however, were another story entirely. I happened to be present when my always dignified husband went scooting down them on his butt as his stocking feet went flying out from under him. Fortunately none of us was ever hurt and of course all that I could do was laugh helplessly as each of us, including myself, took a turn slipping and sliding down those polished death traps.

In case anyone is not yet convinced that I wouldn't make a good nurse then here's a convincing example of why not. When Brooke was five and in Kindergarten, she became very ill. This was a child who was always happy and busy, who suddenly started falling asleep at the dinner table while waiting to be served, and who had to be picked up at a Daisy Girl Scout Christmas party when the leader called and told me that she was running a fever. She would appear to be fine one moment then the next would spike a sudden high fever. I was so scared that she had leukemia that I wouldn't take her to the doctor, choosing instead to play ostrich and hope it would all go away. In two weeks time she had gotten so thin however, I was forced to take her. The doctor sent us straight to radiology where they took a chest x-ray then instructed us to wait in the waiting room for the films to take back to the doctor. We waited nearly two hours! We sat and watched many people come and go and as time drug on, the more convinced I became that she was gravely ill and that I had likely killed her with my reluctance to take her to the doctor sooner. As it turned out, the radiologist wanted to ask me about the clips in her chest. She had had a coarctation of the aorta repaired two weeks before her fourth birthday and the clips were still visible on the x-rays. So what was the final diagnosis? She had walking pneumonia which explained the sudden fatigue and spiked temperatures. I suppose I deserved the punishing wait for the films. Bbut that didn't stop me from wanting to wound a certain radiologist who put me through torture while I waited for the mom imposed death sentence of my child.

All three of my children have broken bones and all three have endured mom's misdiagnoses. Mistie broke her wrist while skating near the end of the school year with her sixth grade class in Texas. When I got to the emergency room I looked at her wrist and decided that at most, she had sprained it. The final diagnosis was one of the most common breaks of childhood. When a child falls they put their hands out to break their fall and wind up breaking their wrist instead. We moved from there to Alabama shortly after and she wore a wrist cast for much of the hot, sticky Alabama summer. Brooke was finishing the fourth grade in Germany when I was called to pick her up at her Judo class early, due to a possible broken collar bone. The Judo instructor's brother had tossed Brooke then landed on her. All described a sickening sounding snap, and she was in obvious pain but being the always caring mother, I looked at her back and said "I don't think it's broken. You'll be fine". The next morning she was still in distress so her dad and I took her to the hospital in Frankfurt for x-rays. She wore a brace for several weeks and of course this was one of the hottest summers that Germany had seen in years. When Stacie broke her leg in a skate board accident I was convinced she may have bruised it but surely it wasn't broken. An ambulance ride from the military to civilian hospital convinced me that I was wrong. In case it didn't, the toe to hip cast for ten very long weeks sealed the diagnosis. At least she broke her leg in the cold of winter so the cast helped keep her leg warm.

There are those who know of my problems handling an emergency and no doubt think I'm a nut case. I prefer to think I'm easily excitable. Still to be safe, if you ever find yourself in an emergency and your choices are to call me or call a taxicab for a ride to the hospital, call the taxi. Trust me on this one.

Jeremiah 49:24 Damascus has become feeble, she has turned to flee and panic has gripped her; anguish and pain have seized her, pain like that of a woman in labor.

Home, A Regular Funhouse Of Laughs

We definitely have our moments where life is tumultuous to say the least, but we also have our fun moments. In fact I often feel as if I live in a fun house with the regular laugh riots around here.

Case in point—Irene who turned 7 a couple of weeks ago and who is finishing up 1st grade is learning about good touch, bad touch, tattling versus telling when someone is getting hurt, etc. She came home recently and reported what she learned that day so imagine our surprise when she informed us that she had learned about body parts. *That* will get your attention fast. The raised eyebrows of shock quickly turned into facial contortions as we listened to:" Boys have penises and girls have Chinas". We nearly exploded as we tried not to burst into laughter. She was deadly serious and could not figure out why we were all suddenly bug eyed and turning blue from holding back the laughs. Alexis picked up on our humor and said, "I thought they're called Japans". I suppose we'll teach her the correct word some day but first we have to be able to say it with a straight face.

Alexis, who will be 9 in July, has recently learned how to armpit fart. What a charming little talent. She loves to play mini-armpit concerts for any unsuspecting audience. My brother, a talented armpit fart musician himself when we were kids would be so proud! Of course she only does this for family members. During one of our deep conversations recently, she made me promise that I"ll never tell her friends about this ability or the fact that she frequently practices the "other" kind as well. I like her mom's suggestion that we keep this information in mind for when she starts dating. We can threaten to tell her date and all of her friends if she doesn't respect curfew. We sure raised her mom right.

Jarod, who'll be 3 later this month, offers up his own fair share of laughs as well. He has developed a parrot like talent of repeating many things that he hears, verbatim. This means we all have to be careful what we say within his earshot. Butthead is one of his favorite words now. He's a happy little guy and wakes up in a good mood most mornings. One day last weekend he woke up in an exceptionally good mood and decided to try and scare me and his Bapa. We were sitting at the computer trying to find some information when he jumped around the corner in a perfect Hulk stance, roared at us then started laughing.

He has several movies that he likes, all on "DDD's". He even has a bag to carry his ddd's in when he goes from here to home and back. Currently his favorites are anything Shaggy and Scooby. We watch them so often that I think I've got them memorized. He has the Scooby movie of course, and recently went to see the second Scooby Doo movie, his very first time in a theater. Mistie tells me that he cries to go and see Shaggy and Scooby every time they pass the cinema now.

Just like any family, we have our conflicts and arguments but thank God we are also blessed with fun and funny moments. We never know what to expect next, and I truly wouldn't want it any other way.

Genesis 49:25 because of your father's God, who helps you, because of the Almighty, who blesses you with blessings of the heavens above, blessings of the deep that lies below, blessings of the breast and womb.

I Ain't No High Class Broad

I'm really not a country fan but I do like Gretchen Wilson's song, Redneck Woman. Apparently though, according to my daughter's as in the song, I'm a redneck woman. I'm okay with that, but I must however insert one caveat to this claim; I do not leave my Christmas lights up all year. The mere thought of leaving them up past the New Year makes me feel sweaty and faint.

I was lounging around yesterday in my new favorite shirt talking about going to the library when Stacie said, "Just don't go out in public in that shirt!" What?! She doesn't like my new denim, short sleeved shirt with the beads, sparkles and shiny threads?! That's... so sad.

What can I say? I love shiny things, especially on my clothes. I particularly like wearing them during the Christmas holidays. My sweaters are so loaded that the only things missing are lights and baubles. I've even considered battery powered lights, but the baubles are a no-go. I'd have to spend all my time standing since they'd be too uncomfortable when I sit. I wore shiny clothes so much for the Christmas play practice last year, that one of the young girls at church said to me, "Mrs. Nagy you sure do like shiny clothes don't you?" My response was "I SURE do!" as I puffed up with pride in my pretty, sparkly, fake jewel encrusted sweater. I wish that I could find shirts like those sweaters for all seasons.

Stacie, in a moment of profound thinking, reflected as she shook her head that "It doesn't matter what era you were born in or what part of the country, you're still a southern woman at heart and a ....I jumped in with "A redneck woman"? She shook her head in disgust as she agreed.

If wearing pretty, flashy and I'll admit it, gaudy shirts makes me a southern, even redneck woman at heart then I accept the label with pride and honor. After all they tend to have fabulous taste in clothes. Why, just look inside my closet.

Isaiah 61:10 I delight greatly in the LORD; my soul rejoices in my God. For he has clothed me with garments of salvation and arrayed me in a robe of righteousness, as a bridegroom adorns his head like a priest, and as a bride adorns herself with her jewels.

I Am A Cowpitter?!

My oldest daughter, Mistie shared this delightful snippet with me when Alexis (now 11) was in pre-school. Her (now ex) husband Joe had been having back problems and after a trip to the military doctor, brought home a pamphlet about lower back pain. It had a picture of a side view of a spine on the front. The following conversation ensued after Mistie asked Alexis what she thought the picture was:

"It's a cow pitter [caterpillar]."

"A what?"

"A cow pitter...you know...with legs."

"Giggle"

"A cow pitter has [gesturing with her hands wildly] FREAK legs."

"Giggle, giggle, did you hear this Joe?"

"It's a cow pitter, with freak legs and it goes [gesturing wildly again] *&&*^^&&[unintelligible sound effects, something like erk erk erk]"

"You mean a caterpillar?"

"NO, a COW PITTER, with freak legs."

"How many legs does a cow pitter have?"

"Three...freak..er..lots!"

"Does a cow pitter have a hundred legs?"

"NO, not a hundred...FREAK."

"Honey, that picture is a spine...it's a picture of what is in your back (as I am tracing my fingers down her spine)."

"(Eyes wild with amazement) I am a cow pitter?"

Thought you might enjoy this. ~~Mistie

Genesis 1:27 So God created man in his own image, in the image of God he created him; male and female he created them.

I Am A Laundry Menace

Let me tell you, the past couple of weeks have been difficult at times not to mention expensive. Unfortunately, I'm responsible for all that's taken place too. I shouldn't have left 2 ½ year old Irene unattended long enough for her to attack the chair with a knife. And I certainly should have made sure the garage door remote was out of her reach since she is used to pushing the button when we come and go. Fortunately the hood of the Jimmy wasn't damaged by the door coming down on it, and the broken garage door was easy enough to fix, though it still has a crease in it.

This latest is also 100% my fault. I would love to blame someone else but it's my own dumb responsibility. I was trying to get a jump on housework last night so started laundry in the early evening. I washed a couple of new shirts for Ernie then put his nice khaki pants in to wash. I noticed they had spots so grabbed the Spray and Wash and doused them good. Imagine my horrified surprise when I took them out of the washer and they were streaked. I grabbed the bottle, sniffed it and realized the S&W bottle had bleach in it! I don't know who did it or when it was put there, but it was definitely bleach. I noticed it smelled funny, but had used it a few times before with no problems. These new pants have only been washed two or three times. I was *so* upset but I didn't say a word to Ernie.

I was afraid he'd ask for them this morning when he got dressed, but thankfully he didn't. However I wasn't taking any chances, so I hid them behind a big bottle of detergent in the laundry cupboard just in case he went looking for them. Bet you didn't know what a coward I am. So instead of doing housework this morning I went to the store for new pants to give him when I tell him about his other ones tonight. I found some nice ones too, made of some micro-fiber. The (now) streaky ones looked good on him, but these will look even better. That's what I intend to tell him anyway.

Psalm 19:12 Who can discern his errors? Forgive my hidden faults.

I Am A True Menace!

I have done it again……..I am a menace. Someone needs to unplug my washer and dryer and lock the laundry room door.

You may recall some time back that I wrote and told you about ruining a pair of Ernie's new pants when I poured something other than Spray 'N Wash on them. (Actually, it was bleach but no one has fessed up to being the culprit who put it there. In fact, everyone has accused ME of doing it! HUMPH!) This is so embarrassing…. I ruined another pair of his pants.

It all started when I accidentally washed something pink with a load of whites. The only things that came out pink was a pair of Irene's shorts and one of Ernie's really nice knit Polo shirts that he got from work. During this same laundry session, I noticed that Ernie had gotten a rather large spot of what looked like ink on the leg of his somewhat new, dark green pants. I tried to remove the ink using pre-wash, quick n' brite and hairspray but NOTHING worked. It didn't even lighten.

We were leaving for Alabama the next day and I wanted to take Irene's shorts with us, so I made a trip to the store to buy a box of Rit dye remover to get the pink out. In my infinite lack of wisdom, I decided to toss his green pants in to see if it would remove the ink. Oh wow, BIG mistake. Once again, you can imagine my horror when I saw those green pants turn maroon (!). Who would have thought green would turn that very unattractive shade of color? And to make matters worse it didn't even touch the ink.

Well true to my own proven cowardice, I took those dripping pants and stuffed them into the trashcan next to the washer. I then asked Brooke, who was having a few friends over from work the next evening, to PLEASE take them to the trash can and bury them the next day after we had left for Alabama. She just shook her head and agreed to the deed, and said that first she was going to show them to her friends. I hope none of them is into blackmail.

Thankfully Ernie hasn't asked about his pants….yet. I'll get to the store to replace them soon. I just can't figure out how to tell him. I don't know if he'll be upset but I suspect he'll say I should have saved them and he could have worn them around the house to work in. I just have a little problem with the giggles every time I imagine him mowing the yard in maroon colored pants though.

The truly sad thing is I sincerely enjoy doing laundry. Why couldn't I just blow up a vacuum cleaner or two? That's a chore I would gladly give up.

Exodus 19:10 And the LORD said to Moses, "Go to the people and consecrate them today and tomorrow. Have them wash their clothes

I Love A Parade!

I was suffering with a case of the "woe is me/poor me's all day yesterday, but that ended at 6:00 PM last night. That was the night of High Point's annual Christmas parade and no one but the worst scrooge could stay in a bad mood in the midst of such sights and fun. Fun because once again the little girls got to take part. For the past two years since she works for them, Brooke has been asked to ride on the 911 float, so Irene and Alexis get to go too. Last year it was so bitterly cold that they were crying by the end. We were so frozen that as soon as their float went by, we gathered them up and went home. We weren't sure they would want to ride again this year but apparently they have short memories. They nearly drove us nuts while waiting for the big day. The mommy's bought warm hats and gloves, and we took blankets to wrap them in. We also took steaming thermoses of hot coffee and raspberry flavored hot chocolate. Thankfully it wasn't nearly as cold this year, dropping down only into the 40's. The hot coffee sure tasted good though and helped keep the chill at bay.

Brooke arranged for us to drop the girls off at their float site along the parade route around 5 PM. She alerted the young cop manning the barricade that we were coming, so we felt "special" when he saw us and moved it, waving us through. We handed the girls over to Brooke and several of the other float riders then went off to find a parking place near City Hall, our meeting place for after the parade. We were so early that we had our pick of parking places and even saved one for Mistie who was meeting us there after work.

After Mistie arrived we got Jarod all wrapped up in hat, coat, mittens and a blanket then stowed him in his stroller and walked the two blocks to Main street. We got there in time to lay claim to a brick wall and sat down to wait. There was so much activity going on with police cars and people, that Jarod was kept entertained watching it all. At 6 o'clock sharp we heard the first strain of band music. Being near the start of the parade, it was just a short time before we saw them marching towards us. By this time the crowds had grown to thousands but we had a great vantage point right on the street so we just relaxed and enjoyed the show.

Last year was so cold that we couldn't even enjoy looking at the floats. We were so miserable that we just wanted "ours" to get there so we could leave. The route is between 2 to 3 miles long and we were at the end of the route so it took a while. This time we got to oh and ah for almost 2 hours. We saw mini-cars and mini-motorcycles, many marching bands and legions of floats. There were over 200 entries, both riding and walking and surprisingly, it went very smoothly. The one exception was when the car

Bonnie and Clyde were riding in broke down and had to be push started. At first we thought it was all part of the "act" when the driver jumped out and started looking under the hood. It wasn't long before they were rolling, and shooting it out with the cops again. (I have no idea what this had to do with a Christmas parade but it was entertaining!). We also saw local celebrities from our favorite news channels and radio stations.

The 911 float was number eighteen in position and we were watching anxiously for them. I spotted the red, white and blue balloons some distance away so we all jumped up in anticipation. The little girls and Brooke were watching for us too and we all waved like maniacs. It was a proud moment for this Nana! I was so thankful that this year was warmer and that they could enjoy themselves this time. The final float held the only Santa in the parade and he was very authentic looking. The girls went nuts calling to him. He spotted them, spoke directly to them, making them suddenly shy and awe struck. I hope they never forget this memory and that it will be just one of many more to come.

Esther 8:15 Mordecai left the king's presence wearing royal garments of blue and white, a large crown of gold and a purple robe of fine linen. And the city of Susa held a joyous celebration.

I Wonder If Possums Bite

Our middle daughter Brooke has a home near here in Halifax, but works in High Point, which is a three hour drive, so commutes on her days off for work. Or at least did commute. She had been doing this for two plus years and grew quite weary of it so moved Irene down to High Point with her and plans to sell her house here.

Her dad being the wonderful, generous person that he is has been working on her house in the evenings and on weekends, getting it ready to place on the market. Being the mom, I get volunteered to assist. I'm generous and wonderful too, but more reluctant about it since I'm not a terribly handy person. My husband is the type who can build or repair just about anything. Not me. I once watched him replacing boards on our deck and felt sorry for him while watching him pull boards up, cut new ones to fit then screw them into place. It was a lot of up and down work so I offered to help him by using the drill, freeing him to pull and cut. It was a nice idea in theory. I couldn't even get the first screw in and tore the top of that screw all to pieces. It should be so simple, just place the driver into the screw head, pull the lever and voila! Not so, at least for a handy incapable such as myself. That drill slipped and slid all over until he took it away from me before I could manage to drill my foot to the deck.

I can paint though. I can also use a manual screw driver, clean and hang curtains after washing them, mop floors and other menial but necessary tasks, so I am able to assist a bit.

Unfortunately when I painted, I got a bit enthusiastic and managed to paint the outlets requiring them to be replaced. My husband is also a very forgiving man and showed great patience as he handed me the screw driver, instructing me to remove the plates then loosen the outlets from the wall so that he could change all six in that one bedroom. It didn't take long to remember why I don't ordinarily perform these kinds of household maintenance chores. I had already removed one cover and had stuck the screwdriver into the screw holding the outlet when it occurred to me that it would be a good idea to confirm that I had indeed killed power to the outlet. I had flipped the circuit breaker, the overhead lights went out so I went to work, assuming that the outlets were now dead as well. Thank God I listened to that small voice in my head. I plugged the vacuum in to the outlet and flipped it on, expecting silence. Wrong again. The outlet was live and I had almost been dead. By the way, for the record I am now firmly convinced that it should be a federal law that all screws have ½ inch deep heads at the very least. For the life of me, I can't figure out how to firmly seat a screwdriver into that tiny little slot on top. It just slips around as if the screw head were made of ice and the screwdriver was feet. Then again, maybe I'm not as inept at household maintenance as I thought. Yeah, that's it. It's not my fault; it's the fault of screw and drill manufacturers. They need to design tools for the handy incapable, something along the line of the chopsticks seen in a Chinese restaurant one time. I simply can't grasp the use of those things either. This particular place had some made just for kids; two chopsticks with a folded piece of napkin between them, held together with a rubber band. They work great for kids and klutzy, inept adults. I know this because I asked for and used some myself, much to the amusement of my family.

But now I have wandered off the point. Where was I? Oh yes, the fixing up of Brooke's house for sale, while trying to not kill myself or cause any major damage along the way.

Her home had not seen much daily living abuse since she got to spend so little time in it, so most of the maintenance chores are straight forward and simple. Ernie does need to replace one window. The former owners had replaced all with double hung, but somehow missed one in the second bedroom. How I don't know, and why they didn't just go ahead and replace it is an unanswerable question. He also needs to tear out the surround in the shower and re-finish the bathtub. The same former owner attempted to paint the tub and did a very sloppy job of prepping, so it peeled shortly after she moved in. Thinking about it, this goes a long way in explaining how he would miss a window. The plans are to replace the cracked surround with ceramic tile and to attempt to sand and properly re-finish the tub since it's otherwise in good shape. Besides, he recently remodeled our oldest daughter's bathroom and spent an entire day cutting her iron bathtub into sections so that he could remove it. I think his arms shook for the rest of that day from the pounding they took. This is an iron tub too so he's trying to avoid the same punishment for being good.

We had gone over one pretty Saturday afternoon to do some painting and he stepped out on the back deck to grab a can of paint to repair a patch in one of the rooms. When he came back inside, he casually mentioned that Brooke had a dead possum in her big trash can that was sitting on the deck. Say what? Now he knows quite well that I was born and raised in Missouri, otherwise known as the Show Me State so I of course *had* to confirm this. I stepped outside and half expecting it to be a big joke where he'd jump behind me to scare me, I sidled up to the trashcan,. Nope, there really *was* a possum inside! Of course being the good born and raised Missourian that I am, I had to lean in to see it better and discovered that he was wrong about one thing; it wasn't dead, it was asleep. The last time I had seen a possum up close and personal I was in the first grade and one ran out of the woods in front of me and my sisters as we walked to school one morning. It startled me so bad that

I almost got to turn around to go home and change my underpants. I don't scare as easily now, especially when one of us is trapped. So of course I had to investigate and it didn't take long to figure out why he'd gone into the can. It held a bag of almost empty dry dog food, and possibly being from Missouri himself, he had decided to jump in from the deck rail to check it out and became trapped in the process. We have no idea how long he'd been in there, but there was still some food so it probably hadn't been terribly long. He sure looked cozy under that dog food bag blanket with his scary looking little feet and tail sticking out. I could sympathize. When I sleep at night I have to have my feet sticking out from the blankets, and if I had a tail would no doubt want it to hang out as well. Even though those strange almost human feet and his creepy little snake-like tail freaked me out, I couldn't resist so gave the can a good shake. That only caused him to crawl deeper under his paper blanket while snoozing on. I was concerned that he was near dead from fear of enclosed places (a trait I share if so) and lack of water then remembered that possums are nocturnal so left him alone. At least for the most part. For the rest of the afternoon I took frequent breaks to go out and shake the can to see if he'd wake up. Every shake just drove him deeper into the covers, which thankfully made his freakily fascinating tail and feet disappear with him.

Finally around dusk and shortly before we quit for the day, I went out and found him awake. I think he knew I was the one who had rocked his world all afternoon because he wasn't all that happy to see me. In fact he was downright rude and mean. He opened his mouth in that pointy little face of his and made hissy noises at me! I tried to explain to him that I meant him no harm, that I'd simply shaken him up to try and send him on his way but he was having nothing to do with my explanation and was holding a grudge. Being as scared of him as he was of me and being quite unsure if he'd suddenly find the ability to jump straight up and latch onto my face with his mean, snarly mouth, I carefully rolled the trash can over to the stairs and laid it on its side. "Run free ugly-little-snake-tailed-creepy-footed-snarly-mouthed-ingrate" I yelled but he simply continued to lie in the overturned trashcan, snarling from his ugly little pointy faced mouth so I decided to leave him mercifully be for a few minutes, to see if he'd leave on his own. Returning all of three minutes later (I did say a few) I found him still in residence and still snarling. This went on for several more minutes with me shaking the can to try and dislodge him. This only caused him to hate me more ferociously so in a final courageous, I'll save you act of heroism, I covered my head with one arm (still fearing his developing a sudden ability to lunge and latching on with his mean little mouth), picked the can up and dumped it. He slid out and was gone so fast that all I saw was a blur. I can't speak for him, but my unmentionables survived this possum encounter just fine.

As for the house, it is looking sharp. If you know anyone looking for a cute home, tell them we've re-painted the master bedroom, cleaned the carpets, will soon replace the window and re-finish the bathroom. That simply leaves cleaning the yard, and then it will be ready to sell. This is a darling little two bedroom, one bath house on a quiet street, located directly across the street from the Halifax County Library. It even comes with its own pet....but you may not want to mention that part.

Jeremiah 8:17 "See, I will send venomous snakes among you, vipers that cannot be charmed, and they will bite you," declares the LORD.

Interesting......

Have you ever watched Maurice Sendak's "Little Bear" on Nickelodeon? With little ones in the house, I have watched a fair amount of shows and highly recommend it to anyone with a sense of curiosity and a strong imagination, even if you don't have kids in the house. Little Bear lives in the forest with Mother and Father Bear, with his grandparent bears living close by. He plays with Cat, Owl, Hen, and Duck, who was separated at birth from her family and was raised by a chicken so she never learned to fly. Duck is flaky, silly and my favorite character. I'd watch the show just to hear her quacky laugh. There's also Emily, the little human girl who visits the forest with her grandmother. She's Little Bear's best friend and has a doll named Lucy who carries on imaginary conversations with Emily and Little Bear. And finally there's No Feet the green snake. I even like him in spite of his being a snake. They all have incredibly creative imaginations that take them from the depths of the local lake in an imaginary submarine to a picnic on the moon. Whenever they learn something new, one of them will frequently say "Interesting..."

While taking Irene to school this morning, I noticed something interesting myself. Irene was uncharacteristically quiet on the ride so I amused myself by paying attention to small details around me. It wasn't long before the car in front of me caught my attention with the brightly colored and shiny items hanging from their rear view mirror. Closer inspection revealed several strands of Mardi Gras beads. This got me to thinking about what kinds of items other people hang from their own rear view mirrors, how many do or don't decorate and why. I don't know the answer to why but due to a quick un-scientific survey performed for the rest of the drive I now have a good idea of some what's and sort of how many. I watched cars, business vehicles and trucks as I traveled south on Main Street and the results are in.....

The number of drivers who decorate their mirrors was roughly equal to those who don't. The most popular item seen dangling were air fresheners of all shapes, sizes and designs. We appear to have some stinky automobiles here in High Point. I even saw two cars, one after the other with the same red white and blue style freshener swinging from the mirror. I also saw everything from sunglasses (the only thing my husband will decorate his truck's rear view with by the way) to baby shoes, chains, graduation tassels, crosses and cell phones. My own Jimmy has a faded red "Stop to Pray" medallion hanging from a string.

When I go to pick Irene from school later, I intend to continue my little survey to see if I can decide if women or men are more prone to have decorations hanging in their windshields.

I wonder who the first person was to decide the mirror needed decorating, what the very first adornment was and why they decided it needed one? I may not know the answers to these questions but I can just hear Little Bear saying "Interesting....." while Duck quack laughs in the background.

Isaiah 3:23 and mirrors, and the linen garments and tiaras and shawls.

Irene And Nana..........

We've pulled another dumb one. Irene got a pair of my old panty hose out of my bedroom trashcan and brought them into her room across the hall, where the computer is currently located. She then gave me one end and she took the other then streeeeetched them out of her room, across the hall and into my bedroom. Those babies look like they were made for a 10-foot tall giant. Well guess what? They weren't old ones from the trash; they are brand new ones I had bought today. Man, I think we both need babysitters.

Proverbs 8:5 You who are simple, gain prudence; you who are foolish, gain understanding.

Irene, Garfield, And Tiny Dancers

I went shopping yesterday with 2 ½ year old Miss Irene in tow. I promised her a treat if she was good. She was and for her treat picked out a book (of course, she LOVES books) and a box of Garfield Band-Aids. She tried to sneak a candy bar in but when I told her to put something back, the candy went. Well that child had a ball with those Band-Aids. She sat and ate her lunch in front of the TV and when I checked on her, had a Band-Aid on at least three toes and one finger. Throughout the afternoon I found several pieces of furniture that had developed "boo-boos", so were sporting colorful Garfield boo-boo covers.

I admit it! I no longer deny I'm getting old. I find few things in life more enjoyable than a short nap before bedtime in my big overstuffed recliner. I took a short but intense nap last night. It took me a few minutes but when I woke up I realized the big toe on my left foot hurt. I looked down and guess what? Remember the Garfield strips? Irene had wrapped one so tightly around my toe it was cutting off the circulation. I also had one on the birthmark on my left leg and discovered one on my lower leg in the shower the next morning.

Speaking of showers taking one by myself is a rare treat. She can be in any room in the house and will come running, stripped naked, as soon as she hears the shower door open. She got so upset the other day when she heard the water turn on that she jumped in with her panties still on. I had asked her if she wanted a shower but she declined because Dragon Tales was on. It went off as I stepped into the stall so she of course changed her mind and came running upstairs to join me.

This morning, for some reason known only to her she decided she wanted a shower in the main bathroom bathtub instead of our shower. This was fine with me since I needed to shave and waste an awful lot of shave cream when she's with me. I've got tell you, there's very little that can compare to the enjoyment of standing in a nice hot shower listening to your 2 ½-year-old granddaughter belt out Twinkle Twinkle Little Star in the other shower. She was really giving it all she had.....at the top of her apparently, very large lungs.

This last incident happened the other day and I still laugh when I think of how she looked. I had a couple of $5 bills sitting on the computer desk next to me while I checked e-mail. I told Irene who was playing with them, that we were going to the store later and I laid them there so I wouldn't forget them so please don't lose them. I looked over at her a couple of minutes later and she had them poking out of her panties like some tiny stripper! Need I say that I nearly rolled out of my chair laughing?

I never know what to expect her to do next or what Mistie will tell me Alexis has recently done. (Like sneaking into the closet and unwrapping all the Christmas presents), but I do know I'll (almost) always find them very entertaining.

Matthew 19:14 Jesus said, "Let the little children come to me, and do not hinder them, for the kingdom of heaven belongs to such as these."

I've Watched Toooo Many Scary Movies

I took a deep breath this morning, and after a week of keeping the door closed so that I wouldn't have to look at it, went in to clean the grandkids bedroom. It's simply amazing what three little kids can do to a bedroom, so I was almost ill at the thought of entering the "pit".

I bagged trash, sorted clean clothes from dirty and fussed the whole time I worked. Finally I reached the point that I could start clearing out from under the bed. Using the broom handle, I started pulling what I could reach then pushing junk out to the opposite side when I suddenly had a near heart stopping moment; I had hit something solid and immovable. I was pushing hard, and though I didn't hear any grunting I was sure that something tugged back on the broom, creating an instant of panic. I gave whatever it was another good poke and when that elicited no sounds, I decided to get down on my knees and look under the bed. Believe me I was praying since it's a huge chore for me to get these knees to bend, so I knew if anyone was under there, I'd be a goner. I would never be able to get up and run away fast enough unless it was a dead somebody. Somehow that thought didn't offer a whole lot of comfort though.

So with my heart in my throat I got down on all fours and nearly screamed when I finally worked up the nerve to look. No it wasn't a body, dead or alive but *was* the biggest pile of junk, pillows and blankets that I've ever seen. I almost wish it *had* been a body. The bed is too low for me to crawl under (or I'm too big to fit but I refuse to admit that) so I was unable to get at all of it. I plan to reorganize the room next week when Brooke is off work so it will just have to wait until then.

Of course keeping in mind all of the really (bad) scary movies that I've seen over my lifetime, I'm going to be very cautions when I do go back to finish the job. That pile of junk could actually be a living entity that I woke from its slumber and it may start to grow again.........

Daniel 5:6 His face turned pale and he was so frightened that his knees knocked together and his legs gave way.

Jimmy Saga Chapter 1,000,000

Ok, so it only *feels* like a million chapters. This would be because we've had so many problems with Jimmy over the years. We bought it new after our first (also new) Jimmy turned out to be a lemon. The repair file on that thing must have been two inches thick with problems ranging from a bad air compressor at six-months of age to the final straw, transmission trouble eighteen months later. We made it clear we would seek a lawyer if the car dealer didn't make an excellent offer on a replacement. They did so we chose another Jimmy, this time upgraded with sun roof and multiple CD player instead of single. We were assured that the first one with multiple problems was a fluke, and this one would be reliable. It was for the duration of the warranty but as soon as we moved from Alabama to North Carolina, the fun began. We never knew when or where it would just decide to quit, then it was anyone's guess when it would start working again. We had that stupid thing towed three times to a dealership, but twice it started up again once they got ready to look at it. Third time was the charm, after stopping mid-way through a turn on my way to school with Alexis one morning. It didn't start again and the dealership was able to determine it was some sort of problem with a black box doohickey. After that was repaired we managed to keep it going with occasional minor problems until our dreaded trip to Georgia when it once again began to fall apart, quite literally. (See Redneck road trip). It wasn't long after that trip that the end finally arrived for dear old Jimmy. A couple of days after we got home from that trip, the thing started making a noise that we tried to ignore. Then just a day or so after this new noise, I was just getting ready to turn into our driveway when it started making a horrendous noise and barely made it into the driveway where I turned it off. When we attempted to re-start it, the noise was so fearsome that we quickly turned it off and arranged to take Jimmy to the vehicle hospital.....

We finally got the Jimmy to the Jimmy Doctor/our mechanic last night and what an ordeal it was. We've wanted to take it all week but Ernie simply hasn't had to chance to get to the U-Haul for the toter. Last night he did so we all assembled out front. By all I mean me and the three grandkids. They were there to watch and I was there to encourage, but as it turned out I was actually there to help. I really wanted to join the kiddy group but I was the only other adult present.

It started out with Ernie backing the toter into the driveway. (The kind that only the two front wheels sit on). The kids were so excited, having never seen one and interested in just what we were going to do with it. Sad isn't it, what gets them excited? Irene insisted on standing in the driveway and after repeated instructions to "MOVE" I finally grabbed her arm to drag her away before she got run over. She stumbled backwards on the uneven brick walk and fell into the brick retaining wall next to the driveway, scratching her back. Suddenly we had one less spectator as she stomped off crying into the house, yelling "Leave me alone Nana!" as I tried to apologize. Ah well better a scratched back than a squashed kid I always say.

Now we have the dilemma of HOW to get Jimmy onto the trailer. If it had been backed into the driveway it would have been simple since the driveway slopes down towards the street. I was lucky to even get it into the driveway when the head gasket (we think—still waiting on that diagnosis) blew and didn't have the foresight to back it in which I often do on a normal day. We live on a very busy street and backing in just makes getting out again sooo much easier. But I digress.

Ernie rolled Jimmy down the driveway and into the street against the curb then backed the trailer back out "into position". He then tried to start Jimmy but it very quickly became obvious that it was a very BAD IDEA. You've never heard such a racket. As much as I have disliked this vehicle over the years, we have had our good trips and long periods of taking-for-granted so it hurt to hear it in such obvious pain. Thankfully our street has a very gentle decline, so Ernie was able to put it in neutral and roll it backwards. He then instructed me to *get inside* so that I could steer (no power steering OR brakes at this point btw) while he *pushed* it onto the trailer. YIKES! I tried to squirm out of it by telling him that he wasn't strong enough to push that thing up a ramp with me inside but he was determined to try, so I got in. I was scared silly too since I couldn't see the ramps to be sure that I was straight with them, but he assured me that I was OK as long as I turned the wheels to the right just a bit. That man is STRONG! He started pushing and suddenly we've got some great momentum going and I'm nearly blubbering with fear that I'll hit the ramp and miss them and some unknown disaster will occur and we're going faster and it looks like we'll do this and we're just touching the ramp when I look up and see *all* three kids sitting in the back of the pick-up watching all of this and I panic and......hit the brakes. Ernie was so aggravated with me that I just know he could have strangled me. In fact he pretty much told me he could and asked WHY did I hit the brakes JUST as we were reaching the ramps? I was soooo sorry to do it to him but I panicked—I just knew when we hit the ramps that something would fly up and hurt the kids. So we got them tucked inside the truck out of harms way and he backed back down the street again, and prepares to push it one more time with the world's biggest chicken driving once again. This is the point that God delivered two angels in the form of workmen hired to do some work for the neighbor who, when they saw what Ernie was preparing to do, came running to help. I didn't have much time to think about anything as I jumped in and they started pushing. They all assured me that I was dead on to the ramps when I asked are you sure I'm dead on to the ramps, as they started pushing. Too late to back out now because we're flying towards those ramps now and Jimmy hits it and...rolls back down. We didn't have quite enough momentum going (probably due to the weight of that huge chicken inside which was growing in size with every scary attempt). So we rolled back a bit and once again here we go faster and faster and VICTORY! We're on the ramps and they're all yelling "hit the brakes now!" I stood on the brakes with both feet just to be sure.

Glory Halleluiah we have a ramped Jimmy, ready to go to the Jimmy Doctor. We all load up in the truck and take off for the Jimmy clinic, joking about how there seems to be a car following us awfully close.

Less than 15 minutes later we're pulling into the vehicle hospital yard and we all pile out to watch as Ernie prepares to take it off the trailer, giddy with relief. Then again maybe we should leave it on the trailer to make it easier for Dr. Eddie to get it inside one of his bays? We can always pick the trailer up the next afternoon. That sounds like a good idea so it's just a matter of unhitching the trailer....It turns out that that's not going to happen. That thing is waaaay to heavy for him to lift off of the truck trailer hitch even if all three kids and I helped. So we prepare to back the Jimmy off of the trailer into the yard. Ah oh—it won't budge. The wheels are sitting down in a well with a lip on it soooo.....Ernie instructs big chicken to get back in the driver's seat while he pulls the truck forward. This time I'm to hold the brakes on with it in neutral and it should roll backwards, over the lip and off the trailer. Theoretically speaking this sounds like a great idea. In reality it was a sucky idea. It's getting dark, chilly, we're hungry and the stupid Jimmy just won't give up without a fight but we're just as determined to win. One more time Ernie tells me to get ready to roll, has me put the parking brake on then pulls forward. Eureka!!! Mission accomplished as I roll backwards and gently brake to a stop.

I left the key on the front seat with a note telling Doc to call us as soon as he has a diagnosis. I expect a call any time this morning. I just hope the diagnosis isn't terminal. Ok I admit it I allllmost hope that it is terminal.

We did finally get dinner last night at almost 9PM, after dropping the trailer back off at the rental place which was still open. I had thankfully fed the kids earlier so they were in good shape. I on the other hand was ready to dine on a tire, had I had some salt and pepper with me. Thankfully our dinner was already cooked so all it needed was re-heating. It tasted mighty good after a hard evenings work of loading then unloading that pitiful Jimmy.

Final diagnosis: a thrown rod or some such disastrous disorder. That was the proverbial straw for these backs—we went out a few days later and bought a new Honda Odyssey mini-van. I have wanted one for years and love it. We had needed more seating for a long time since we frequently carried all three grandkids, and several of their friends a good portion of the times we roll out of the driveway. The mini-van has a DVD player and so much glorious room that the kids have trouble finding things to argue about now.

We ultimately put the Jimmy in our front yard with a 4-Sale sign in it once it was finally released from the car ICU complete with a rebuilt engine. When we brought it home, we discovered the air conditioning compressor had quit so we came down on the price. It sold within a week (it really is a pretty vehicle) to a young man headed to college. A couple of months later we heard from his mom that the transmission had gone out. We sincerely hated it for him but were in no way responsible since he'd had it for so long. This sealed our decision to never, ever buy another GMC Jimmy.

Jeremiah 2:21 I had planted you like a choice vine of sound and reliable stock. How then did you turn against me into a corrupt, wild vine?

Ladies And Gentlemen, Please Welcome The Gatlin Brothers!

Wee haw! I got to attend my first ever concert last night, and what a great time it was. The Gatlin Brothers are fantastic! We laughed, we cried, we laughed, clapped, laughed, sang and laughed some more. My mascara and eye liner were probably smeared all over my face afterwards, but I didn't care since I was having so much fun.

Our evening got started as we arrived just shortly after 7 PM to an already packed reception area. All of my earlier concern about having to make small talk was for nothing; we didn't know anyone there. It tickled me too as I looked around. Stacie has kidded me about the upcoming Gaither concert in Chapel Hill that I want to attend with my church. She said she can't believe her Mom wants to go to an old geezer concert with a bunch of old church geezers. This concert last night was good practice because the hall was packed with geezers! It's no wonder though, since the Gatlins have been performing for over 40 years now making them somewhere in their 50's. I want to know how someone I listened to in my youth can be that old.

Having never been to a concert before, I wasn't real sure what attire was appropriate. It turns out pretty much anything goes. I was dressy casual in a (per Irene) beautiful black blouse and dress pants. I saw women there in everything from long, pretty dresses to sequined tops and leggings with heels. One thing that struck me after the concert though was all of the fur coats. I've never seen so much fur outside of Humane Society Cat cages. I've never had a desire to own a fur coat myself, since I feel it's a horrible waste of animal life but being in such close proximity to so many last night I had to literally fight the urge to reach out and pet some of the ladies as they walked past me.

We decided to hang on to our coats to avoid the crush at the coat check afterwards and juggled them as we grabbed some food from the more than plentiful buffet. It wasn't fancy food but there was lots of it. We noshed on cheese and crackers, chicken salad, meatballs, fresh fruit, tiny little quiche tarts and far too many other finger foods to list. I was disappointed that the only beverages they offered were sugary fruit punch and coffee. When asked about sugar free drinks, the lady serving apologized and gave me a cup of ice for the water fountain. I just want to know, haven't the organizers ever heard of diabetics?

At 7:25 we decided to beat the rush and head for our seats that turned out to be center stage, seven rows back! We were close enough that we could have shot spit balls at the Gatlins with dead on accuracy had we been so inclined. We settled in next to a couple of other people from Georgia Pacific, and chatted while I people watched. I'm a dedicated people watcher and last night was a people watcher's smorgasbord. There was a whole lot of kiss, kiss and hug, hug going on since we were seated in the VIP/Corporate Sponsors area. Fortunately Ernie isn't so far up the VIP ladder that he has to participate in this so I just sat back, relaxed and enjoyed the "pre-show entertainment".

Then it happened. You may or may not recall my stories about attracting everything from creeps/perverts to yak-ety blondes to people with big heads when I go to movies, which is why I rarely go to movies. Tonight was to be no different; a group started filing into the row in front of us and sure enough a very tall man sat right down in front of me. Ernie told me to think positive as I groaned and I told him "I am—I'm positive I'm not going to see anything". My neck was getting sore from all the twisting I was doing trying to see around Mr. Stinky—my nickname for him since he was also obviously a smoker, yuck, so shortly after the show started I scooted over two seats (four of the GP seats went unoccupied) behind a blessedly short little kid. Ernie said he'd be lonely without me so he moved too, and was able to see fine around the young man in front of him. We then happily settled in for the fastest 1 ½ hours I've ever enjoyed.

At one point they asked all veterans to stand and be recognized and I was so proud of all the guys who stood, including my dear reluctant-to-stand and be noticed husband. I doubt there were many dry eyes as they sang a song dedicated to all military, active and retired. Steve Gatlin dried the tears though when he jokingly told us, "General Schwartzkoph (supposedly) said recently: It's up to God to meet and forgive Saddam Hussein and it's the job of the United States military to arrange that meeting".

Growing up, my siblings and I were force fed Country music. This is all my parents listened to so when we went anywhere with them in the car, this is all we heard. I grew up believing that I hated country and as soon as I had my own car was never caught listening to it again, until Brooke and Stacie went through a short-lived Country phase of their own a few years ago. Last night I learned that my old country roots still run deep. I couldn't force my left foot to stop tapping as it took on a life of its own. My hands hurt from all the clapping and the smile hasn't left my face. Last night was so much fun that I'm glad my first concert at the mature age of 48 was this fabulous Christian Country trio.

I'm planning to see the Gaithers in March for sure now. If it's as much fun as this one was and I fully expect it to be, then I am going to give serious thought to becoming a geezer groupie. Stacie will be so proud.

---

*Sadly I did not get to attend the Gaither concert as planned since there wasn't enough interest in our church to support the ticket cost. But I am determined to see them some day and look forward to that opportunity.

1 Chronicles 15:16 David told the leaders of the Levites to appoint their brothers as singers to sing joyful songs, accompanied by musical instruments: lyres, harps and cymbals.

Life Lessons And Ill Gotten Gains

The following is from Rich Rowand of Recipe du Jour, my story follows.

Rich's Note: Indiana Rich and the Golden Egg

The woman had such a long, sad face she reminded me of a horse. She said, "When I say go, everyone six and younger spread out and look for Easter eggs. When you find one, stop and put it in your basket, then look for more eggs. We'll have a prize for each age group for whoever finds the most eggs." As she said this she held up a colored cellophane-wrapped, candy-filled Easter basket. Our little eyes got bigger. "Also," she continued, "we have two special eggs for you to find. One of them is silver. If you find the silver egg, you'll get this basket." She held up another cellophane-wrapped, candy-filled basket tied with a silver bow. It was easily twice as big as the previous one, chock full of chocolate and multi-colored candy. I wanted it. There were five of the other baskets, but only one with a silver bow. Then she said, "And if you're lucky enough to find the GOLDEN egg, you'll win THIS basket!" Someone handed her the granddaddy of all Easter baskets. It was easily the hugest Easter basket I'd seen in all my six years. It had a gold bow tied to its handle. I could have sat in that basket it was so big. Forget the silver one, I wanted to find the golden egg.

It was a warm spring morning and we were in the field outside my grandmother's union hall on the Saturday before Easter. There must have been a hundred kids behind me. Looking out across the field I saw hundreds of pastel-colored eggs nestled in the new mown grass. I saw eggs in the bushes and eggs balanced in the crooks of the branches of trees. They were all over the place, more eggs than I could count. I squinted against the sun, scanning desperately for a sign of the golden egg. The only advantage we smaller kids had was that we'd go first. I decided on a strategy of ignoring the pastel eggs and concentrate on finding the golden one.

I'm going to make a long story short since there's no use describing a bunch of screaming kids scattering over the field like famished locusts cheered on by adults who probably wished they could look too because they wanted that humongous basket with the gold bow themselves. I passed by dozens of blue, yellow, orange, red, purple, and green eggs in search of the golden one. I looked in trees. I looked under boxes and bushes. I looked all over the rusty tractor surrounded by weeds. I searched and searched and searched with my empty basket until I heard some twelve-year-old scream that she had found the golden egg.

Too late I realized I had nothing to show for my efforts. All the eggs had been found.

My grandmother tried to turn it into a lesson of life, but I didn't listen. I knew the next year would be different.

Jayne's turn:

I don't recall my age at the time but the memory is still clear in my mind. There was a church sponsored egg hunt at the park up the street from our house. As kids we spent many hours hanging out in this park. This is the same one where the pervert followed me, my sister and best friend home one day; but that's another story. (Mad Dogs And Children).

The prize was much smaller than the one in Rich's story but at the time it seemed wonderful. Three lucky children would receive a solid chocolate bunny, encased in a brilliantly colored box *if* they found the brightly colored marshmallow egg with a slip of paper inside the cellophane. We all took off on command and scattered all over the park, searching desperately to find all the candy eggs we could and hoping to find one of the special ones. I found several and my basket was filling up fast but no special egg yet. Just as I was ready to give up, Eureka! I found one of the eggs! I made a beeline for the table to collect my solid chocolate bunny. My twin sister, who is 23 minutes older than me but the shy one, followed me over. Being the extrovert that I was and am I was always protective of her, as if she were the younger sibling. I felt awful that she hadn't found an egg with the slip of paper. There was hope though since there was still one more out there.

Once you found the egg you were supposed to trade it for the bunny but the lady forgot to collect mine. I slipped it back in my basket and told my sister to follow me. I then discreetly dropped it back on the ground for her to "find" it. She grabbed it up and ran to exchange it. I was happy and all was well with my world.

Then the third egg was found. Oh dear that hadn't occurred to me. There were no more solid chocolate bunnies! Someone had made a mistake! They asked if someone had not turned in their egg by accident but I didn't speak up, just stood there guilty as sin, knowing that the bunny was ill-gotten gain but refusing to 'fess up. They finally gave the boy a $1 bill so that he could buy one.

On the way home my dad gave a little min-speech on how it's wrong to lie and that they knew *someone* had. I just knew HE knew it was ME but I still didn't confess. I ate the bunny but as I recall it didn't taste nearly as good as I had anticipated.

My face still burns in shame all these many years later. I have never shared this story before so I'm hoping the telling will help exorcise the memory as well as the feeling of guilt. I need to finally forgive the little girl who so badly wanted her sister to share in the bounty that, she shamelessly lied to help her win.

Leviticus 6:3 or if he finds lost property and lies about it, or if he swears falsely, or if he commits any such sin that people may do-

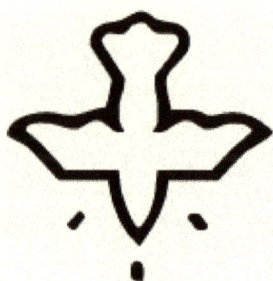

Little Old Woman

We are so happy and content at our new church! Everyone is so friendly and we love the minister who, by the way looks like he's about 20 years old. Even Irene, 8 at the time (now 9) shortly after we started attending, asked me "Nana, that guy up front, what is he maybe 17?" However, he has much wisdom to share that belies his youthful appearance.

One thing that really tickled me was when the preacher announced recently that he was accepting questions from parishioners for his summer long "You asked for it" series. I had suggested this very thing to our last minister but he never got around to it before we left. At any rate our preacher chooses a question each week that he then incorporates into his sermon.

I had submitted a question myself but was losing hope that he was going to get to it, and then he preached on my submission today! I was so tickled when I saw the question posted on the overhead that I nudged Brooke and whispered "Hey! That's my question!"

I would regret this very quickly as some of the first words out of his mouth were: Every church seems to have *a little old woman* who wants to know what happened to the Amalekites.......Oh no. I knew that I was in for it then. Brooke started snickering quietly then not so quietly. In fact she was so loud that it's a miracle the preacher didn't hear her. That was probably only because we were in the balcony. I whispered at her to hush while trying not to laugh myself and resisting the urge to slide under the pew since I was sure others around us had heard me say it was "my" question.

The preacher went on to say that some might be tempted to view the question as the type that (again with the reference!!) little old women, that every church seems to have would ask but please don't as the question being posed was an excellent one. Of course Brooke was totally missing this because she was busy making scratching noises and giggling under her breath. I glanced over to see her writing "Little old woman" with an arrow pointed my direction. It was all she could do to keep from snorting with laughter. Mistie, who was on the other side of me and running video today, was struggling hard not to lose it. She said later that her shoulders were shaking so hard she must have looked like she was having a seizure.

What a family. Here I was pleased to have offered an excellent question and all they heard was "little old woman". I shook the preacher's hand as we left and thanked him for the great answers followed by thanks for calling me a little old woman and showed him the note that Brooke had drawn. He thought this was very funny and said how he was happy to have offered them fodder for their fun with mom. I just laughed and told him, "As if they needed any" as I hobbled my way down the hallway. For the record, I think that the little old women in the church are simply precious.

Exodus 17:16 He said, For hands were lifted up to the throne of the LORD. The LORD will be at war against the Amalekites from generation to generation.

M&M's And Little Blonde Girls

Have you heard the joke about the blonde who took forever to make chocolate chip cookies because it takes so long to peel all of those M&M's?

Many of you know that Irene's nickname is Reenee; she's even known by this name by all of the teachers at her pre-school. You also know by now what a very funny and bright child she is. It seems nearly every day that someone says, "Do you know what Reenee did?" (We now call these Reenee dids) A recent day was no different, and I just have to share this story on our girl.

Ernie, Irene and I went to the Farmer's Market that morning for fruit and vegetables. The kids had so much candy over Christmas break that they were bouncing off the walls. I declared candy off limits so it's fruits, veggies, no sugar-added ice cream or nothing until further notice. While there we got a great deal on red bell peppers so bought a bunch to put in the freezer. I was standing in the kitchen cleaning and chopping the peppers while Irene sat at the table chattering away at me. I was deep into my chopping and thinking of other things while only half listening to her rattle on. I perked up quick though when I heard her say, "Now I have 2 cuts Nana, so I'm going to go get some tissues" I whirled around and saw her finger had blood on it so hollered for her Bapa to come look. She got scared and took off to hide, but we coaxed her out and she started sobbing "Am I not in trouble?" We assured her she wasn't and Ernie checked her out and convinced her to tell him how she cut herself.

Welllllll......do you know what Reenee did?? She had been using my vegetable peeler to peel mini M&M's..........We have laughed about this for days and she now understands that you don't peel M&M's with anything for any reason. I doubt she'll want to eat any for a while either.

Update:
Brooke and Irene were out shopping later in the week. This is normally a great time for heart to heart talks with her since this is "alone time" and this trip was no different. Irene worries about Nana being diabetic, and asks about foods that I can eat. She confided to her mommy that she was peeling those M&M's because she wanted me to be able to eat them too. She thought taking the shells off would make them ok for me. Ahhhhhhhh I almost feel bad now for laughing at her.

We spend a lot of time laughing at all of the grandkids. They are adorable even when being rotten. As far as we're concerned, they are all the smartest. Most gorgeous grandkids ever. Most days anyway.

Psalm 119:103 How sweet are your words to my taste, sweeter than honey to my mouth!

Mad Dogs And Children

Sometimes I think back to certain incidents in my childhood and shudder. Truly it is a wonder how parents or kids survive the trying times of safely raising and being raised.

I am currently reading the Book "To Kill A Mockingbird" and just finished the part where Atticus Finch shot what everyone presumed was a rabid dog, in February. Until that passage I had completely forgotten about a close encounter that several of us kids in our neighborhood had with a rabid dog of our own. I grew up in a neighborhood where everyone knew who you or your parents wer,e so they had ways of keeping us in line. I remember several occasions when phone calls were made to parents, my own included. If we got fresh with someone who knew us but weren't friends of the family, word would get passed to the barber shop up the street where it then got passed to your dad so punishment would be levied. We used to cover a lot of territory just walking and riding bikes and would wander several miles from home. We always felt watched but safe.

The neighborhood dogs roamed freely, but we knew them all so played with them secure in the knowledge that their families took care of them. I remember helping Leslie tease her dog Tippy once while he was chewing a bone. He growled at us but we weren't scared since he had never attempted to bite anything other than a tire of the cars he tirelessly chased. One day though, a strange dog wandered through and it's a God given miracle that none of us was hurt.

He was a medium sized brown and black dog, just a mutt really. What we all found amusing about him was the funny way he walked and the foam covering and dripping from his mouth. We chased him under a neighbor's car, then tried to coax him out to get a close-up look at his amazing behavior. I suppose we'll never know how close we really came to disaster because he started growling low and mean. I've never said we were the smartest kids in town but we knew enough to back off and run before he could charge at us. I recall running home to tell my mom but memory fails me now as to the outcome of our near disastrous run-in with that poor, probably rabid dog.

I do remember the outcome of an encounter with another kind of mad dog a few years later though. This animal was of the two-legged variety and all the more dangerous because he did try to come after us. My twin sister Jayme and I were twelve at the time, and Leslie was eleven. She lived across the street two doors down and we had played together since the ages of three and two. This particular day we were bored and had wandered to the neighborhood park a few blocks away to hang out on the swings and discuss problems unique to adolescent girls. We hadn't been there long before a dark haired man (At the time we would have thought of him as older, but I'm sure now he was in his 20's) drove up with his little girl. We had a vague idea of who he was because we recognized his pale blue pick-up truck. He didn't live in our actual neighborhood, but more on the outskirts in a small rented house. He spoke to us so we started talking to him, probably flattered that this good-looking "older" man had noticed us. Being caught in the angst of pre-teen adolescence, it wasn't long before we got bored and started walking home.

We lived several blocks from the park and had just gotten back to our house, which was located on a corner. We were sitting in the side yard when we saw his blue truck drive up. He had apparently taken his little girl home because he was now alone. He stopped his truck and called us over to him. We felt safe since we'd already spoken with him in the park so we ran over to talk through the passenger window. I've long forgotten what all was said but I do remember being asked our names. We grew up in a safer time, but still our parents had cautioned us over the years to be cautious about talking to strangers. A red flag went up when he asked for names. The next sentence out of his mouth clinched it for me though when he asked, "Would any of you like to hop in and go for a Popsicle?" I nearly fell over as I jumped back and yelled, "Get back! He's a kidnapper!" In retrospect I think now he was more of a pervert, but these were simpler more innocent times. Jayme and Leslie jumped back away from the truck too as he took off fast. Leslie's little brother Mike rode up on his bike at that moment so we told him what had happened. He took off pedaling as fast as he could to chase the creep. I have no idea what he intended to do, but he almost got seriously hurt. The creep in the truck slammed on his brakes and Mike slid sideways almost under the truck before he stopped. The weasel took off in his truck again while we ran home to tell the folks.

Leslie's mom called the police who came to take statements and she filed charges against him. We were eventually called to court. In the weeks before court we would look out the windows several times to see his blue truck being driven slowly past our houses by his wife, with a female friend in the passenger seat. Another call to the police brought the stalking to an abrupt halt. We were a little nervous but being kid's life went on much as usual.

This incident took place during summer break, and we spent as much time at the community pool as possible. We in fact planned to go swimming immediately after our court appearance so I wore my black 2-piece swimsuit under a pretty, green skirt outfit. I was a kid so what did I care that it showed under my sleeveless top? I still laugh thinking about it because it embarrassed my mom.

We all had turns on the witness stand and testified about what had taken place that afternoon. The judge listened intently and handed down a ruling before we left court. His Honor decreed that he believed our version and not Mr. Creep's, nevertheless since he hadn't succeeded in convincing us to go with him that there was nothing he could do regarding punishment. He did however fine him for a long-standing violation of some sort that was found when they charged him with the attempted kidnapping. He also admonished him to change his ways and stay away from young girls.

It wasn't long before they moved from the little rental house and we never saw him again. I don't think about him very often but when I do I wonder if he learned his lesson. In my heart though I fear once a pervert, always a pervert.

I believe God has angels assigned to watch over kids as they journey through each day and that ours spent a lot of time on full alert status, especially on those two days. How else could we have survived our own stupidity?

Exodus 21:16 Anyone who kidnaps another and either sells him or still has him when he is caught must be put to death.

Making Memories

Ernie and I got to take the kids trick or treating, together for the first time last night. I know some folks don't like the idea of Halloween, but we couldn't bear to disappoint the kids. Besides, we believe that any night can be made into something evil and it ultimately comes down to the way you believe. I'm not attempting to justify our decision to allow trick or treating, but want only to convey the innocence of children.

The two little girls were ready to go as soon as they got home from school at 3:15 and had been counting down for days. Long before we were ready to leave they had plastered themselves to windows, watching for other trick or treaters and offered us regular updates. Jarod had no way of knowing what was up but joined in the excitement and ran around laughing, while we waited to leave the house.

Ernie got home in time to go and as soon as he could swallow a cheeseburger nearly whole (the kids were VERY impatient) we took off. The girls fairly danced across the yard as eighteen month old Jarod, who refused to ride in his stroller thank you very much, chased after them. He had no idea what we were all up to in the dark but he was game for anything. We went to the next door neighbor's house first where Mr. Neighbor greeted them and handed out their candy. We had "practiced" at our own door so Jarod already knew to hold his bag out. After we left, Mistie who stayed home to hand out treats and work on a project for Alexis said Mrs. Neighbor came over with "special treat bags" for all three. She had them all made up but hadn't told the Mr. We then walked over to the neighbor on the other side of us where the girls were so excited they could barely contain themselves. Jarod was running after and holding his bag out like a little pro at this point. He's SO smart! I don't think he knew it was candy being tossed in yet so it was safe there. He has a sweet tooth bigger than he is so we watch his candy intake.

We tried putting him in his stroller about then but he slid right back out and took off running. He never did ride in it so I pushed it, appreciating it later when we had to walk back up the hill across the street. I was huffing and puffing and would have fallen over if not for being able to lean on it.

Alexis and Irene are very patient with Jarod and would wait excitedly for him to catch up then they would all run to the next house. They all looked so sweet in their costumes: Irene a Unicorn in a gorgeous plush outfit, Alexis a sweet angel complete with wings, and Jarod a cowboy in the outfit his Aunt Brooke made him, complete with chaps. She even made goodie bags from Halloween cloth for them. They must have looked cute to everyone else because they frequently got "extra" pieces of candy tossed into their bags. Ernie eventually declared that Jarod had enough candy so he quit taking his bag to the doors. This didn't stop Jarod, who held his hand out and got candy this way. The girls finally got to the point where they would run ahead and be done by the time Jarod and Bapa were half way up a walk. Jarod didn't care. He had figured this scam out and was determined to hit the door anyway. I would wait in the street at curbside with the stroller, holding a flashing colored strobe light. I still almost got run over by a driver who apparently wasn't paying a bit of attention. I haven't heard any news of a child being run over so hope they woke up after that.

We spent about 45-minutes walking to a few of the neighborhood houses then came home to relieve Mistie so she could get ready for work. We had already been warned that we not only live on a busy street but also are in "the rich section of town" so to be prepared for LOTS of kids. That part was no exaggeration. We had kids coming even after we turned the lights out at 8:00. Every time the doorbell rang, Jarod would run chattering to the door and try to squeeze out to follow them. He knew the game plan now and wanted *more*. Alexis and Irene had their loot so were content to help pass it out now. Alexis even offered hers in case we ran out. What a hoot. It was frequently aggravating trying to keep him inside but it was fun at the same time. I was proud too of the girls for being so generous and polite with all the little tricksters.

I am so happy that we got to take those kids out. The little girls were so excited and kept giggling about how much fun it was. Jarod just delighted in being out, running around in the dark and getting candy to boot, chattering and laughing all evening. He was also wired the rest of the night. I was freezing at 9:00 so decided it was bedtime. We took him to bed with us thinking he'd wind down. He finally did around 10:00. Bapa has declared NO sweets for Jarod after dinner tonight. In fact I'll have to move the canister that we keep candy and treats in. Jarod has a habit of pushing a barstool over to that counter, climbing up and getting into it. More than once I have found him sitting on the stool, legs swinging as he digs through the canister as if it is some kind of candy buffet.

It's times like last night that help you forget the aggravating spills and shoes, socks and toys left all over the house. Who needs a clean house if you've got happy grand darlings? Some day I'll have the immaculate house so want to make happy memories to warm its rooms when that time comes.

Psalm 45:17 I will perpetuate your memory through all generations; therefore the nations will praise you for ever and ever.

Meet Desdemona, My Grandkitty

For those who don't know who Desdemona is, allow me to introduce you. She's Stacie's (Shakespeare fan) cat, otherwise known as my grandkitty. She's been staying with us for the past year and I have fallen head over heels in love with her. I haven't had a pet since all of ours died years ago, had no desire for any, but this girl has worked her way under my skin much to Ernie and Stacie's regret since (1) Stacie wants her back and (2) Ernie hasn't desired another pet either and still doesn't. She's a funny girl who used to be near feral but after a year of living with us and though she can get a tad moody (she is a cat after all) she's no longer a scaredy cat., unless of course Jarod decides to go after her.

Ms. Des is a very pretty, tiger-ish striped cat with the stripes on her sides sort of swirling so she's unique looking as well. She has such pretty and expressive eyes which she uses to communicate so that I can tell when she's feeling insecure and when she's just plain mad. Of course, her ears flattened against her head are a good indication of mad as well and that usually happens when Jarod is around. She started out as pretty much the runt of the litter and stayed tiny for some time. Her huge siblings Titania and Oberon (I did say Stacie is a fan of Shakespeare?) would hog the food dish and Oberon would hog Stacie's attention so poor Des sort of melted into the background. Stacie finally had to give Titie and Obie away (both to the same good home) and Des's growth took off. Suddenly she had food! I think the previous lack stunted her tail and head growths though, as both seem sort of short and small for such a now big cat. Honestly she borders on looking like a small cow at times and likes to stomp through the house eliciting yells of "Yee ha! It's a kitty cow stampede!" Stacie gets really upset with me when I let her gain too much though so I do try to watch how much I feed her. This is not always easy as she's very adept at herding me into the kitchen to her food dish. She runs in front of me then between my legs as I walk through the room, herding just like a good cow cat should.

Dessie or Desperate as some of us sometimes call her is a very talented kitty. She can entertain herself tirelessly with bugs before killing them and has no compassion whatsoever for butterflies as demonstrated when she attempted to rip the kids butterfly net house to shreds while trying to get to the butterflies housed within. She occasionally plays prestidigitator (magician for those who don't like big words) and stuffs her large kitty butt into my small napkin basket. She is endlessly amused by her trick of stealing the desk chair any time a certain someone (me) gets up to do something else. She's stubborn about giving that chair up too.

Her greatest talent though never repeated left us all with mouths hanging open in awe. I had left a box of dog biscuits on the dining room table from having treated the neighbor dog who likes to come over and mooch. We got up the next morning to find one of the bones on the table half eaten. Laughing as I cleaned it up, Stacie pointed out a small pile of biscuits next to the box. Then we spotted another small pile on the floor under the window and yet another small pile next to the buffet. All were neat and tidy little piles too. These were not small dog biscuits as the neighbor dog is quite large so it must have taken that little pile maker extraordinaire all night to make her little stacks. Did I mention that she's good at entertaining herself?

Desperado (another pet name) is not overly affectionate most of the time so it's a special treat when she decides to grace your lap by sitting in it. This usually happens when a person is using a Carolina Blue lap blanket so we'll all try to be the first to grab it when it's chilly. The feeling of her in your lap quite simply makes you want to purr along with her. I like to sweet talk the big baby buttercup and say things like "Here pretty, pretty, pretty!" and tell her how sweet she is and how much I love her. Stacie says I insult her intelligence when I talk to her like this. All I can say is Despot seems to eat it up and I'd say from her love of Carolina Blue that she's a darned smart cat so I think she'd know intelligence insulting sweet talk when she hears it.

Desdie looks so much like my old Tiger (some of you know the story of his otherwise embarrassing name of Booby) that it hurts some times just to look at her. Just as Tiger did, Dessie has fat flabs that flip-flap when she runs, which we all find endlessly amusing to make fun of. Tiger had the prettiest tummy I've ever seen on a cat and he loved to lie on his back with it exposed. If you dared to touch it he'd rip your hand right off of your arm too. Desbo doesn't mind a good belly rub as long as you don't get toooo personal about it so even though her tummy isn't as pretty, I can now rub to my hearts content.

As I mentioned earlier she can be a bit moody, another trait shared with Tiger. Jarod, her least favorite person already, learned the hard way about her moods recently when he innocently tried to love on her. I had taken her to the vet that morning to have her claws trimmed as she had a bad problem of getting velcroed to the carpet and furniture. Let me just say that she was not a cheerful traveler and was happy to be home though quite grumpy. Jarod wanted only to express his sympathy with a hug, but she took offense and swiped him across the forehead which he clutched as he cried and yelled "Hey, she's still got claws!" (His cats are both de-clawed and he thought we had had hers removed in the three minute trim procedure). I swear Des smirked as she ran away.

Some firsts for Des

Des is "in a mood" lately but it's a fun mood. I was folding clothes in the bedroom earlier today while watching some TV and she came over to "watch" by lying down on some of the clothes needing hanging. Aggravating sure but she's so cute who could get upset? Besides, I still had some to fold and sure enough, predictably Irene came in and annoyed her off of them before I needed to hang them. I finished up then sat on the chest at the foot of my bed to finish watching the show I had started. Before I knew it she came over and nudged me into petting her.! She has never done this before and I was delighted to oblige her. When she got her fill of being loved on she proceeded to clean herself. Then it hit me—she hates it when I pet her while she's washing herself and will actually snap at me like a dog which is another of her talents. It never hurts because she never bites hard, and it tickles my funny bone to make her do this. She's so darned smart; I suspect she did this to keep me from petting her while she washed. Didn't work, so when I started tickling her leg she turned around and laid down on my hand, completely trapping it then continued washing herself. My favorite smart aleck stunt was last night though. We (Ernie and I) were headed to bed at 10 PM as usual and she ran ahead as she often does, where she'll wait on the bed then jump on the vanity to walk around and rub on me while I brush my teeth. Not last night though. She was waiting on the bed and walked over to Ernie where she encouraged some petting by sniffing his hand. (She's a true scent addict like me and will smell anything at least once). Ernie has resisted petting her for the past year that she's been here in order to avoid bonding, but he's starting to fall for her too and has been petting and talking to her. After he pet her he walked over to the sink to brush his teeth and she followed him. HEY! She's not supposed to make up to him like that, that's supposed to be "our" time! She just kept looking at me as if to see if I'd intervene. I just laughed at the little snot. What finally got me though was when the brazen little hussy jumped on the bed and laid down between his feet all the while looking at me as if to say "Try to do something about it". All I could do was laugh at her. Next time I know just what I'll do though. I'll totally sic the kids on the sassy little sauce box.

Genesis 1:24 And God said, "Let the land produce living creatures according to their kinds: livestock, creatures that move along the ground, and wild animals, each according to its kind." And it was so.

Update—Desdemona is now residing with Nana and Bapa permanently. I told Stacie that it was just going to be too hard on Des to move since she was so comfortable here. Bapa agreed to let me keep her, and even he has started to fall for her. She is so tame now that I can pick her up and carry her around while she snuggles and purrs softly. I call this our cuddle time and it appears she enjoys it as much as I do. Yesterday evening she was sitting on Ernie's dresser and meowed at me every time I walked past her. She finally hopped down and ran across the hall to Stacie's old bedroom. When I walked back up the hallway she followed me, meowing at me so I turned around and followed her into the bedroom to see what the problem might be. She promptly hopped onto a box sitting in the corner, next to a chair and waited for me. I sat down and picked her up for some cuddling. We were having a great time; she was purring and I was sweet talking her when Jarod then Irene found us. Oh boy, her two "favorite" people. Cuddle time was over but it was fun while it lasted.

Merrily We Sing A Song

Oh how I love having grandkids! I just wish I was quicker with answers to some of their more off the walls questions. Take this morning for instance. I was taking Irene to school when she tossed a question right out of left field. Irene: "Nana how can we get to the North Pole?" Nana: "Ummmmm start driving north? Maybe by sled dog or hitch a ride with Santa? I don't know. Why don't you ask Bapa?" Bapa of course, has lots of answers to some of life's most pressing questions and is usually quick with a smart (aleck) reply. I don't know for sure where this question came from but it could possibly have something to do with the car heater. Most mornings I take Alexis to school at 7:30 then take Irene to her pre-school an hour later. Since neither destination requires me to get out of the car, I generally just throw a pair of shorts and T-shirt on and will do so at least until the snow flies. This morning was no different and since it was a little cool out, I turned the heater on. I guess this got her little mind turned towards winter things so before I knew it, we were driving down the road singing Jingle Bells and Rudolph. We sang them over and over making for a very enjoyable 15-minute ride to school.

Exodus 32:18 "It is not the sound of victory, it is not the sound of defeat; it is the sound of singing that I hear."

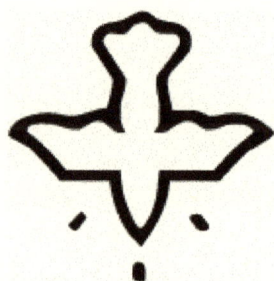

Mohawk Cat

It's highly doubtful that I will ever forget the time I woke up at 3 o'clock in the morning to find a strange looking Mohawk-cat-thing sitting in my living room. Yegads, it turned out it was *my* cat now sporting a Mohawk haircut.

Maybe I should start at the beginning. First and foremost, Brooke and Stacie were both night owls when teenagers and loved to stay up all night then sleep all day during summer vacations. I never really minded since they had no real responsibilities outside of chores, which they did daily. Besides, I always knew where they were, which was either sleeping or somewhere in the house thinking up more mischief. All three daughters still prefer nightlife to daylight, but I digress.

This was when we were still owned by both of our cats, Midnight our "special needs" cat that would hide in the nearest cabinet when the doorbell rang, and Tiger formerly introduced as Booby. But we won't go there again. Midnight was horribly allergic to flea bites and needed a steroid shot about every 6 months to control the awful reaction she would develop to the bites. Over time she developed a fat tumor at the site of the injections. The tumor grew so large that her veterinarian suggested we have it removed during another scheduled surgery. I was happy to oblige since it was yucky feeling when my hand would accidentally rub over it. The tumor was benign thankfully, but Miss Midnight sported a shaved side with purple stitches for a couple of weeks making her look like some sort of Frankenstein cat with a purple zipper

Brooke and Stacie both swore that not only was Midnight self conscious about her conspicuous new hairdo, but that Tiger was also laughing at her. They swear they would catch him sitting and smirking at her, which leads us to the Mohawk haircut. When I woke up as I usually did at some point in the night when the kids were young, I went down stairs to the living room to see why the lights were still on. Yikes! My gorgeous tiger striped cat looked like a freak and both girls were laughing, having a wonderfully bad time. Being the rotten kids they were (are) they decided to give poor booby a haircut so that Midnight would feel better about herself. Tiger was named this for a reason, and put up quite a struggle when they brought out the grooming clippers. I still can't figure out how only two of them were able to hold him down AND scalp the poor baby. Frankly I was amazed they still had hands intact. As I stood in open mouthed amazement one of the girls held up a paper grocery bag and said "We saved the hair!" I don't remember what else was said when I saw poor Boob, but the girls tell me now that they thought they were really going to get it come the light of day, but instead I laughed at him when I saw him in broad daylight. I don't think the new look even bothered him. He did however keep a wide berth of "those girls" for a while and the fur re-grew with no further haircuts. Midnight's self confidence did seem better after that. I swear I even saw her staring at Tiger with a big smile on her face.

I never knew what to expect from those girls (and still don't). Brooke had shaved her own hair some time before this. She put it up in a ponytail then shaved the underneath side so it wasn't obvious when her hair was down. She sported this look for several days before she finally told me. Stacie was her willing accomplice in that hairdo(n't) as well.

Brooke was also fond of dressing our spaniel dog Lucy in people clothes, complete with headscarf. On one particular occasion Lucy ran out of the house when someone opened the door, and took off down the street. Mistie's best friend was visiting that day and a hysterically funny few minutes ensued while we all tried to catch that dog before any neighbors spotted her or us chasing her. One time she dressed her up, and then we took her shopping with us. We still laugh about the elderly lady who "showed" Lucy to her dog when she spotted her in our car.

I think that maybe Brooke missed her calling. She should have opened a salon/boutique where people could come and bring their pets for matching haircuts and outfits. Stacie could have been her design associate and haircut assistant.

On second thought I'm not sure the world is quite ready for them.

Leviticus 19:27 Do not cut the hair at the sides of your head or clip off the edges of your beard.

Mommy I'm Blind!

Most parents harbor bad memories they'll never forget no matter how badly they may wish to put those memories behind them. I have one in particular that still haunts me, and no doubt will till the day I die, and all because of a moment of weakness.

Stacie was about three years old and we were stationed in Germany at the time. She and I had gone to the P-X for some long-ago forgotten item. While there I wandered over to the perfume counter. I have a weakness for perfumes and scents that borders on illness. I am simply mad for perfumes, colognes and scents. I have a collection sitting on my dresser now that I have no hopes of ever using up and I continue to buy more. Expensive or cheap (most are) I love smelling good. Anyway back to my sad tale. I had sprayed and splashed myself to the point that I had run out of room unless I started on my feet. I'm no contortionist so I decided to use Stacie's chubby little arms. She turned to object just as I sprayed a new one at her and I sprayed it directly into her eyes. Well of course she immediately started screaming and crying, causing everyone within the vicinity to stop and stare and some to come running. There I stood, guilty as sin with the bottle still in hand while I tried to comfort (shush) her. Someone suggested I try to rinse her eyes so we took off for the nearest bathroom, located behind the office. She screamed every step of the way while the ladies in the office glared at me, making it clear what their opinions were of my mothering skills. The poor child continued to scream no matter how much water I splashed in her eyes. I was convinced I had blinded her, and feeling guilt such as only a mother can feel, decided the only thing to do was get her to the emergency room post haste. She sat behind me in my van and wailed every inch of the way there. Every time I would ask her how she was doing, which was every three or four seconds, she would cry hysterically, "It hurts! I can't see!" I had visions of Seeing Eye dogs, white canes and felt white hot guilt every time she opened her mouth. I had blinded my darling little girl! I kept assuring her that we would be at the emergency room soon and that all would be fine. I fully expected to be locked up the moment we arrived, to have all three of my children removed from my care for such a horrendous mistake in judgment and that they would call my husband to tell him his wife was being sent back stateside due to sheer stupidity.

I took the final turn into the ER parking lot on two wheels and as I did my sweet...precious.....dear child suddenly stopped crying and exclaimed, "I can see now!" I didn't know whether to laugh or cry. Instead through clenched teeth I told her, "Tough! You're going in any way!"

I didn't get locked up or deported, my kids all stayed in my possession and thanks to my carelessness, she got her eyes flushed with water for the next very unpleasant 30 minutes. I am far more careful about sampling any scent now and to this day Stacie isn't much of one to use perfumes. Imagine that......

Matthew 26:7 a woman came to him with an alabaster jar of very expensive perfume, which she poured on his head as he was reclining at the table.

Movie Madness

Mark this date on your calendars. My honey and I went out to dinner and a movie tonight, and I actually made it through the movie without incident.

I am a living legend in this family. Everyone from husband, kids and friends know not to take me to the movies with them. I attract every creep, moron, bubble headed blonde and pervert within five city blocks, and they ALL sit around me. I am a human creep magnet.

I have sat in front of a blonde who talked so much she never had time to realize she was in a theater. I guess she was so dense it never occurred to her the lights were off for a reason. She giggled, tittered, and chattered so much that I was ready to pull her bleached hair out by the roots long before the movie was over.

On one trip to the movies we had the misfortune of sitting in the same row as a group of young thugs who thought it was funny to throw coins around the theater after they ran out of popcorn to throw. To make things even more interesting, the young girl in front of them apparently knew them (at least I hope she was acquainted) and kept reaching behind her to put her hand between the legs of one. She was sitting with a friend and her mother, but they either chose to ignore the hanky panky or truly did not see it. I finally got fed up and went and got the manager. Of course all involved behaved as long as he stood behind them.

I'll never forget going to the movies in Germany to see Space Camp. An adult woman sat behind us with at least six kids. One of the brats kept kicking the back of my seat and talking, to which I would respond by politely asking her to not kick my seat. The woman had smuggled canned sodas into the theater and the final straw came when one of the little darlings knocked it over and it ran all over my foot. I went and got the manager and he came and spoke to her. Things pretty much quieted down after that. After the movie we all stood to leave, and Mrs. Grown-up looked at me and stuck her tongue out at me, in front of all six children. I told her I hoped she felt much better and that I now realized why the kiddies acted the way they did.

Poor Ernie feels big screen deprived occasionally so hauls me to the movies with him. I am dragging my feet the entire time reminding him that I am the kiss of death on a good time. "Remember me? I'm the creep/jerk/moron/blonde magnet!" Being the brave one that he is, not to mention his amazing ability to tune the distractions out, he'll insist. So many months ago we went to the movies..........I thought I'd fix them all and sit in the very back row against the wall. No one can sit behind you there, right? Have you ever seen the cartoon Rocko's Modern Life? Mrs. BigHead from this cartoon has nothing over the woman who sat in front of us that night. Over half the theater was empty, yet she and her tiny headed husband (who sat in front of Ernie) and her young child scooted right into the row in front of us. I could have wept. She spent the entire movie moving her big head around as she reached into her husband's popcorn bucket repeatedly, effectively making sure that my view remained obstructed by her oversized cranium. I've been asked why I didn't move and the answer is simple, it was a matter of principle...I was there first.

So tonight we wanted to go to dinner and a movie. I usually insist on waiting on the video to release, but hated to disappoint my man. Besides I wanted to see Galaxy Quest as much as he did. If you haven't seen it, I sincerely recommend it. It has cheesy special effects but it's *supposed* to be cheesy. Great movie, especially since I was able to sit through it without peering through some large headed woman's big hair, or having to listen to a dumb blonde act blonde, or have to watch the Alabama teenage pervert perform her thing with the thug behind her.

After tonight I think I've finally hit on the trick to enjoying a movie. No I didn't stand in the door. Once again we sat in the very back, spaced a seat between us and leaving one seat open on our end, assuring that no couples would sit beside us. Once the movie started, we scooted over to sit together. We also placed our coats over the seats in front of us. Several people paused, saw the coats then kept going. Eureka! I can enjoy a movie again. All I need to do is be sure to take a coat with me, even if it's 90 degrees outside, but that's a small price to pay to be able to enjoy a show.

If all else fails I can always take my shirt off and drape it over the seat. That ought to keep the seats empty for several rows around us.

Titus 3:2 to slander no one, to be peaceable and considerate, and to show true humility toward all men.

Moving Saga

Well the moving part is over and the real fun has begun. Unpacking, yuck. You'd think after all the moves we made as an Army family that we would have an organized system, or at least be philosophical about it all. It's still the most hated part of moving, and most time consuming since we spend a great deal of time trying to decide where things will fit and look right. Ah well, we figure it should all be done in a couple of weeks with of course, several desperate moments. I already want to walk away and start fresh but once it's all done we'll be able to relax and enjoy being around our old possessions in a new home. At least I finished the kitchen yesterday, relieving a lot of stress. It's no fun trying to cook around piles of boxes.

We were fortunate with this move because the only breakage we've found so far is a computer speaker and a glass panel for the china cabinet that one of the moving guys knelt on. When the Army was moving us we never knew how many would show up for the packing and moving but usually found them short staffed. This move was orchestrated by Georgia-Pacific and they are efficient if nothing else. We had three very efficient packers. The loading crew pulled up Friday and I held my breath since the movers (Army arranged) only sent two the day we moved into the house in High Point. They wound up going to hire a temporary helper with that unload job. I started to breathe easier as I watched the third guy get out and relaxed as a fourth guy roll out of the truck. I was nearly jumping up and down when I saw a fifth guy get out! Even with all that help it took them from 9 AM to almost 6 PM to load it all. When they delivered on this end we had the same guys with the exception of one, and I think the new one was sorry he signed on for this job by the end of the day.

We just simply have TOO MUCH stuff! I told Ernie I'm not sure if his last job working for a furniture manufacturer was a blessing or a curse. I do know we will be having a furniture sale in the very near future; we just need to get everything unpacked and situated so we know what to sell. One of the movers (I think it was the new guy) even commented on how much stuff we have. I jokingly accused them of slipping someone else's household in with ours, but sadly it's all ours.

We have a huge side-by-side Frigidaire that I've never been happy with since we got it home from the store. It looked gigantic there but it actually doesn't have a lot of fridge space. I no longer have to worry about it since it is now sitting in the garage, to be used as a second fridge, something we have long wanted. They had to take one door off just to get it through doorways only to find it is too wide for this kitchen by about 4 inches. We have a huge upright freezer and now this one for extra storage so considered buying a fridge only unit (yes they make them. Sears has them) but decided against it since we would no longer have an icemaker. I am headed to the local Sears appliance store today to order a fridge that includes icemaker and that we know will fit since we have measured and compared. In the meantime we are thankful that the other one is available even if it does mean a trip to the garage every time we want ice, milk, cheese,.......

As difficult as any move is, there are always moments of hilarity, even when we have to make our own. The day before we moved in I brought the kids over while Ernie worked on the pool. Of course they had a ball running around the empty house screaming to hear the echoes. Irene managed to get herself locked in a room and was hiding in the closet when I found her. I couldn't figure out how she managed to lock herself in until the next day. Stacie came out of the front bedroom with this doorknob cover thing in her hand. It fits over the knob and you have to push pressure points to make it work, which explains why Irene's little hands couldn't open the door. (I sure felt guilty about getting impatient with her the day before) Stacie asked, "What kind of evil parent would put this on the inside of a bedroom door?" We now know. We had set a small TV and a VCR up in the master bedroom so the kids could watch cartoon videos and theoretically stay out of the way of movers who were incredibly patient with them. Being kids and of course excited about all of the activity, this plan didn't work as well as we had hoped. About five minutes after she asked the evil parent question, Stacie herded the kids back into the bedroom and stuck the doorknob cover on the knob then shut the door. We were resting in the living room while we waited for their reaction, giggling in anticipation. They discovered the problem quickly and completely overreacted. What we hadn't planned on was the new guy being in the hallway when they started pounding on the door and screaming "Hey, let us out of here!" He stopped dead in his tracks with a seriously funny look on his face and took off back down the hall to check on them. He realized he had been had when he heard me and Stacie laughing uncontrollably. We laughed so hard our sides ached. He mumbled something at us as he went back outside and we decided we had better not try locking them in the bedroom again until there were no witnesses.

Speaking of evil.... Roanoke Rapids now has a city employee who is probably convinced that I am dangerous. We had a moving truck sitting in front of this house all day Monday and we now live on a very busy street so I think everyone in this town, population approximately 16,000 drove past at least once during the day plus a few lost travelers from I-95. This house has sat empty for a couple of years from what we know of the history. The people in the water/sanitation department are neither the friendliest nor most helpful as the only information they offered as they collected the mandatory $60 deposit is that trash pick-up is on Fridays. Yesterday, one day after move-in I answered the door to find a city employee standing on the porch. He pompously informed me that the pile of leaves at the curb has to be bagged for pick-up. OK fair enough. In High Point we didn't have to bag so when we saw several piles of leaves in neighboring yards on their curbs, we naturally assumed it was ok. The termite inspection guys were here to inspect and if necessary treat the house as part of the closing deal. I was trying to finish the kitchen so was hot and tired and this poor guy made a very bad mistake when he told me that, technically he was supposed to write me a citation but if I took care of it today he wouldn't. I kind of went off on him then, pointing out that we had *just* moved in as was made obvious by all of the boxes stacked in the open garage, not to mention that the house had been empty for the past two years. I told him if he dared write me a citation that I "would tear this town apart" and was even in the heat of the moment planning my calls to the city manager, mayor and anyone else I could think of. He nervously glanced over at the termite guys (I think he was hoping for help or at least witnesses) and said "OooKay". I then told him that I have a house to unpack alone since my husband was working and that I had three little ones to watch as well (he could see them standing inside the door) and that I would most definitely not be taking care of it immediately. He was very agreeable as he walked away. I told Stacie later that I felt kind of bad for him but he just pushed me too far when he made that citation comment. Today I am going to go rake the leaves back from the curb and dare him to say another word. I can have anything I like in my yard. Besides the other neighbors who had the leaves piled curbside still have them there so I may take pictures. We don't want trouble with the city and certainly not right from the get-go but let's be reasonable. I did call the city public works department and told the supervisor about the incident. She wanted the ma's name but I declined to offer it, telling her that I had effectively handled it and just wanted to let them know that their employees may need some training in non-pompous relations with the citizenry. I think I may just have to run for a city council position some day,

I spoke with our High Point realtor yesterday and the house back there is ready to go now. We had new carpet laid top to bottom Monday. We won't get to see it but she assures us that it's gorgeous and that the house will show really well since we also painted and thoroughly cleaned. I just have to tell you what our neighbors did though. Kris and Dana live across the street in our High Point neighborhood and have always been wonderful, Christian neighbors. They showed up at our door Saturday morning with paint rollers and brushes in hand and said to point them to the rooms that needed painted and cleaning. I can't begin to express our appreciation since we would never have gotten it all done in time for the move without their help. What an incredible witness! I just hope some day to be able to pass it on. Even with their help, I was so exhausted by day's end that I got on my own nerves. I was trying to mop my way out of the house but kept tracking back over the wet floor when I needed to rinse the mop. Ernie finally took the mop from me, sent me outside to cool off and finished it by rinsing the mop in the outside faucet. Duh! I was so beat that I just hadn't thought of that.

That nasty pool is almost ready and in fact we plan to use it tomorrow on the 4th. I suspect that it will be icy in spite of the almost 100 degree weather since we have dumped and replenished most of it. Oh well with heat like this it should feel good.

Have a safe and happy 4th of July celebration and if you're in the area please stop by. Just give me a couple of weeks to finish unpacking first, OK? Maybe by then the little ones will have settled and quit crying to "go home".

Genesis 13:5 Now Lot, who was moving about with Abram, also had flocks and herds and tents.

Never, Ever A Dull Moment

Lowes had fire logs on sale today so I asked Stacie, who had left for Rocky Mount with Brooke at 4 AM this morning for Black Friday shopping, to stop and buy me four cases.

While they were gone, Mistie and I assisted the little girls in cleaning their bedroom and they did a wonderful job. We cleaned, pulled out, vacuumed, sorted and tossed. Their room looks so nice now.

I took them to lunch at Ryan's (Alexis' favorite restaurant) as a treat for working so hard and doing such a good job. Afterwards we stopped at Dollar Tree where we bought among other items, some marshmallows.

It is cold outside so the kids asked if I could build a fire in the fireplace to roast some of the marshmallows. They've been especially good so I said sure. Irene and Jarod went out to Aunt Stacie's car to get a couple of logs. Irene decided it was easier to bring the entire case in so was trying mightily to lug the box in with Jarod's little four-year-old manly assistance. Just before they went out, I had turned the TV to "Tremors" a movie that we're almost embarrassed to admit that we like. Jarod wanted to see the monster worms so I ran to the door to tell him the commercial was over. He heard me and dropped his end of the box to take off running to the house. Irene started hollering "Hey! I need a little help here!" It was one of the funniest unexpected scenes I've ever witnessed, and I laughed till my sides ached. Mistie was sitting in the dining room and though she didn't look out the window, could tell from the conversation just what had happened and was laughing too while telling me that I was mean for doing that to Irene. I just laughed and told her it wasn't on *purpose*. Alexis went out to help Irene get the box to the porch where I took over getting it inside (barefooted which is why I hadn't gone out). I was impressed with how well they'd done getting that heavy box to the door. WOW it weighs a lot!

So I get the starter logs into the fireplace and start them right up with one match and they're blazing away. The kids are getting their marshmallows and sticks ready when I realize—the house is filling with smoke. I grabbed the key to the flue only to find it won't work—too big. We lost the original somehow so Ernie bought this one, but it's too big. I ran out to the garage for a pair of pliers to turn the knob and by this time one of the smoke detectors is announcing what we already know—it's smoky in the house. Really smoky. We're gagging and opening windows and doors while the kids keep running outside to check the chimney for smoke. Just as I think I've finally got the flue open, the smoke alarm starts announcing that I'm wrong.

Soon all three smoke alarms are going crazy and by this point, so am I. The kids all want to call 911 but decide that we should wait until after they toast their marshmallows. Apparently we've done a wonderful job teaching them to set priorities. Since we don't see any more smoke, I tell them it's OK to toast and they have a ball. It's finally quiet so I decide to take a short nap, only to be woken by the stupid kitchen alarm again. Then the other two alarms chime in but this time I remember the attic fan and turn that on. The two hall alarms are quiet now but the kitchen one keeps beeping periodically which of course encourages me to try to fiddle with the flue some more and therefore start the entire smoke-window-door-beep-crazy process all over again.

I think I've finally got it open now, but I'm not sure since it's hard to see through all the lingering smoke. Jarod is passed out on the couch and we're hoping it's for a nap and not from being overcome by smoke.

With all of the smoke pouring from our open doors and windows, we're surprised but thankful that the neighbors haven't called 911 themselves to report a fire.

The fire logs are almost burned down now and I've assured the girls that they had better enjoy those marshmallows since those are the last ones until their Bapa comes home next week from his hunting trip with his dad. God be willing, I may even have the smoke smell out of the house by then.

Psalm 31:22 In my alarm I said, "I am cut off from your sight!" Yet you heard my cry for mercy when I called to you for help.

Night Owls And Pumpkin People

Alexis loves to spend the night with Nana and Bapa and will ask to regularly. Irene, who lives here, likes to spend the night at Alexis'. Go figure.

Alexis spent the night last night and slept in Stacie's room. Irene decided to sleep with her, rather than in her own bed alone. This morning I had to get Alexis up at 7 AM since it's a school day. She is definitely not a morning person so I started out gently rubbing her arm and calling her name. She just snuggled deeper under the blankets. Irene, who is a morning person, lifted one eyelid to see what was going on. In a flash the other eye popped open and she was up and ready to go, offering to help wake Alexis who was in the meantime flailing at us and telling us to leave her alone. I finally had to pick her up and stand her on the floor all the while threatening her with never being allowed to spend the night on a school night again. Sigh.....I hate having to do this to her. I know from years of experience, having raised three daughters who were also not addicted to mornings, how painful it is to be woken. Poor Alexis is just like them. Ernie and I are both morning people though he doesn't bounce around happy to greet the day as I have been known to. He's much too dignified for that. I am a certified nutty morning person A.K.A., a pumpkin person. I love getting up in the morning and getting my day under way. When I worked most of my co-workers were night people and hated me for being so chipper each morning. This of course means that I start turning into a pumpkin around nine at night though.

I know all of the night owls who worked the day shift with me didn't start functioning well until afternoon, which makes a day job interesting for them as well as for observers like me. I got a fair amount of laughing in each day when I worked with non-morning night owl people. They just looked so funny stumbling into desks with red rimmed eyes. There is however, a down side to being a pumpkin person. No matter how I try sometimes I just can't keep my eyes open in the evening and miss the ends of many good shows and movies. This is when night people in the family get their laughs; they all swear that I snore even when I nap. Hmmmph... Of course I recognize this as a big fat lie made up by bitter night people trying to have fun at the expense of us pumpkin people, but that's ok. I get my revenge every time I cheerfully wish them a bright and early "GOOD MORNING!"

Genesis 1:5 God called the light "day," and the darkness he called "night." And there was evening, and there was morning—the first day.

No Not Nana

Before I share I'll admit right up front—I'm a baaaad Nana.

Friday evening Mistie and the kids were here for a little while, and Jarod was running wide open as usual. I tried to sneak off to the bathroom at one point but knowing all three kids well, I locked the door behind me. Sure enough a short time later Jarod was trying to follow me in. He beat on the door then started sticking his fingers under the door. Normally I'd play with him by "squashing" his fingers but this time I turned the bathroom lights out and had some fun. He could see under the door so his immediate response was Nana turn the lights on! In a very deep voice I said No not Nana! Nana not here! Jarod: (laughing) Naaanaaa stop that! Turn the lights on! Me: (always speaking in the very deep voice) No Nana not here! Jarod: Nana stop that! Me: Not Nana. I'm going to eat you little boy!! I laughed so hard my sides ached as I heard him jump up and run away. I found him across the hall, hiding with Stacie in her room. He looked a little unsure and said "Nana you creeped me out!" That was the whole point my little man.

ROFL!!!

A short while later Mistie was trying to herd Jarod and Alexis out the door for home. It was chilly out so we told Jarod to get his coat only to discover he'd left it in the car. He assured us that he'd be fine and as they started out the door he stopped and said "Man it's freaking cold out there!" Mistie and I were laughing so hard we couldn't breathe and my sides ached even more. I finally gasped "That will teach you to leave your coat in the car!" I'm such a sympathetic and maternal Nana.

This kid is a hoot. He's wild and he's wide open much of the time, but he sure is fun.

Judges 13:12 "When your words are fulfilled, what is to be the rule for the boy's life and work?"

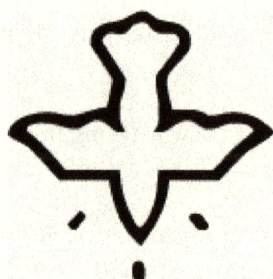

Oh My Achey Breaky Feet!

I hate my feet. I have so many problems with them without injuring them that, many days I wish I could just cut them off. I've suffered with plantar fascitis, bunions (removed) Hagland's Deformities on the heels (also removed and *ruined* my feet forever) and had a neuroma under my toes that required a shot of cortisone into the site. I was even hard on them as a kid, fracturing one once while visiting my grandparent's farm. I was just plain hard on bones as a child, a real klutz. I cracked my ribs when I fell into Monkey Bars at the park, sprained my ankle severely enough to be on crutches for weeks while skating, and had a concussion when I fell backwards and hit a rock at the neighbors. The worst pain though comes from the neuropathy that started a few years ago. My feet burn, sting and just plain *hurt* nearly 24/7, with some days worse than others.

I've always said that God doesn't make mistakes but sometimes I have to wonder about feet.....they're UGLY and not very efficient. I really think He designed feet as a big joke on us. Take your shoes off (or someone else's if your own feet stink) and take a gander. Aren't they hideous things? In many cases they aren't very big and even when they are large, in comparison to the rest of you, they seem to shrink since these little things were designed to carry us. See what I mean by joke? I'll bet God chuckles every time He thinks about them.

In my case I probably deserve all of the foot problems since I wasn't very kind to my feet for many years. I worked in hospitals and wore heels a good deal of the time. Apparently I wasn't very smart either. I worked in jobs that required me to sit for long periods, but that also required lot's of walking throughout my shift. Talk about abuse. Oh but I loved the way my ankles and calves looked in those heels (I've always had nice compared to the rest of me—go figure). Yet I recall many a day that I could barely wait to get to the car and take them off. One day I didn't even make it from my desk. I had a brand new pair of shoes on that had me in near tears by the end of the day. A co-worker loved them (and fortunately for her, she wore the same size) so I took them off and handed them to her as we left, and walked out in my nylon stocking clad feet. Gee that brought back a sudden memory. I was working 2nd shift (in a hospital of course) and worked on the surgical floor, 3 flights up. I am terrified of elevators so always took the stairs unless in a huge hurry. One day I had a brand new pair of panty hose on (as I recall "No Nonsense" brand, what a laugh. It was Nonsense all night long!). They were defective though and the seams, instead of straight went diagonally so they were constantly slipping no matter how I tried twisting them into shape. I was headed up the stairs at one point when a male co-worker joined me. Those things started slipping and I thought I was going to lose them! I was praying like crazy to make it safely upstairs, fearing they'd slip to my ankles at any moment. Prayers work and I made it to my floor, excused myself and made a quick dash into the ladies room to once again rearrange them. By the end of my shift I was worn out and I hurt. Those dumb things had worn my inner thighs raw from all the twisting. I had complained all evening to my co-workers, and told one on the way out that I was taking them off the instant I got into my car. She just laughed at me. When I passed her on the way home and waved my pantyhose at her she started howling and beating on her steering wheel, tears rolling. She never doubted me when I said I was going to do something again though. But now I'm rambling......

I have broken my little toes several times and even broke one of my big toes once when a can of vegetables fell out of the fridge on top of it, hitting the toe with the rim. I don't recall now why a can of veggies was even in the fridge but I *do* recall the pain. The women in my family all have problems with breaking toes. My older sister walked into a brick and a trash can breaking toes on separate occasions. My mom has broken her toes so many times that they are all crooked and twisted now. I broke my first one when Brooke ran in front of me as we made a mad dash to the front door when Alexis was little. She was about eighteen months old and playing outside while her Bapa mowed, when she started towards the street. Brooke and I both looked out and saw her so took off for the door at the same moment, where I caught my toe on her sandal strap. OUCH and Ewww. I hated that sound. As it turned out, Bapa was in control of the situation and had her safely in hand before we even made contact. I re-broke it a few weeks later, just after it had healed, when I walked into a baby swing sitting in the floor. Jarod took a turn then and broke one of my toes last year. The kids, Brooke and I were upstairs lounging on her bed watching Trading Spaces while Jarod romped on the bed in the way. Aunt Brooke told him to "SIT DOWN!" so he did, right on my toe. OUCH and Ewwww again.

Yesterday my friend Carol wrote about how she had just broken one of her toes THEN dropped a marble rolling pin on it! I guess I felt so bad for her that I broke one of mine again that night, in fact the same one Jarod broke last year. We have a large and very well made Lexington wicker basket sitting in the front hall for shoes. One of the kids drug it out from under the table and forgot to push it back. I walked through in the dark and kicked it. OUCH Let me tell you, my marble rolling pin is staying put for now. I'd hate to carry sympathy that far.

I love to go barefooted and always have. As a kid my feet were tough as shoe leather from going barefoot outside. In fact they still are tough and rough. I once shredded the foot area of some silk sheets with them simply by sleeping on them with my sandpaper feet. As soon as I walk in the door whatever shoes I have on come off and straight into that basket. (Don't listen to Ernie who would tell you they go all over the house). I've even got the little grandkids doing this. It's so much fun to watch cute 2 ½ year old Jarod kick his shoes off and toss them at the basket. I even take my shoes off when visiting friends. However I'm tired of broken toes, no matter how pretty the bruising gets. My poor feet have suffered enough, so I'm now thinking of designing some cement shoes. I can design a whole line of sandals, casuals and dressy. I'll even include a pair of house slippers for Carol and the other women in my family.

I think I'll pass on swim shoes though.

Ezekiel 16:10 I clothed you with an embroidered dress and put leather sandals on you. I dressed you in fine linen and covered you with costly garments.

The Trials, Tribulations And Joys Of A Young Child In The House!

I must say, "Oh Irene!" fifteen times a day. (This is a conservative estimate) She is one active, bright and imaginative two-year-old, who keeps her Nana young at heart, which is a good thing since I come close to having a heart attack at least once a day.

Poor Irene has been sick with a slight cold or allergies. She had a runny nose a couple of days ago, so I sent her to the bathroom for some tissue. This was a BIG mistake on my part. I was doing laundry and mere SECONDS after I sent her off, I walked by the bathroom in time to hear her flush the toilet...about a millisecond after I noticed the loooooooong trail of toilet paper going into the toilet. Need I say I panicked? I ran over just as the water reached the top of the toilet, yanked the lid off and pulled up on the du hickey to stop the water from running. Great, now I have a new problem! I'm all alone and I'm sure the water is going to overflow if I let go. It's only 2:30 in the afternoon and Ernie isn't due home for nearly four more hours. I can't stand here and hold the thing all that time, so I streeeeeetch across the room and grab the can of Wizard. I then try to stick it in the tank to hold the bar. Darn! It just flips on its side and floats. By this time I'm so flustered, I've forgotten to be mad at the child. Then, good golly but with great relief I realize that the rubber flapper thingy is down so the only place the water is going to go is into the tank. Boy am I glad no one was home to watch THAT episode! I was still aggravated when I had to go to the store the next day for a plunger to unclog the darned toilet. Exhausted too, since this meant every trip to the bathroom had to be made to the upstairs toilets, and we make a lot of trips to the toilet with a two year old in the house. Lesson learned: NEVER send a 2-year-old into the bathroom alone. (This is a lesson I should have learned with my own kids, especially since her own dear mom was the tiny queen of clogged toilets at her age.)

Just as soon as you get mad enough to lock her in a closet, she'll do something cute. Ernie came home later that evening with our new couch. We had to shove, push and cram that thing in the door. THEN we had to get it through the kitchen area. Ugh.. Well, willing helper that she is, Irene got right in there under my feet and helped push it saying, "I'm helping, right?!". Now I ask, who could get upset with such a big helper? Certainly not me.

Just a few minutes ago, I walked into my bedroom to find little white bugs all over my bed. Well not actually bugs, it just looked like bugs. It was actually little white wax potpourri pellets that *had been* in a cup on my dresser. The upside of this is my bed now smells nice and lemony.

Dinnertime means it's almost time for Bapa to get home and this is fun time for me. She dearly loves to set the table so I set the plates out and she gets the forks, knives, etc out of the drawer-all 15 pieces, for 3 people. She then proceeds to lay the plates out wherever she has decided we'll sit. What a sight! Silverware is lying every which way. Oh well, if we drop anything during the meal, we've got lots of extras to choose from.

I dread the words, "I brushed my teeth Nana!" because I know I'm going to go into the bathroom and find at least a foot of blue, bubble-gum flavored tooth paste snakes in the sink. At least it is easy to clean and sure saves on cleansers. It's the oddest thing though, every time I go in there my mouth starts to water and I have this urge to start chewing.

Last night, her Bapa and I were doing some work on the computer while she sat out in the hallway and entertained herself. I looked out to check on her and found her sitting at the top of the stairs, rolling her ball down the stairs. And here I had been thinking we needed to buy her some educational toys. When she saw me watching, she tried to get me to go after the ball for her. Yeah right kid, in your dreams!

Shopping trips turn into real treats, especially when she throws a temper tantrum as only a two-year-old can. Yesterday she got mad at me when I told her she would have to wait until I was through shopping to ride the dinosaur inside Wal Mart, since I didn't have any change with me. This did not go over well with her and she took off running after me, screaming at the top of her lungs. It's not easy to stay cool with a wild child drawing everyone's attention. I had to stop walking to allow someone to walk in front of me and when I did, Irene ran smack into the backs of my legs and fell back on her butt. Some woman, who only saw her fall shook her head and said, "That poor child". Yeah right lady! If you'd seen the entire episode you'd have been saying, "That poor woman!" It's just a good thing for us that there were other witnesses.

There are no bad days with a young child around. There ARE days that are more hectic, chaotic, confused and well you get the idea. There are also times that are more fun than others. Times like the other evening when we went out for pizza buffet at a local pizza restaurant. Irene was in a terrible mood when we first got there because she had fallen asleep in the car and had to be woken up to go in. Hint: Always try to allow sleeping two year olds to waken on their own! Anyway, her Bapa had taught her a new trick recently and she finally remembered it, bringing the tears to an abrupt halt. This trick is to blow the paper off of her straw. Of course I am her very most favorite target for shooting practice. I didn't mind though, since it got her to stop yelling at us for waking her. However being the incredibly bright child that she is, (I've read kids get their smarts from the mom's side of the family) she took it a step further this evening. Her Bapa had made her a plate of spaghetti and pizza and after she ate her fill, started to patiently stuff spaghetti noodles into her straw. When she had it full, she proceeded to shoot the noodles at her Bapa. I'll take the paper hits over a soggy noodle assault any day.

When Alexis still lived close, she and Irene would stay in constant "trouble". What one couldn't think of to do or get into, the other could. Alexis is coming to stay with us for a while starting in January and I am so excited that I can hardly stand it. Still, knowing these little ones the way I do, I think I'll start taking a daily mega dose of multi-vitamins. Remembering the gray hairs they can cause, I think I'd better stock up on my favorite hair dye on my next shopping trip as well.

I originally wrote this for my friend Cindy, who had recently found out she was going to be a first time grandma. She has since had two more grandchildren so has no doubt discovered her own joys, trials and tribulations. I myself now have three grandchildren. Jarod is 5, Irene is 9 and Alexis is 11. Our days hold a never ending supply of fun and funny moments which of course makes them all well worth it.

Grandchildren truly are God's reward for not killing our own.

Proverbs 17:6 Children's children are a crown to the aged, and parents are the pride of their children.

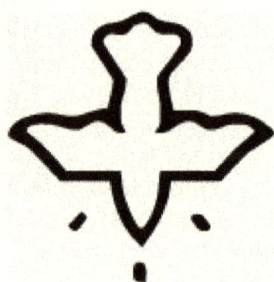

Old And Young

Alexis and Irene accompanied me to evening church services last night, for a concert being performed by a visiting gospel group. Unfortunately the group cancelled at the last minute due to weather, but I was still glad we went. I'm ashamed to admit it but I don't normally attend the evening service. I enjoyed it immensely and the reward I received afterwards just rounded out the evening.

While waiting for services to begin Alexis and Irene played and talked quietly in the pew. Alexis suddenly declared that she "wants to be a kid forever!" I laughed and told her that we don't have that choice and that she would actually enjoy being an adult some day and that we adults have fun too. The conversation was put on hold as service started, but we continued it on the way home and this is pretty much the way it went:

Irene asked if adults play with toys and I told her there was certainly nothing to stop us and that some do enjoy playing with toys. She then pointed out that "40 would be good because you can stay up allll night!" I laughed (I laugh a lot with these kids around) and told her that it's a lot harder to stay up alllll night at 40 than it is when you're a teenager. This led one of them to ask how old I am and I replied "I'm 49. I'm OLD!" They both responded in unison, "Woooooaa!!". "Yeah Nana is old", I laughingly responded. Being the wonderful and sincere little girls they are, they immediately started saying things such as: "Nana you're not old! I think you're perfect! I like the way you look! We like you the way you are!"

There is nothing quite as uplifting for the spirits as the innocent yet sincere compliments of a young child who loves you. Who needs toys when you have grandkids around? They're more fun than any toy ever made. I highly recommend them to anyone wanting to stay young at heart. In fact I'd loan you mine, but I'd miss them and my daily dose of laughter.

As the saying goes: "Grandchildren are God's reward for not killing your own!" And a precious reward they are.

Genesis 43:33 The men had been seated before him in the order of their ages, from the firstborn to the youngest; and they looked at each other in astonishment.

Oooooooooh It Was Soooooo Embarrassing!

When we lived in High Point, we had one of the best postal carriers we've ever had. His name is Eddie Noble and he sets the standard for postal delivery in town. (This per one of his supervisors, an opinion I strongly endorse). Eddie is a big, laid back (not that it matters, just trying to acquaint you too) black man with a marvelous sense of humor. Even then I was a freebie fan and did a lot of buying on Ebay, so he delivered a lot of packages to the door. He used to laugh and tell me that he was tired of delivering packages, and had just seen the moving van up the street and it was headed to our house. We got to be friends, so it was a sad day when I told him that the moving van really was coming to our house. He adored the little girls (having a little girl of his own about their age) and gave them a hug on their last day. He then turned and gave me a hug too all while Ernie watched and laughed. He knew what a great Christian man Eddie is. We all still miss him!

Our temperatures reached the high 90's today. I still refuse to turn the central air on, preferring to tough it out for as long as we can withstand it. I feel like a prisoner all winter in a closed up house, so thoroughly enjoy opening the house up to fresh air even when it's hot. We have an attic fan that goes on first thing every morning as I walk down the hall, immediately followed by the opening of all windows in the front of the house. I also leave the front door open with the screen door latched.

So why am I telling you about two seemingly unrelated stories? Because it was really hot today and one of the most embarrassing moments of my life transpired and Eddie Noble came to mind.

I had cleaned house all morning. It was a mess and I worked hard. I was hot and sweaty when I got done, so went back to the bedroom to get ready for a shower. I've always had a problem with forgetting that I'm not alone in the universe and today was no different. I took my shorts off and still in underwear and t-shirt, went back into the living room to check something on the computer. Of all places to sit half-naked while your house is wide open. The phone rang as I sat down at the desk. I answered and it was my oldest daughter, Mistie calling to confirm that we were still going to look for new eyeglasses for me. I told her yes that I just needed to get showered. It was about this time that the doorbell rang. Here I am sitting in the front room with the windows next to the front door open, so whoever it was knew I was there. I jumped up and made a mad dash through the dining room into the kitchen whispering to Mistie that "someone is at the door!" She said something to the effect of "so answer it!" When I told her how I was dressed she started to laugh and told me to run to the bedroom. When I told her I had to pass the OPEN front door to get there she started to laugh harder. I ran to the laundry room to look for something, ANYthing to toss on. Wouldn't you know there was a huge basket of clothes but they were *all* the kid's clothes? I was trapped like a rat.

In the meantime the person kept leaning on that doorbell. After all, they knew someone was in here since I had been sitting at the desk talking just moments before. I told Mistie, who was laughing hysterically by this point that it was tough; I was just going to ignore them. THEN they started to knock AND ring the doorbell. I couldn't take it anymore so yelled in my sternest voice, "Who IS it??!!" "It's the postal carrier! I have a certified letter for Paul!" was the response.

Rats. Now he not only knows I'm here, but has important mail needing my signature. I then said, "I have a little problem. I'm not dressed". He politely responds "That's ok I've already waited 3 days, 4 hours and 20 minutes, I can wait a little longer!" (This is when I thought of Eddie Noble and wondered if they could be related.).

Ooooooooh.....he doesn't seem to understand my predicament so I have to explain. I got as close to the wall as possible and poked my head around the family room corner to the front hall and see that it's the really nice mail man, the one who always delivers all of our mail to the door whenever he has a package to deliver, unlike the rest who only bring the package. I say, "Well you see... I have no clothes so I need to get to the bedroom and to do that I have to go through here." He looks thunderstruck, says "Oh I'm SORRY!", and turns around while I make a mad dash from family room to bedroom hallway. I was dying of embarrassment and wouldn't allow Mistie, who is laughing like a loon, off of the phone. NO WAY am I going to face him alone even if it's only virtual support. I toss on my shorts and go back to sign for the stupid letter all while still holding the phone and refusing to make eye contact with my mail carrier. I was soooo embarrassed and my face must have been flaming red. He told me to have a nice day as he walked away. I would have cried if I hadn't been laughing so hard.

It was a tough day for me all around, so when Ernie suggested we go out to dinner tonight I jumped at the chance. I was telling him about the most embarrassing moment of my life and said "The poor man will probably put in for a transfer now!" I swear I could hear Eddie Noble's big, hearty laugh in the background as I said it.

I wish I could say that I've learned my lesson and will never walk around half-dressed again. Knowing me though, I'll forget that I'm not the last person alive and pull another dumb stunt eventually. I just hope I have the front door closed when I do, and definitely plan to leave some clothes hanging in the laundry room from now on, just in case.

Job 31:19 if I have seen anyone perishing for lack of clothing, or a needy man without a garment,

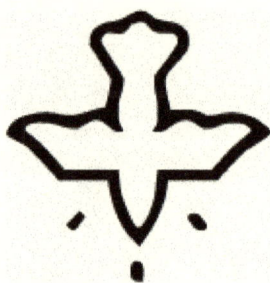

Peee Yewww What A Stink!

I believe that almost all memories are precious. Some are sad, some funny and some touching, but nearly all are precious. So that said, I'd like to share some laughs and a precious memory from a not so precious time of my life.

Many of you know that I was once trapped in a very unhappy marriage. I left that life behind when I met my husband Ernie. He is my own Knight in Shining Armor, and we celebrated our 25th anniversary on November 6, 2006. I very rarely even think about my old life due to being happy now, and because so many of those memories are bad. However the story I am sharing today is a funny one, though at the time it was more aggravating than funny. You may even learn something from our mistake.

We had recently purchased a house in a new development. This was still a very new area and some of the wildlife hadn't figured out that they had been displaced yet. It wasn't unusual to find scorpions on your patio, or that raccoons had ravaged your trash. This was nothing compared to what happened to me one day though! Our washer and dryer pair was located in the garage which is also where we kept bags of overflow trash between trash pick-up days. The door to the garage was just off my kitchen, and I went be-bopping out there one day to start a load of laundry when I came face to face with a skunk. I don't know who was more startled, but I do know I screamed and slammed the door shut as I ran back into the house. After I calmed down a bit my now ex accompanied me back out to the garage, not quite believing that I had indeed seen a skunk. We started poking around looking for it when sure enough; there he came running out of a bag of trash! We ran for the door and the skunk ran towards the wall. We stopped to see how he had gotten in and saw him run through a hole that had been chewed into the plastic dryer vent hose. Unfortunately, he got confused in all the excitement and turned towards my dryer instead of the outdoors and freedom. That darned skunk wound up inside my clothes dryer. We didn't have a clue how to get him out, so went inside and called the animal control people through the police department. It was a weekend so we got a cop instead of animal control. He was as baffled as we were as to how we were going to get rid of our new pest. To this day I don't know how or why they decided to move the dryer, but they did. With my ex on one side and the cop on the other, they moved the dryer from the garage to the driveway. Mr. Skunk was not happy with this new arrangement so he let loose with all he had and sprayed the inside of my clothes dryer. P U, what a stink. I guess he couldn't stand his own smell and ran out and off across the yard, never to be seen again.

I had only had the machines for a year or so and was not a happy laundress. I immediately called our homeowners insurance company and inquired about replacing it under our policy. I have never heard a professional person laugh so hard in my life. After he calmed down, he assured me that he would call me back after researching the problem. Well he did call back and after thanking me for a great laugh (I could hear others in the background still laughing) he explained that they had never heard of this happening before and unfortunately, could not help me since they were viewing it as an act of God. This left me with few options, so I started calling fumigating companies. I got so tired of explaining the problem and hearing people laugh. It sure wasn't funny to me. Most said they could sell me a solution to soak old rags in that I could then run through my dryer. However they couldn't guarantee results and it was going to cost me approximately $30 to experiment! Being poor and living paycheck to paycheck, I decided to try my own concoction. What did I have to lose? I said a prayer, then mixed up pine cleaner and vinegar (PU, a whole new stink). I soaked old rags in it, then tossed them into the dryer. I ran the dryer until the rags were dry then re-soaked them and ran them through another cycle. I held my breath as I opened the dryer......It didn't stink anymore! I had no faith in my recipe so was totally surprised. Never let anyone tell you there is no power in prayer.

Deciding we needed to find out how that little stinker had gotten into the garage, we went to the side of the house where the dryer vented to the outside. There we saw tiny little footprints in the dirt...right under the open vent. The ex cut a piece of sheet metal to fit, poked holes in it and screwed it over the opening. We would check every few days and would find little footprints until our unwelcome guest finally figured out his favorite restaurant had closed.

Though not very funny at the time, in retrospect the entire thing is hysterically funny. I used that washer and dryer for many more years without a problem. I also learned a valuable lesson. Whenever I move into a new home, the first thing I do is check the dryer vent to be sure it has some sort of cover over it. I've also long ago forgiven that insurance agent for laughing at my very difficult and somewhat embarrassing problem. I've even given up secretly hoping he finds a nest of skunks in his clothes dryer, while filled with his clothes.

Genesis 27:27 So he went to him and kissed him. When Isaac caught the smell of his clothes, he blessed him and said, "Ah, the smell of my son is like the smell of a field that the LORD has blessed.

Peeeeyewwwwwwww!! What IS That Smell???!!!

I ran across a website once, where people posted embarrassing things that had happened to them. Some of the things listed were kind of lame to say the least. I mean, come on, sneezing three times in a row? My dad hardly ever sneezed less than five times in a row, but always seemed more aggravated than embarrassed. Or how about putting on your pants and realizing they're too tight in the thighs? What woman hasn't experienced that?!

One thought though, found way down the list, not only caught my attention but also caused a flash back to Food World (grocery store) in Enterprise, Alabama several years prior. It was early afternoon in the canned fruit and dessert aisle to be exact. In retrospect, it's quite funny recalling the short encounter but it was also such a malodorously unpleasant experience that every detail is forever burned into the olfactory glands of my memory bank. What's the bad thing listed you may ask, that triggered this odiferous memory? "You fail to silence a fart in public".

Noooooo this didn't happen to me. Gosh no. What did happen was almost as bad though. Brooke and I had been out running errands with a few weeks old Irene when we stopped for some dinner items at Food World, our last stop before heading home.

Normally my kids accuse me of being related to the camel family because I can go for hours without needing a drink where as they need to stop at the first gas station for a soda the instant the car backs out of the driveway. This day however I was really thirsty. I was painfully parched in fact so deciding that I couldn't wait until we got home I grabbed a small bottle of chocolate milk out of the dairy cooler and chugged it down then tossed the empty into the cart with the rest of the groceries. I was so thirsty that I drank a little too fast and started feeling a bit queasy. Unfortunately this happened just as we went around a corner and entered the canned fruit aisle where one of the most horrific smells we'd ever experienced smacked us right in the face and made our eyes instantly start to water. Several other people were entering from the other end of the aisle and we could see them start to grimace as the smell assaulted their senses. Someone (I fear it was me) exclaimed "Oh my gosh! What's that SMELL?!! I'm going to be sick! I shouldn't have drunk that milk so fast!" I quickly started to check Irene's diaper and it's at this point that we all look down to see an elderly gentleman squatting to look at some items on a bottom shelf; the comically horrified look on his face said it all. It was obvious to all that he had to put it quite bluntly, passed gas, cut the cheese, dropped a stink bomb..... farted.

I don't know about the rest of the shoppers but it took all I had in me to keep from bursting out laughing but since that would have required breathing I fought the urge. Not another word was said as we all hurried out of the fogged area. As we rounded the corner to fresher air space I gasped to Brooke that someone needed to check their britches but it wasn't any of us, and that I really should have waited until we got home for that drink.

1 Corinthians 12:17 If the whole body were an eye, where would the sense of hearing be? If the whole body were an ear, where would the sense of smell be?

Pinkie Up Dahling

Maybe it was because of the tea related freebie notice that I sent out in my freebie newsletter the day before, or maybe it was because I've been promising Alexis that we would do it. Whatever prompted it, both of the girls and I decided to have a "tea party" last night after supper and showers. I've had a couple of impromptu parties with Irene who invited a few of her stuffed animals to join us, and a good time was had by all. Alexis has always been at her house when we've had them so missed out. Told that they could have the party if showers were taken early, they jumped at the chance.

Alexis wanted to play hostess so set out three of my good china cups and saucers. Jarod, always up for a good time especially if it involves food, decided to join us. There was no way that he was going to agree to using a mug (I tried) so we got one of my mismatched sets out. He didn't notice a difference, and as it turned out was wonderfully careful. In fact all three were very careful with the dishes and acted so very grown up.

No one was in the mood for hot tea so Irene and I had iced tea in our cups, Alexis started with water (she no longer likes tea and drinks LOTS of water) and Jarod asked for tea as well. We discussed school activities for a while then I remembered that we had Chips Ahoy cookies in the cabinet. (I'm a more modern grandmother. Why bake if you can buy?). Then I recalled the quart of chocolate milk in the fridge. Alexis and Jarod dumped their drinks and went with the milk. The cookies probably tasted better in milk, but Jarod seemed to enjoy them dunked in my tea as well.

I finally just sat back and watched. What a sight. The little girls got along so well and Alexis loved playing hostess. Irene, having hosted them enough that she is now a pro in the tea party set, was happy to allow her the experience. Jarod used his cup and saucer like a true gentleman and all cleaned up after themselves.

We had such a good time that we've decided to host a tea party this fall for a few friends and their mommies, or in one case, grandmother. We'll choose a day that they're out of school for a teacher work day, and make little sandwiches and tea cookies.

Being the lazy person that I am and a modern kind of grandmother, we'll make it a casual, come as you are kind of affair. I think I'm as excited as they are and really look forward to our little party. Now I just need to look at a school calendar so we can set the date.

Maybe I'll even be able to answer Irene's question about why etiquette says you should hold your pinky finger up while sipping tea before then. Care to join us?

Genesis 21:19 Then God opened her eyes and she saw a well of water. So she went and filled the skin with water and gave the boy a drink.

Tea Etiquette per "What's Cooking America"

http://whatscookingamerica.net/History/HighTeaHistory.htm

Pick up your cup and saucer together — holding the saucer in one hand and cup in the other. The best way to hold a tea cup is to slip your index finger through the handle, up to almost the first knuckle, then balance and secure the cup by placing your thumb on the top of the handle and allowing the bottom of the handle to rest on your middle finger. Hold the cup lightly, by the handle — your pinky doesn't have to be extended (Contrary to popular belief, the ring and pinkie fingers should not be extended, but should rest by curving gently back toward your wrist). Hold the saucer under your cup while you sip your tea (lest you should spill or dribble). When stirring your tea, don't make noises by clinking the sides of the cup while stirring. Gently swish the tea back and forth being careful no to touch the sides of your cup if possible. Never leave your spoon in the cup and be sure not to sip your tea from the spoon either. After stirring, place your spoon quietly on the saucer, behind the cup, on the right hand side under the handle. Pick up your cup and saucer together — holding the saucer in one hand and cup in the other. The best way to hold a tea cup is to slip your index finger through the handle, up to almost the first knuckle, then balance and secure the cup by placing your thumb on the top of the handle and allowing the bottom of the handle to rest on your middle finger. Hold the cup lightly, by the handle — your pinky doesn't have to be extended (Contrary to popular belief, the ring and pinkie fingers should not be extended, but should rest by curving gently back toward your wrist). Hold the saucer under your cup while you sip your tea (lest you should spill or dribble). Milk is served with tea, not cream. Cream is too heavy and masks the taste of the tea. Although some pour their milk in the cup first, it is probably better to pour the milk in the tea after it is in the cup in order to get the correct amount. When serving lemon with tea, use lemon slices, not wedges. Either provide a small fork or lemon fork for your guests, or have the tea server can neatly place a slice in the tea cup after the tea has been poured. Be sure never to add lemon with milk since the lemon's citric acid will cause the proteins in the milk to curdle.

Power Ball Fever

Lottery fever hit the Nagy household Friday morning. I mean, who can resist the chance of winning nearly $300 MILLION dollars??? Apparently we can't so Brooke and I loaded Irene and Jarod in the Jimmy and took off for West Virginia Friday morning. I drove, and remorse for ever undertaking the trip struck about half way there. I knew the odds of winning were something like 1 in 80 million so regret hit me about the same time Irene started whining about how she didn't even want to go on this trip and how it was taking too long, etc. Ever been on a trip with a 4 year old whining, "Are we there yet?"? It isn't fun for your ears, trust me. As Brooke pointed out, it would all be worth it if we won. If not we had our memory of the trip.

We took Highway 52 to West Virginia which was a straight shot up. If you're not familiar with Highway 52, trust my description of very curvy and mountainous. It's also some of the prettiest country you could hope to see, not that I saw that much. I was too nervous driving on those curves. I used to be such a risk taker when driving, before I started driving an SUV that is prone to roll-overs when taking curves too quickly, something my kids like to remind me of when I'm taking a corner a little too fast for their taste.

If you're into old antique stores (as in been there a long time from the looks of things) then Highway 52 is the place for you. I have been trying to organize a trip with Mistie, Brooke and Stacie (NO kids!) for some time now. We want to just go and spend the day wandering through as many as we can squeeze in during a day. Some day we'll all get our schedules coordinated to go. Ernie has already said, "Have a good time and don't bring home any old junk!" (*His* term for antiques)

We finally made it to Bluefield, WV 2 ½ hours later. It seemed more like 6 hours since Jarod got bored about ¾ of the way into the trip and started yelling "Are we there yet?!" in 4 month old baby language. Of course he was all smiles when we finally stopped for tickets and I was able to take him out of his seat. Babies are so forgiving. That smile made it all worth the howling that we had endured.

We stopped at the first sign that said they sold tickets and Brooke got in line, while I attempted to find a place to park. People were lined up from the store nearly to the street. Fortunately another car drove up and the driver tried to tell everyone there was another store up the road where there was no line. Brooke was the only one who listened, so we took off following his directions which were a little off in distance but accurate otherwise. Sure enough there was no line (we did see a taxi pull up with 3 people who were there to buy tickets) and Brooke was in and out in no time. When we went back by the first store people were still lined up, and the line had barely moved.

By this time I was nearly ready to explode with need of a potty break and so hungry I thought I would perish. I had eaten two rice cakes just before leaving home and a few crackers that Brooke brought. Brooke checked the map and said it would be easier to travel Highway 77 home since, though it was still mountains, it was interstate till near Mt. Airy. We figured we'd stop somewhere along the way for a quick drive-through meal. We stopped at her usual spot on 77 to purchase Virginia lottery tickets and while there Irene and I used their filthy restroom. Desperation and toilet seat covers will make you do things you wouldn't do otherwise. We went next door to another Snappy's location (that is as old and rundown as the original) only to find them closed. I don't eat gas station food after a bad experience with a moldy sandwich several years ago, but the food back at that station was sure starting to sound better....We decided there must be another place along the way and drove on, which was a mistake since eating places (that offer fast food for a fast trip) are few and far between on this road.

Brooke was driving this last leg of our trip. I should have more confidence in her driving, but she has a tendency to drive too fast. I like being in control, especially when driving in high places. We rounded one corner and off to our left was a magnificent view of mountains and valley. Unfortunately, I suffer with a severe fear of heights so wanted to throw up when I saw it. Brooke on the other hand was saying, "Look at that view!" I was yelling, Noooooooooo and YOU QUIT LOOKING TOOOOOOO!" She found this hysterical, the rotten brat.

Irene was still cranked up with the boredom blues and was now hungry on top of it all. Jarod had finally cried himself out and was taking a hugely appreciated nap. He slept all the way to Winston-Salem where we finally found a fast food place at 1:30 in the afternoon. I think we all inhaled our lunch. Jarod woke up just as I finished eating and made it clear that he was hungry now too. Brooke took the next exit and pulled over so I could move Irene's car seat to the front and take the back seat with Jarod. He had the biggest tear that I'd ever seen running down his cheek by the time I got his formula mixed and the bottle in his mouth. Babies have a ways of looking at you that cut to the heart and his look said, "Why were you ignoring me?" I felt guilty for the rest of the trip home which was only a merciful thirty minutes.

We finally made it home and just in time to pick Alexis up at school. The trip took us a total of 5 hours driving time and we spent most of it planning what we'd do if we won. We bought Stacie two tickets and decided if she won, we would demand 5 million apiece just for the aggravation we went through getting there and back. When informed of this, she didn't appear to see it our way, asking whose fault was it that we took two little kids with us.

We checked our numbers this morning and we didn't win. Not that we expected to, but we didn't even come close. All of our wonderful plans went to nothing. Oh well we still have our memories of the trip.

Hebrews 13:5 Keep your lives free from the love of money and be content with what you have, because God has said, "Never will I leave you; never will I forsake you.

Prepare To Be Pelted

It's a whole new kind of dangerous outside today. The schools are on a 2-hour delay start, so we didn't leave home this morning until almost 10AM when the sun was shining and it was warming up fast. So fast that the ice is falling off of trees and power lines at such a furious rate, that it's like being pelted with rocks when you walk under them. It sort of gave a new meaning to ice storm.

It has been many, many years since I've lived in ice country. I lived in Oklahoma back in FULBBWLWE (Former Unhappy Life Before Blissful Wedded Life With Ernie) Days, for several years and lived through a long winter of major ice storm after major ice storm. I was so tired of ice by spring. I'll never forget the day I walked out of my front door to go somewhere, and fell on my rear. The ice was about 3 inches thick on the ground and I slid all the way down my gently sloping yard to my car which was parked in the street. I had dead-on aim too, stopping right at the driver's door. Being much younger then I quickly got to my feet and, happy to find I had hung onto my keys, unlocked the door and hopped in hoping that none of my neighbors had witnessed my slide down the slippery slope. As I started the car I said a prayer of thanks that I didn't live on a mountainside.

We noticed on our drive to school this morning that several trees had broken and fallen under the weight of all the ice. What fascinated me though was that nearly all of the fallen were young trees that had either split down the middle or were uprooted completely. Some older trees were bowed under the weight and a few had lost limbs but had withstood the pressure of the heavy ice. What a great metaphor for the human condition.

I'm just glad that I don't need to leave the house again until time to go pick the girls up at school this afternoon. I'm not even going to brave the trip to the mailbox since the path is under tress all the way. I'll just pull up to the mailbox when I leave the driveway and check mail from the relative safety of Jimmy. I'm more than happy to let it take the pelting.

Ezekiel 1:22 Spread out above the heads of the living creatures was what looked like an expanse, sparkling like ice, and awesome.

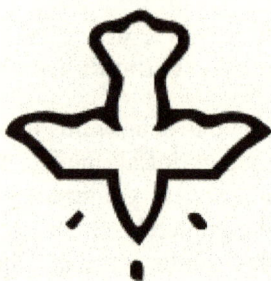

Pretty Little Girl A In Fur Coat

We were stationed in Hanau, Germany from 1984 to 1987 with the Army, and lived on the economy in a tiny little town called Huttengesass for the first half of our stay. We met a wonderful woman there by the name of Bridget whom we all called Oma, German for Grandma. She knew most everyone in this tiny town, and being a frugal person asked one day if I was interested in some clothes for three year-old Stacie that a friend had given her. Of course I said yes, having been the recipient of other beautiful, castoff clothing for the kids. She brought a trash bag of items over, one of which was a gorgeous white fur coat with red fur buttons. Stacie looked darling in this coat.

She was wearing this coat one-day when my friend Darla and I took our kids to lunch on Fleigerhorst Kasern, one of the small military posts around the area. We each have three kids, all fairly close in age, so they entertained each other while the mommy's had a nice lunch. As we were leaving the building, Stacie ran ahead of us down the stairs and towards the street. We saw a car coming around the corner, and we all started screaming for her to stop but on she ran. We could only stand and watch in horror as she ran out into the street and straight into the side of the car. Darla and I ran like we probably hadn't since high school and got to her almost before the car stopped. I grabbed Stacie up and checked her over. With the exception of a now filthy white fur coat and dirt under her fingernails, she was fine. I think the dirty nails were what undid me and I hugged her as hard as I could then turned her over to warm her behind. Things were happening so fast that I hadn't even noticed who was driving the car. I looked up as I started to whack her backside and saw a bewildered young Lieutenant standing by the car looking devastated. He fully expected to find a dead child lying in the road and instead found her mother bent over whooping her. I apologized profusely as we left with her firmly in hand. The poor guy was so shattered by this near death incident that he couldn't even drive. Fortunately his wife was with him and drove him to his destination.

I think about him occasionally and wonder if he has nightmares of pretty, little girls in white fur coats with red fur buttons, running into the street as he turns the corner, and wonder if he's able to stop in time in those nightmares.

Psalm 5:11 But let all who take refuge in you be glad; let them ever sing for joy. Spread your protection over them that those who love your name may rejoice in you.

Rainbow Colored Memories

I was looking at a collector's tin of crayons recently and while reading the back of it, flashed back to my childhood. The back say's "Whether you're 9 or 99, the brilliant rainbow of hues in the familiar yellow and green Crayola Crayon box is one of the most identifiable symbols of childhood. Both young and old alike can remember their first box of Crayola crayons and their favorite color".

This got me thinking and I realized that, though I don't recall my first box I do remember the excitement of opening a new box. I was dazzled by all of the pretty colors and the not quite pointed, perfect tips. I can still recall the way a new box of crayons smelled when you opened it while reaching for a coloring book. Yet as excited as I was to have it, I was a little slow to use them so that they would stay perfect. What fun opening a new box and trying to memorize where each one was placed so that you could return it back to its proper position. The big fat ones were so easy to handle for small hands then one day, you graduated to the box with the sharpener! That was such a neat feature that you hoped to use but not toooo soon since you wanted to keep the crayons new looking for as long as possible. I loved looking at the colors while choosing my favorite amongst the rainbow of colors inside.

Then I recalled the disappointment when the first tip broke, how ugly one became if you managed to use it long enough to dull the tip without first breaking it in half, how the paper would sometimes need to be peeled off, and trying to just cram them back into the box, forget trying to get them back in a neat and tidy row in their proper order. Just getting them in was a chore. Sometimes no matter how carefully you treated them you would come up short a crayon that had mysteriously disappeared, and it would invariably be the favored red crayon. Eventually all of the crayons, both whole and broken just got tossed all together in a box, no longer special.......

Then mom would bring a new box and I would be dazzled by the beautiful colors, the oh so pretty, sharpened points, the way they smelled and how they sort of resembled a boxed flower garden of colors........

Revelation 4:3 And the one who sat there had the appearance of jasper and carnelian. A rainbow, resembling an emerald, encircled the throne.

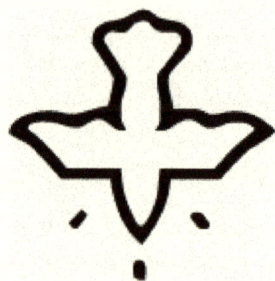

Red Wagons, Troubles And Blessings

One of the most "interesting" times of my life took place over a two-month period several years ago. While a very trying time it also proved to be a growing experience, one that showed I am strong and can survive.

It started in November of 1987. We had just transferred back stateside after being stationed with the Army in Germany for the past three years. Due to unexpected circumstances, my husband and I were forced to find a house to buy when the plans we had made to stay with relatives while he was away in school for a few months, fell through. This was our first home purchase and we had one week to accomplish this awesome task; we did it too.

We moved into the house the week before Christmas, put the tree up the day before Christmas Eve, finished shopping for Christmas and unpacked the house all that week. The reason for all this rush? My husband was leaving the 4th of January to drive to Ft. Leavenworth, Kansas for his two-month long class. I was not looking forward to this since we had just returned stateside and I knew *no* one in the area. If I had only known what was waiting for us, I may have let all the air out of his tires and hidden his car keys.

Two weeks after his departure I had to take care of the closing on the house. I had noooo idea what I was doing and was scared silly. The mortgage people nearly drove me insane with requests for this or that document, copies of his ID, which of course he had with him, etc. Somehow I survived that ordeal and managed not to sign on any wrong lines or to sign my soul away.

I had been fighting a sinus infection since we stepped off the plane the week of Thanksgiving. I tried treating it with over-the-counter meds but it wasn't getting any better, and in fact just kept getting worse. Ernie had been gone for about a week when I woke up during the night with such a headache I thought the side of my head would blow off. I woke Mistie up (who was in high school but wasn't old enough to have a drivers license yet) to tell her I was going to the emergency room. I had to drive through snow flurries to the military hospital in Aberdeen, the next town over, and arrived around two in the morning, which fortunately was a quiet time for them. The doctor got to me right away, took one look in my ear and announced that it was no wonder I was in pain since my eardrum was bulging from an infection. She then gave me meds and sent me home. On the way my ear started oozing so I called her when I got home. She told me the pressure had undoubtedly caused it to burst. What joy. I spent the next two weeks changing cotton balls and taking medicine for the still excruciating pain. I would ultimately require numerous follow-up visits since the infection, in the words of one doctor, was "blooming like a flower garden" in a subsequent outer ear infection. This of course required special ear medication suspended in thick liquid since a thin liquid could seep into the rupture and carry the infection to my brain. The new medicine naturally had to be special ordered.

Approximately a week later, just as I started to feel human again, the nursing home I had applied to for a Unit Clerk position called me for an interview. I was hired and started working immediately. I had been there for about two weeks when we had a small snowstorm. It wasn't much of a snowstorm but the schools still closed for the day. Around 2 o'clock in the afternoon I received a panicked call from my kids. The snow had melted by afternoon so Brooke and Stacie decided to go outside and let the dog pull them together on the skateboard. They hit a bump, Stacie went down, Brooke went down on top of her and well.....Mistie called and said Stacie had hurt her leg and she thought it might be broken. When I got home I took one look at her leg and declared "it doesn't look broken to me!" but since she was in so much pain I loaded them all up and took her to the emergency room at the army hospital in Aberdeen. I don't know *what* I thought a broken leg was supposed to look like, because the doctor ordered some x-rays then called for an ambulance. It was broken and he was sending her to the civilian hospital in Havre DeGrace to have it set. I went into an immediate panic. I had no idea where this hospital was much less how to get to Havre DeGrace! God was looking out for me that day because a man dressed in Army uniform was standing at the desk checking out and overheard my dilemma. He explained that he lived there and said he would show me the way. I sent Mistie to ride in the ambulance with Stacie while Brooke and I took off to follow this perfect stranger. I was nervous but I had to trust that he was honest. He pointed us to the hospital as he drove past and we arrived just as the ambulance did but the desk clerk wouldn't allow me to go back until I finished her paperwork. I still wonder if she realized how close I was to going across that desk after her. When I finally got back to the treatment area, the doctor was already putting a toe to hip cast on her leg. I felt like a failure as a mother for ever doubting her. My due punishment was about to begin though...

I was referred back to the army hospital the next day so we could have Stacie measured for and instructed in the use of crutches. She absolutely refused to even try and cried hysterically with each urging since she was still in a lot of pain and terrified of falling. So we took the crutches and went home where things got even more interesting. Stacie was in Kindergarten and was too heavy for me to carry with this huge cast on. Most shopping carts were too short to accommodate her and her unbendable leg, so her sisters would take turns staying in the van with her whenever I needed to go shopping. Since this was winter in Maryland, I would need to leave the vehicle running to keep them warm. This prompted me to also take our dog

Lucy with us each trip so that we would all feel safer. Not that she was such a deterrent, even though she was a good sized dog. Brooke had a penchant for dressing her in human clothes and scarves making her look pretty silly and harmless. If someone caught a glimpse of her in the windows, they were usually too busy laughing to be scared of her. Anyway this arrangement got old very quickly so in my desperate situation, I got the idea to buy a wagon. Of *course* the toy store would put it together for a fee which I would gladly have paid, but they told me it would be a week to ten days! I bought it and went knocking on a new neighbor's door. What a great way to meet new folks. I introduced myself, explained the situation and begged for mercy. He kindly put it together for me and even delivered it to me. Everywhere we went then, someone would comment on how clever it was to pull her around in the wagon. They had no idea the desperation that had driven me to this.

Of course with this full leg cast she wasn't able to get on and off of a bus so we had to go to home tutoring provided by the school. This meant I took off at noon every day and picked Stacie up at the babysitter, arriving home just in time to meet the tutor. Since I had to be at work well before they left for school, Brooke would deliver her to the babysitter on her way to the bus stop, using the wagon to get her there. One morning I forgot to leave the wagon, which was in the van. Brooke is and always has been very bright and didn't miss a beat. She stuck Stacie in the motorized jeep we bought her for Christmas and "drove" her to the babysitters. I was very impressed by her ingenuity and would have enjoyed the sight of them driving down the street. Ultimately Stacie did learn to use the crutches and could move quickly on them which was great, since she kept a toe to hip cast on for ten very long weeks.

During the time my husband was gone we had several little crises. The heat went out, but fortunately it did so before closing so the still current owners had to pay for repairs. We spent a few chilly moments though until it was fixed. Another time I came home from work to get the kids together for a trip to the grocery store. I turned the dishwasher on before we left and for some forgotten reason, stepped out onto the patio. I'm so glad I did because when I came back into the kitchen the dishwasher was spewing smoke! I quickly turned it off and stayed around to make sure it wasn't "on fire". Oh goody, after three years of no dishwasher in Germany I was back to doing dishes by hand. A few days later my oven went out. NOW I had no way to bake! Meals made on top of the stove get tiresome so we had a good excuse to eat out frequently. On the upside, when my husband got back from school we bought new dishwasher and oven.

We also had a several week period where we had to deal with near daily power outages. We never knew when it would go off or for how long.

Sometimes the entire neighborhood would go off, sometimes it was just our house. At times it would be for minutes, others for hours and one time overnight. On one occasion a minister from the church we had recently visited had just arrived to call on us when the power went out. Stacie was playing in the windowless family room when the power went off and was thrust into total darkness. *Of course* we all laughed hysterically when she started yelling and still do when reminiscing. Baltimore Gas and Electric finally tracked down the problem and fixed it but we had some nerve-wracking moments during the problem. This was made worse by the fact I read a newspaper article just days after Ernie left about the local "Phantom Fondler". Apparently Edgewood where we lived had this pervert running around town who would gain entry into people's homes in the middle of the night by way of unlocked doors or windows. He would then lie on the floor or stand over the female in the home and fondle her until she woke up. Many times it took them several minutes to realize it wasn't their husband! Once they were awake he would then run out before anyone could react fast enough to catch him. He never hurt anyone physically but he sure made a lot of people nervous. After I read that article, I don't think I slept a wink all night long. I was CONVINCED he was going to find my house and get in spite of the fact I had triple checked all of the doors and windows before going to bed. I'm happy to report that he never did find me and that they did eventually catch him, several years and fondlings later.

During our four years in Maryland we also survived Mistie getting a driver's license and a car and of course the requisite car troubles that went with it, which usually occurred while dad was gone. The worst we faced though was the two months he spent in Saudi. Being a former helicopter pilot himself, he had helped develop a new gas mask for aviators. He was there fielding and training pilots in the use of them when the war was officially declared. I believe that is the most scared I've ever been in my life, but we survived with the help of friends and lots of prayer.

This was just an inkling of what I could expect over the years. It got to the point that the kids and I knew we could expect some disaster to occur while hubby was gone on one of his very frequent trips throughout the rest of his military career. I knew we could handle it though because I knew I was and still am a strong person. I had to be. Besides I had and have God on my side. How could I not be strong?

Occasionally over our years spent as a military family, I would be asked how I was able to manage all of the problems. All I can say is it was worth it every time I saw his truck pull into the driveway. It still is and praise the lord will be for many years of marriage to come. Besides, for every problem there were countless blessings. Who could ask for more than that?

Recent: There is a young mom with a son in Jarod's Kindergarten class who frequently pulls her son and his little brother to school in a red wagon. I smile every time I see them in it, and memories of Stacie's time in her own red wagon come flooding back. It wasn't a fun time but there *were* times of fun while she was down with the broken leg. I still laugh when I think about her and Lucy playing tug of war with an old dish towel, Stacie's leg stuck out to one side and Lucy snarling and playfully growling. I smile when I think of how Stacie would scoot up and down the stairs on her bottom, and how she thrived under and loved her home tutor. I even chuckle when I recall how she would run stiff legged, as if still in a cast for several weeks after its removal. No not a fun time but certainly times of fun.

Now when I see the mom from school I sigh. She has one of the tiniest waists I've ever seen and is pretty and slim. If I had thought for a single moment that I could at least have a waist like hers, I would still be pulling Stacie around in a wagon eighteen years later. I also want to smack myself in the head and say "WHY didn't I ask for a wheelchair???!"

Psalm 71:20 Though you have made me see troubles, many and bitter, you will restore my life again; from the depths of the earth you will again bring me up.

Ringing Telephones

The telephone has an incredible ability to make us jump when it rings. Few can resist when it calls out to us. However I've no doubt we've all had moments when we wished we hadn't picked it up. Be it telemarketers, perverts spouting obscene words or just people you'd rather have avoided speaking with, we've all been there. I have fielded my share of all of these types of intrusions, but some very specific calls are burned into my memory. None was pleasant and in fact all were sadly life changing.

The first time I ever regretted answering a phone call happened during summer break, the year I was twelve years old. My sister and I were home watching TV when the phone rang—I was nearest so I ran to grab it, assuming it was a friend calling. The caller identified himself as my Uncle Elwood then asked to speak to either of my parents. I didn't even have time to think it strange that he was calling my parents in the middle of a weekday as I quickly told him they were both at work. His next words will be with me for the rest of my life: "You need to get hold of them because your Granddaddy has been killed". He then hung up. I spent many years resenting him for being so callous and cold in the way he handled this call and only recently realized that he himself was probably in shock. I called my mom at work and told her what my Uncle had said. She called me back mere seconds later, crying and essentially begging me to tell her that I had made a mistake. I assured her that this was exactly what Uncle Elwood had said, then did as she told me to do and called a neighbor to ask her to help locate my older sister who was spending the day with friends. I then went outside to the side of our house, leaned against it and started sobbing and praying that I had misunderstood or even dreamed the call. Time felt as if it stood still as we waited to find out if I had been wrong or it had all been a bad dream. In the meantime my mom called our minister who went with her to meet my dad at his carpool drop-off point. I will never forget watching them as they walked into the house and my dad went to the kitchen to set his lunch bucket down, then started to empty it. When he broke down I realized that this was the first time I had ever seen my dad cry. I also knew then that it was true— Granddaddy was gone. I thank God above though that Granddaddy was a wonderful Christian man so I know I'll see him again.

Many years later while working for the Girl Scouts in Alabama I would have reason to regret answering the phone once again. Our beloved Spaniel dog-child Lucy had been sick for a couple of weeks, and though obvious that she was sicker by the day, we kept up the hope that she would recover. We had taken her to the vet's office the day before and had left her overnight for observation and tests. Ernie had gone to visit her and I was planning to go visit our baby within the hour as well. I shared this office with one other person who was rarely in so when the phone rang it was up to me to answer. Hearing Ernie on the other end, I assumed he was calling me with an update on Lucy's condition. Instead he was calling with the heartbreaking news that our girl had died just minutes before. Our sweet, smart and oh so funny girl was gone from us. All I could think about as I started to cry was that I was so thankful that Ernie got to see her before she went. Lucy loved each and every one of us but as her "daddy" Ernie was her paws down favorite. She simply adored him as he did her. We brought her home that afternoon and buried her in the back yard with her favorite toys and the blanket from her bed. I would later cry when I found her leash in the closet. How she loved seeing that leash come out because it meant she was going for a run with her daddy. As we buried her the memories overwhelmed us. This was the only time I'd ever seen Ernie cry, as we hugged and agreed how much we would miss her. We would grieve hard for her and even now, over nine years later I am crying as I write. We still miss her terribly. However I sincerely believe that God blessed us with our pets and believe that He will once again bless us with a reunion with them in heaven. I can easily picture her jumping for joy and whimpering in her excitement at seeing us again.

One of the worst phone call and out of all possible bad calls was the hardest to absorb. Ernie's cousin Andrea was on the other end. I was somewhat surprised to hear from her and my mind raced ahead to figure out why she was calling, while at the same time dreading finding out since I knew her folks had been out of the country on a short, fun and much needed vacation break. I was terrified that something had happened to them but before I could voice the question she stunned me with the news that her younger sister had died. I couldn't get my mind to wrap around the idea and kept hoping it was some sort of cruel joke. Andrea is a wonderfully caring person but I kept trying to convince myself that she was pulling a bad joke on us. Dear Lord, how could this be?! Ericka was only 22 years old! I kept asking Andrea how, why, telling her she must be kidding. After she broke the news her mom Terry asked to speak with me and once again I knew that it was true. I felt as if I had been kicked in the stomach and started to cry. I can't even begin to imagine the pain that her parents Terry and Rick and her sister Andrea must feel and always will. Ericka was such a special person—wounded young in life but trying so hard to overcome and making such wonderful progress and was standing at the edge of new beginnings. Always a sweet and loving girl right to the end, she was like a sponge taking in hugs and love yet always returned them back to you with sincerest abandon. Attending her funeral was without a doubt the most difficult thing we've ever had to do yet it was the only way to accept her death and say our good-byes. At last she is free from all the awful stuff she had to deal with in this life and for this I thank you Lord even while admitting that I will never understand why you felt the need to take one so young. Lord she will be missed by us all but I trust you are taking wonderful care of her.

Yet another time I came home to find the answering machine urgently flashing with several messages. A quick glance at the caller ID told me it wasn't going to be fun messages since all were from my siblings back in Arkansas. I reluctantly hit play and listened to the devastating news that my dad had died in ICU a few hours previous, while I was at church teaching a VBS class. He had been failing since having a foot amputated a couple of months earlier but we were all hopeful that he would bounce back as he always had with previous illnesses. Sadly it was not to be and God called him home where he is no doubt having a wonderful reunion with family and friends who had gone ahead of him.

Last year I was the one who answered the phone to the news that Ernie's mom had died. We knew the call was coming since she had cancer and had been in a coma for the past week, but that didn't make it any easier to take the call. Ernie wasn't home so I had to break the news to him when he got home a short while later. That sort of job never gets any easier even with all of my practice.

I know that this won't be the end—that for as long as we live we will continue to regret that we answered some calls. There's no getting away from this fact. I just pray that I don't have to answer another such sad call for a very, very long time.

Psalm 112:7 He will have no fear of bad news; his heart is steadfast, trusting in the LORD.

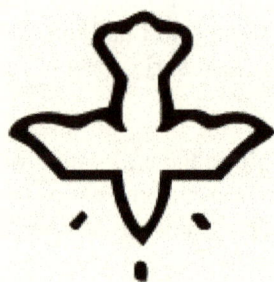

Road Trip!

Before I start my sad tale of woe about allll of the problems that we encountered with Jimmy (ok not THAT many but it sure felt like it) let me say this: we had a wonderful visit with Terry, Rick and Andrea. For those who may not know, Terry is Ernie's cousin and Rick is her husband, Andrea her daughter. We hadn't seen them in over a year—when we went home for a very sad reason. Their youngest daughter Ericka had died very suddenly due to medicine interaction, at the incredible age of 22 years old. The kids were out on spring break and this was just a perfect opportunity to go visit. I love Terry like a sister and just needed to confirm that she's hanging on.

We could not have asked for better weather once there. (The trip there was another story). We got into town just in time for dinner so gathered at their house and visited for a couple of hours before heading back to the hotel. The next morning after a nice breakfast at the hotel, we headed out to shop then back to Terry and Rick's. Terry, Andrea and Alliana, a little girl that Terry watches then took us to the River Walk in downtown Augusta, next to the Savanna River. What a glorious day it was! The sun was shining, we had a light, warm breeze and no crowds. We enjoyed sitting and watching as the kids played on the playground located near the end of our stroll. Afterwards we all went for lunch at the Cotton Patch, a small bar and grill where I had my first ever shrimp po boy sandwich. YUMMY! We then drove over to the cemetery to visit Ericka. Her gravesite looks so pretty with the flowers and tree that Terry had planted and that her friend Karen helps her maintain. We took another leisurely stroll around the garden area (this is the biggest and prettiest cemetery I've ever seen) where there were lots of trees and azaleas in bloom. The kids all picked up fallen blossoms to place on Ericka's marker. They were so sweet! Finally we took the kids to feed bread to the geese in a fenced area of the cemetery. We all got tickled at one that Mistie declared must be a low carb fan. It wouldn't touch the bread being offered, opting instead for the dry leaves lying on the ground. When the kids started putting green leaves and grass through the fence that goose acted as if it had been let loose in a buffet! We were hot and tired when we returned to the house but all in all, it had been a very nice visit and I'm so glad that we got to go.

That said, let me tell you all about the not so fun part of the trip.

We got a late start out of town the morning we left home (nothing new there) but still tried to take it slow since it was pouring rain. I'm talking rain so heavy at times that I could barely make out the tail lights of Brooke in her dad's truck in front of me. (We borrowed his truck since her Jeep would have eaten her alive in gas cost and there weren't enough seat belts in the

Jimmy for all of us going.) Shortly after that we had to slow down for a very bad one-vehicle accident. I sent up prayers for that one since it looked nasty.

If you've ever driven south on I-95 then you're familiar with a place called South of the Border. You start seeing signs advertising the place around 106 miles out and every twenty feet after that. It's a HUGE tourist trap where they obviously sink all of their money into advertising and none on equipment and buildings. Their bathroom house is old and their gas pumps are ancient. They should also be prosecuted for highway robbery since their gas was a good twenty cents higher per gallon than any of the gas stations we passed on our way down. Still, we promised the kids that we'd stop again on the way back home IF they had any money left. They did.

So between getting a late start, needing to stop for potty and food breaks (when the kids get bored they like to break the monotony by begging for food and drinks) and the horrific rain in North Carolina, our mapblast.com projected 5 hours of travel time turned into more like 7.5 hours. It was with a great sense of glee on all our parts when we pulled off of I-20 in Augusta and spotted our hotel just up the road. We got checked in and unloaded then took off for Terry's house, this time all of us piling into the Jimmy for the trip. Brooke drove since she lived in Augusta for a short time and knew her way around. She's also calmer in heavy traffic than I am. I took the position of backseat driver.

We were within a mile of their house when Brooke looked down at the dash and saw the *Check Gauges* light lit and the temperature gauge maxed out in the red zone. She pulled into a parking lot and stopped, while we tried to decide what to do. The light went out in a few minutes so we were off again. Unfortunately the gauge came back on then started a game of peek-a-boo, going off and on. I just KNEW Jimmy would pull something on that trip and it didn't disappoint me. Brooke called Auto Zone after dinner then drove over to have them check it. The conclusion was it was slightly low on antifreeze and that could be due to a slow leak in the radiator, or a leak in a hose or loose seals around the water pump that we had changed just two months before. We simply had to wait and se if we could detect a leak and if so, where. That stupid light continued to go on and off the entire time we were there, yet we could not find single spot of antifreeze on the ground. We were on our way back to the hotel the evening before we came home when the check gauges light went on again, and the temperature gauge flew up to HOT so once again we pulled into a parking lot where we sat and waited for the light to go out, when it finally occurred to us that even though the gauge was showing hot, there was not even a sign of steam or hot smells so we decided to drive on to the hotel. I had already spoken to Ernie on the phone about it and he'd told me it was probably a wiring issue. Brooke called Justin, one of her co-workers who enjoys working on cars and he confirmed this for us. This was good news and we were finally able to relax as far as this issue went.

After a good night's sleep I got up early the next morning, showered and started packing my suitcase then tackled the kids (suitcases, not the actual kids) after I woke Brooke up to take her shower. I decided to save some time and start taking suitcases down to the car while she showered so we could check out as soon as we finished breakfast then head on down the road to home.

This is where the real fun began. I couldn't find my Jimmy keys. I looked in my purse, Brooke's jeans that she had worn the night before and all around the room. When she (finally) got out of the bathroom, Brooke informed me that she had given them to me the night before. What a goof— she had done no such thing. I'd remember if she had! (I insisted). We tore the room apart looking. I took things out of the suitcase and nearly emptied my purse three times. Still NO keys. I then decided that she must have locked them in the Jimmy the night before when she was outside calling Justin. She insisted that she had done no such thing, but that was the only answer I could think of and pray for. We have wonderful insurance coverage with USAA and they provide lock-out service so all I needed to do was call. Naturally all of my insurance paperwork was locked inside Jimmy in the glove box so, we did the only thing we could think to do—we went to eat a warm hotel provided breakfast. The hotel has a computer in their lobby set up for guest use and thankfully it is hooked up to the Internet, so as soon as I finished a quick scrambled egg and sausage meal I started to get up and head for the desk. As if he had been waiting for that move, a man jumped up, hurried over, and beat me to it. I was already disgusted with the missing keys situation so I sat and shot dirty looks at the back of his head until he finished. I then got up and again, another man jumped up and tried to race me to it but I was quicker this time. Brooke tells me that he gave me some nasty looks of his own. I logged onto USAA's web site and called their number, moving to the couch so that the "gentleman" I had beaten to it could have his turn. USAA quickly arranged for a locksmith (Pop's Keys) to come break into Jimmy. I was praying that the keys would be there so that I could laugh at Brooke and her smug insistence that she had given me those stupid keys the night before. They weren't there of course.

I again called USAA only to learn that they had done their part in paying a locksmith to open it. If I needed a key (and I did) then I was on my own. At least they were very nice about telling me this. I hung up and told the guy that I would need a key and held my breath as I asked him how much. Only $75 say's he. Ouch. OK I have no choice so tell him to make it. But wait—there's a small problem: the dealership's computer is down so he can't get a code to cut the key! "Oh GREAT!" I utter, "What else can go wrong?!"

Please allow me tell you what else can go wrong.........

I stomp off to go check the room ONE MORE TIME and to tear the bags apart ONE MORE TIME in hopes of finding those blasted keys. While I'm doing this, Mistie called back to her work and got the phone number for our local dealership then called them for the code. Pop's was already busy cutting a key when I got back down stairs so the situation appeared to be improving.....

I grudgingly paid him the $75 fee (no tip) and clutched that should-be-solid-gold key in my fist as we went back upstairs to get the rest of the bags. What else could possibly go wrong?! As we headed for the stairs, the strap on my purse broke and my purse thunked to the ground. I had never seen even a loose stitch in the thing up to that point. Heaving a heavy sigh as everyone else laughed hysterically, I slung it over my shoulder and huffed onward. Not FIVE minutes later as we're making one last sweep of the room for any other missed items, Mistie decides to look in the night stand. I'd already looked in there three times but what the heck, it was worth a shot. This is when she spotted something between the nightstand and the head of her bed. You guessed it, my keys. I can only think that everyone else thought it was funny since it wasn't them who'd just laid out $75 for a worth-its-weight-in-gold key not five minutes before.

Oh well we're finally loaded and ready to leave. We make a quick stop at Dunkin Donuts two doors up for a large cup of their wonderful coffee and a sour cream donut for me. I know, I know I'm not supposed to indulge in things like that but I hadn't had one since our last trip there and after my morning, felt it was deserved, especially since I had remembered by this point that I had locked myself out of the Jimmy during our trip to Augusta just the year before when we were home for Ericka's funeral. I had been out shopping with the little ones while Ernie, Brooke, Stacie and her friend Audrey went to see the latest Lord of the Rings movie. I had left my wallet in the Jimmy and needed to pay for some shoes for the kids so I ran out to retrieve it. I laid my keys down on the console and remembered that little fact just as the door clicked closed......I hate when history sort of repeats itself.

It's with a great sense of relief that we finally start up the ramp to get onto I-20 for the first leg of our trip home when out of the blue, and once again with no warning, my driver's side mirror falls off. Literally it is dangling outside my window by the power cord. Mistie started laughing, near hysterically. I'll give her credit and admit that she tried to hide it, but still she was laughing. I wasn't. I tried to call Brooke on the cell but got no signal—at all. It was as if forces were aligned against us so I finally got her attention the old fashioned way—by honking and flashing my lights at her. Augusta is right on the Georgia/South Carolina border so we pulled off at the Welcome Center for South Carolina where Brooke attempted to tie it in place with a rope. *That* wasn't going to work so we stuffed the mirror inside the window and drove to a gas station at the first exit and bought some duct tape. In the Army this stuff is green colored and called *100 Mile an Hour tape* and I can now attest that it holds strong, at least up to 80 mph. Brooke then proceeded to tape my mirror back on. I was horrified. Here I am driving a nice looking at least, Jimmy with a redneck patch job mirror. The upside is, once home I didn't stand out in our little redneck town.

While her Aunt Brooke was busy taping, Alexis chose to unfortunately utter the same question that I had earlier: "What else can go wrong?!"

Well, let me tell you what else can go wrong.......

Mere moments after she said this (and we all hollered and asked WHY she had said such a thing), I asked her to hand me something out of my purse. Instead she handed me my entire purse since the zipper pull broke off...while my purse was still closed. A couple of miles down the road, Brooke calls me on the now working cell and tells me that the truck's ABS light has now gone on.... Then the air conditioning goes out on the Jimmy. It's blowing but only warm air. Then it's blowing cold again.... then it's not. This went on for the rest of the trip. Finally, we stopped at exit 70 in South Carolina to gas up. Brooke called me on the cell to tell me that the moment we re-entered the Interstate the truck ABS light went out. In what I consider a God moment I noticed that my check gauges light had also gone out at that same location. It stayed off for the next several hours. At last the strange occurrences had stopped.

Mistie and the kids were tired and stretched out for naps so I turned the radio on. There was a gospel station on that was coming in crystal clear so I kept it there, and was blessed by some wonderful gospel singing for the next fifty miles or so. When the station finally started to lose signal, I hit the seek button and it immediately stopped on yet another gospel station. I left it there and was blessed once again when shortly a preaching program came on, and for the first time in my life I got to listen to an old time religion type black country preacher. He tickled me to no end with his straight forward no holds barred preachin'. Some might say that since it was in the south, running across two gospel stations wouldn't be unusual. I say though that these were more God Moments. Those stations came in clear as a bell for a combined 100 miles or more while driving the Interstate, and were obviously small time radio stations. I wound down and relaxed as I listened to the music and felt as if I was being hugged and was able to smile as I realized that in retrospect, it was all pretty funny.

I made sure to keep Ernie abreast of all the problems that Jimmy was creating, you betcha. I'm hoping he'll come home from his trip tomorrow and tell me that it's time to look at trading Jimmy in. Or running it off of a cliff. Whatever. I just know that I'll REALLY be smiling when that time does arrive, whichever option he chooses.

And for the rest of that story be sure to read **Jimmy saga chapter 1,000,000**

Psalm 54:7 For he has delivered me from all my troubles, and my eyes have looked in triumph on my foes.

Run Child Run!

Yesterday, as is every Tuesday was our homeschool gathering in the park where a growing number of homeschool families meet and let the kids play and socialize while we adults sit, talk and relax knowing that the kids are secure and within sight. Over the summer many of the families have dropped away with so many other activities, but Leslie has remained faithful to attend with her son Anthony. I look forward to visiting as much as the kids. Yesterday I offered her an extra ticket for the final library summer event/party to be held this Thursday, promising to give it to her when we were ready to leave the park.

It was hot, very humid and the kids were cranky, due in part to the lack of the usual kids as much as the heat so we decided to leave early. I remembered the ticket as the kids were loading up in the van. Leslie and Anthony were getting into their own van, so I quickly honked the horn then slammed mine into drive and took off to catch and give them the ticket. (As if I couldn't simply have met them at the party or even taken it to their house). As I spun off I heard Alexis yell "NANA!!!" and looked over to see her running as hard as she could on the other side of the fence next to the van. That girl was hoofing it too. I was in such a rush to catch Leslie and Anthony that I forgot to make sure everyone had made it inside. Seeing her running alongside was such a startling but FUNNY sight that I immediately started laughing and the tears started running. The funniest part is, I don't recall stopping until I got to Leslie's van.

Leslie sort of chuckled (probably too stunned to do much else) and said "Next time you'd better do a headcount!"

I laughed all the way home. Alexis didn't see much of the humor and got tired of my snorts and guffaws and finally said "oKAAAY Nana!" which only made me laugh harder.

I'll say this—that child has a future as a sprinter and since I've said it many times before I'll admit it again....I'm a baaaad Nana.

2 Kings 5:21 So Gehazi hurried after Naaman. When Naaman saw him running toward him, he got down from the chariot to meet him. "Is everything all right?" he asked.

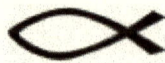

Ruuun!!!!!!!!

I have a funny memory stored away in my brain that makes me laugh every time I think about it. It involves a neighbor and me being chased by a ferret. Of course at the time we didn't know it was a ferret, we just knew it was hairy and monstrously weird looking. And most importantly it was chasing us.

We were stationed in Germany, near the end of our 3-year tour and living on the first floor of government quarters in New Argonner. These buildings are referred to as "stairwells" and this one had three stairwells of apartments with four floors. Each floor had 2 apartments facing each other across the stairwell. The doors were metal so the echoes were unreal in these places. If your neighbors argued or yelled at their kids, you could choose sides and root for your favorite from behind your own closed doors.

This building had two basement laundry rooms with use split evenly down the middle between the stairwells. We hired a local woman (German) to clean the laundry rooms and basement for us since a handful of residents would have had to clean up after the majority. That situation doesn't make for good feelings towards your neighbors so it was a good solution for all concerned.

Our neighbors across the stairwell were actually folks we had been stationed with in Texas. They had three boys while I had three girls. (There is a story about how my youngest daughter, then five, managed to scar their oldest son for life when she answered his knock at our door just as I made a mad dash down the hallway from bath to bedroom …um..not dressed as in naked. Groan). I can still see them all plainly as if I had last seen them yesterday, but can't recall their names. It's just on the tip of my tongue but trying too hard to remember makes me also relive the memory of the boy and the glazed, shocked look on his face as I made that naked dash. I wish I could block that memory as effectively but I'm straying.....

The Mrs. Neighbor and I were standing in the basement by the stairs talking one morning. The cleaning lady was there and we waved and spoke to her. The neighbor kids were still in bed asleep as were my own I'm sure. Suddenly the cleaning lady starts hollering "Misses! Misses!" and we look down the gloomy hallway to see this strange, long hairy creature run away from her—straight towards us. That thing was moving fast and grew longer the closer it got to us. We started screaming at the tops of our lungs and flew up those stairs. We looked back, and that *thing* was hot on our trail, sort of slither-jumping from stair to stair. We screamed louder and prayed for an unlocked apartment. We hit hers first so she threw herself against the door and we tumbled in—with that thing still chasing us. Her kids came running out of their bedrooms with their eyes wild and wide open hollering "What's wrong?!!" We both continued to scream and pointed at that monster chasing us. When one of the boys scooped to pick it up, we screamed even louder, "Nooooooo it's a monsterrrrrrr!!!" They started laughing and said "No it's not—it's the neighbors' pet ferret! (I forget their name too—after all this has been 17 years ago. But this memory sure lingers).

Boy did we feel DUMB. The cleaning lady came running up to make sure we hadn't been eaten alive by the thing chasing us and we apologized for scaring her half to death. We swore though that the thing looked monstrous as it chased us up those stairs and into the apartment. I still feel bad about that day. I think I must be a bad influence—this woman had three boys and wasn't easily scared or shocked and I think she just got caught up in the excitement of the moment. I wonder if she has ever lived that one down. She probably hates me to this day. After all I scarred her oldest for life shortly after causing her to be humiliated in front of her sons. *I* would hate me.

I try always to be a good neighbor; nonetheless if you move in next door to me you should always be on alert and expect the unexpected. However you won't have to deal with ferrets in this family. To this day they give me the creeps and make me want to run when I see one. I do try to suppress the urge to scream though.

Romans 15:2 Each of us should please his neighbor for his good, to build him up.

Secret Ingredients

I subscribe to a newsletter whose author encourages you to "try adding secret ingredients" when cooking. I felt compelled to write and tell him that he should add cautions for cooks like me, since I tend to be dangerous in the kitchen, even without encouragement. Just ask my family.

I'll never forget my cooking flubs because the family won't allow me to forget. Flubs like lemon fish. Who knew when a recipe calls for fresh lemon juice and you're out that you should make the effort to go to the store and buy lemons instead of using reconstituted lemon juice? I swear the bottle says it's made from Realemons! The family was just thankful for the huge can of Beefaroni in the pantry.

Another time I decided to surprise my husband with a special dinner when he came home from a business trip. I was dieting at the time, using an old Weight Watchers cookbook. I found a great sounding recipe for Lime Scallops, and knowing how he loves seafood decided this was the perfect surprise meal. I went to the grocery store and bought some lovely scallops and some REAL limes. We had an un-used electric juicer so I decided to use it to juice my limes for the dish. We sat down to a wonderfully fragrant dinner of scallops floating in a pretty, light green sauce. We all dug in, ready to enjoy those big, juicy morsels. We got about two bites down before someone said *how* did you make these?! Who knew you are supposed to remove the rind before you juice limes?

I'll also never live down my "plastic pancakes". I was making pancakes for breakfast one morning when my children were young. The apartment we were living in was all electric, so I had pre-heated the stove while I got the batter ready. I set the plastic bowl down on an un-used burner and went to set the skillet on the other burner. Unfortunately I got my burners mixed up. I'll never live that one down. I'll also never see the end of the teasing about the watch that I cooked on my toaster oven. I forgot that I had placed the watch on top of the toaster oven shortly before I turned it on. A Timex may take a licking and keep on ticking, but it sure can't take the heat.

This last incident was not my fault, at least not entirely. I just forgot to let everyone know what was sitting on the cookie sheet in the kitchen. A friend, who knew Jarod was teething at the time, sent me a recipe to make homemade baby teething cookies. The recipe is basically dry baby cereal, flour, oil and water. I finally had banana-flavored cereal and time to make them so made a batch. No one was around to tell, so I just left them on the baking sheet to cool. Later I found one half eaten and figured someone had decided to try them. One of my daughters got curious later, asked me "what are those round things in the kitchen", and before I could answer Ernie piped up with "Awful!" I can't blame him, they did smell good.

My husband and my daughters have been the victims of my cooking flubs too many times to let me forget. But personally I'm beginning to think they're all related to elephants.

The Sequel

After the fiasco with the plastic pancakes you'd think I'd learn. Of course it has been a few years since that happened, so it appears I'm doomed to make the same mistakes over again. And my husband is a Safety Manager! One of the ladies on one of my Internet lists posted a recipe for homemade hot pockets and I decided to make them for dinner recently. Unfortunately things did not go quite as planned and this is what I posted on the site.... Wellllllll I made the hot pockets that Jeannie posted and they're baking as I type. Unfortunately I didn't *quite* make them according to directions. I set the bowl that I was kneading in, on top of my smooth top stove right beside my plastic canister, which was sitting on another burner. I turned the oven on, started kneading the dough and was about half way through when I started smelling smoke. I opened the oven thinking I had left something in it but no, nothing there. It was then I noticed the smoke was coming from my plastic canister! I had bumped the control knob with my enthusiastic kneading (I was *really* looking forward to those pizza pockets), and turned the burner on that the canister was stupidly sitting on. I grabbed everything up before complete disaster struck and started scraping melted plastic off of the burner, then kneaded then scraped some more. My husband finally decided to come see what all the commotion was about (As you know I'm not good in emergencies and tend to be loud too), and pitched in to help. We got it all under control and the pockets rolled out and filled. They look lovely browning in the oven and I hope they taste as good as they look. I'm happy to report that the pockets were delicious and the stovetop is clean once again. Jeannie even thanked me. She said she's shopping for a new oven and that I helped her decide what kind of new range she ISN'T going to buy.

Job 11:6 and disclose to you the secrets of wisdom, for true wisdom has two sides. Know this: God has even forgotten some of your sin.

Sharing Some Thoughts

I am soooooo in love with my husband!! We have been married for 25 (!!) years now and this wonderful man still makes my heart do jumping jacks simply by walking in the door every evening after work.

He can make me angry, hurt my feelings like no one else on earth and just annoy the heck out of me, but he's still my best friend and I think he's the greatest.

He always treats me like a lady, whether at home or out on the town. He never leaves me to fend for myself while he goes to yuck it up with the guys and holds my hand to show he's proud to be seen with me. He's always gentle and soft-spoken. What a true man.

He knows what I look like doesn't define who I am. This, in my view is what a real man is all about. I in turn still think he's the most handsome guy alive today and he gets more handsome as the years go by. I have never met a man who comes close to him in attractiveness, both on the outside and inside. He isn't even aware of how good-looking he is, and I really like that. All it takes is a certain look or expression, often one he doesn't even know he's making, and I melt into a big old puddle.

He's incredibly thoughtful and creative too. I can't count the number of times that he has surprised me with a bouquet of flowers after a trip to the store. One of my favorite memories of him and flowers occurred on our nineteenth anniversary. He had called on his way home from work to let me know that he was in route so that I could start getting ready to go out for dinner with him. I knew how long it would take him to get home so messed around on the computer for a few minutes, while talking to my daughters. I finally got up to go upstairs to shower and dress for dinner. I nearly fell over in shock when I entered the hallway and there sat my hunky husband on the stairs, holding a bouquet of red, long-stemmed roses. I quickly got over my shock and hugged him ferociously for the roses. To this day I consider it one of his most romantic gestures.

We've been through some tough times raising kids but he's never faltered in setting an example for them to follow. He continues to be there for the girls even now, as grown adults. He may not always be patient, but he is always fair and that is just one of the many things I love and adore about him.

He has a wonderfully dry sense of humor that is never cruel and he can make me laugh faster than anyone I know. This is another of the many things that make me love him. He never reminds me of my past and never talks about his. He is a true giant in my eyes.

I don't mean to brag about my life. I just wanted to share an almost overwhelming love that I still feel so blessed to have found. I still wake up after all these years and think, what if it was all a dream? What did I do to deserve this? I don't know the answer to that one, but I sincerely thank God that it's reality.

Ephesians 5:33 However, each one of you also must love his wife as he loves himself, and the wife must respect her husband.

Slip Sliding Away

We received our first (and possibly last in this area) big snowstorm the first week of January, 2001. We had a total of eight inches when it was over, and I found it to be beautiful as long as I could stay inside, all toasty warm in front of the fireplace.

The following took place a few days later when the snow ice was still on the ground, having thawed and refrozen several times.

Stacie asked me to go to Wal Mart with her that evening after dinner. Ordinarily I would have declined because as I've been known to say on many occasions, I hate cold. However I needed some socks so decided to go along. If you've ever been here, you know there is only one street in and out of our neighborhood and it involves a very steep hill to the main road. This hill gets VERY slick when it snows. Brooke got home from work just as we were leaving and warned us the hill was indeed slick and that she'd had trouble getting up it moments before. I almost chickened out on going but decided I would be brave and give it a try. We had a great time at the store where I even found a reasonably priced shirt to go with my socks.

Around 8:30 I finally realized how late it was and told Stacie we needed to get home or we were going to get into trouble on slick roads. Unfortunately as we were to discover, we were already too late.

Driving like some old person, (highly unusual for me) I finally made it to the turn for the hill where I saw the neighbor kids sledding on one of the driveways. I was concerned that they would get out of the way in time, but they needn't have worried since we didn't close to them. I got half way up when the wheels started spinning and we started sliding backwards. Never good in a crisis, all I could do was chant "Oh crap, oh crap, oh crap!" all the way down. Have I ever mentioned that I don't cope well in emergencies? I got to the bottom, stopping to gather my wits, but soon had to move so a neighbor could give it a shot. I fully expected him to hit the half way mark and sled back down as well. He drives a Cadillac though so I suppose the weight of it helped him scoot right on up. Show off. I decided to give it another shot, took off and again got half way. This time I started sliding fast. I was really yelling "Oh crap!" this time! I simply could not stop, and just as I'd get control would start slipping another direction. I thought I was going to have a heart attack which is silly since there wasn't anything but flat yard behind me. In my panic, I must have decided that a chasm had opened up back there. I finally regained control, backed it across the intersection to even ground and had Stacie call her dad on her cell phone to request he come rescue us, before I wore tires and brakes out from all the spinning and brake slamming.

Ernie drove his truck to the top of the hill, parked and skated to the bottom. He has always been and remains my hero. Stacie and I climbed into the back seat and fastened our seat belts while Ernie backed waaaay up and took off. I was scared silly we'd hit the top of the hill and keep going right into the house at the top, but Ernie assured me there was no ice at the top. Thankfully he was right. He shot up that hill as if it were a warm summer evening, and then asked if I thought I could get it the rest of the way home. (smart alek) Being just a short three blocks away on a flat street, I said yes and drove Jimmy home where it will sit until the snow melts. If it leaves before that time it's certain that I won't be driving. Instead I'll be the one cowering in the back seat.

As we pulled into the driveway Stacie laughed and said, "You have to admit it was an adventure." Lucky for her I was still shaking too hard to smack her

Psalm 121:3 He will not let your foot slip— he who watches over you will not slumber;

Snappy's Famous Pork Chop Sandwich Jayne Style

Ernie and I decided to take Irene (the other two were at home with their mom) and get away from home this past Saturday morning. Brooke who is on night rotation this week, was sleeping. I whipped through house work since I know me well enough to know if I waited until we got back, I would not have done it. The moment I was done we took off for Mt. Airy, about 45 minutes from here.

Anyone familiar with this area knows this was the inspiration for Mayberry and the old Andy Griffith show. The historic downtown area is even called Mayberry. We took a walk down Main Street and visited some of the shops, the best of which was the pet store. It was small and had no kittens or dogs but they did have a ferret, a chinchilla and a 9-FOOT python named Helga. The sign on her tank said she loves kids. I don't know about that, but she got excited enough about Ernie to lift her ugly head to get a closer look at him. He hasn't shaved in several days and I call him fuzzy face. Maybe she thought he was a rat. The store provided lots of information on the animals they do carry, making it an interesting and informative visit. They have a huge fish—the name of the variety escapes me now, whose name is Bull, and he loves jelly beans! He is in a tank with an extremely large red tailed catfish named Elvis, which will eat anything, to include ham and chicken and well, anything that will fit in his mouth. Bull is safe since he's big enough to eat Elvis. Interesting note: if you were to grab hold of Elvis' tail, the red would come off and stain your hand. Needless to say we didn't grab his tail, as much from fear of turning red as his trying to eat our fingers.

I can hardly wait to go back to Mt. Airy with my daughters and visit some of the thrift stores. Ernie is a man and just doesn't get into the same kinds of stores I do. Namely he likes any store that has tools and I like any that don't.

We eventually wound up at Snappy's diner, the main reason for our trip there. Snappy is famous for a pork chop sandwich, and apparently it was even mentioned in the Andy Griffith show. This has assured they will be a tourist stop until the day they finally close the doors for good. When you walk in though, all you see is a dump! This place is tiny, crowded, *old* and crammed with tables. There are pictures and drawings of scenes and the characters from the Andy Griffith show all over the walls. They also happen to deserve their fame for this sandwich. I don't think we were either one disappointed in it and enjoyed every bite. Irene in her usual fashion provided us with the entertainment. When the waitress brought our drinks in Styrofoam cups, she asked Irene if she needed a lid for hers. She looked askance at her and said, "Yeah cause I'm just a little kid!"

Thankfully we timed our visit right and got there while a few tables were still empty on the backside. When we left, people were lined up out onto the sidewalk and a tour bus had just stopped in front.

Personally I wouldn't mind working there. The waitresses all appear to enjoy their jobs. And who wouldn't since they come to work dressed in shorts and a Snappy T-shirt.

The sandwich was simple, good, and easy enough to figure out. I don't know if it will taste as good at home though since it won't have the atmosphere of the Snappy diner. Maybe it would help to turn on a re-run of the Andy Griffith show.

Snappy's Pork Chop Sandwich ala Jayne

Boneless pork chops (tenderloin, steak, etc)

Tomato slices

Sweet Cole slaw

Beanless chili

Egg, beaten

Hamburger bun

Seasoned flour

Dip pork chop in egg, then dredge in flour, fry in hot oil until done; drain. Place on hamburger bun, top with small amount of chili, slaw then tomato slice, serve with chips and a pickle on the side. My mouth waters as I type.

Isaiah 63:1 Who is this coming from Edom, from Bozrah, with his garments stained crimson?

Sometimes You Just Want To Staple Your Own Mouth Shut

I've no doubt every family has its own stories to tell, stories that will never die no matter how innocent or embarrassing the circumstances.

My family has many and unfortunately most involve me. I am my own worst enemy since I tend to not only tell on myself, but also forget at times that I'm not completely alone in the universe.

My cat Tiger is now long gone but when he was alive, he was my big old fur baby. I had several nicknames for him and my favorite was "boob" since he was such a big old softy and kind of silly at times. Boob sort of naturally evolved into booby and from there (shuddering with embarrassment now) to Titty. You know... kitty, boob, booby, titty...........oh my.

This is a story of one of those times when I forgot I wasn't the only person alive and stepped out on my back patio to call my Tigie inside. I started out with " Tiiiger!! Here Tigie!" Soon that became "Boobers! Come on Booby!" to "Booby, Booby! Here titty, titty, titty!"

I quickly remembered I wasn't alone when I heard my (Christian) neighbor, who was apparently in his own backyard start laughing. Loud. Guffawing even. I *ran* inside, slammed the patio door shut and immediately told my family what I had done. You'd *think* I'd learn better. This story has never been forgotten by my family and will probably be told for generations, becoming part of the family lore.

Proverbs 25:28 Like a city whose walls are broken down is a man who lacks self-control.

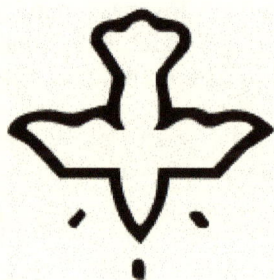

Spontaneous Human Combustion

(Or How To Avoid Becoming A Crispy Critter)

When I was a young girl, I'd guess around 10 years old, I thoroughly enjoyed snooping in my brother's bedroom. He is six-years older than me and at that time owned an amazing collection of the most interesting junk I had ever seen. He had pipes, tobacco, sin-sin mints, marbles, hair grease and a variety of odds and ends important to sixteen-year-old boys of that era. I have no idea if he still does since I'm far too old and mature to be snooping in his bedroom now. Besides I suspect he'd have booby traps set in memory of the aggravation he endured all those years ago such as the pipe that mysteriously filled itself that was left half burned in his drawer. I still gag thinking about the taste. He of course couldn't rat on me since the folks would then find out that he had a pipe and tobacco.

One of the more fascinating things he had was a pile of magazines. The names are fuzzy after all these years but I think one was named "True Stories". I sat down with one once that had the captivating title of "Spontaneous Human Combustion". As long as I live I will never forget the article or the graphic pictures. I had no idea that people could just burst into flames and burn up, leaving only ashes yet burning nothing around them, including the chairs they may have been seated in at the moment of eruption. I was positively terrified! To think that at any moment we can just burst into flames was one scary idea for a ten-year-old. So scary in fact that I don't have any memory of ever snooping in my brother's room again. It took me many years to convince myself that it just isn't possible. Still over the decades I occasionally think back to that article and wonder.......I just laugh and tell myself to "Quit being ridiculous! You know this isn't possible" then I feel better and sleep more soundly at night.

There are some good reasons to hate the Discovery Channel as I discovered a while back when they aired a show about "Spontaneous Human Combustion". Ahhhhhhh!! It was like reliving the horrors of "True Stories" all over again. They had all of the graphic pictures and even live eyewitnesses to round it all out. Of course I watched it; I had to find out if it was fact or fiction. It turns out this depends on whom you are talking to, and I will admit the ones pushing the theory had stronger arguments than the ones who don't. Hello old friends, sleepless nights and worried days.

Since this is an internal problem the old rule of "stop, drop and roll" doesn't apply. However by listening closely I think I figured out a way to avoid becoming a crispy critter. It seems one theory is some people tend to expand with a gas called diphosphates. This can occur with constipation (forgive me for being so personal but I feel you should have a fighting chance as well). When this gas reacts with air, you have instant combustion. This combustion is so hot it cremates the host body in a matter of minutes! My remedy is so simple it boggles my mind that no one has thought of it before. In fact, I'm going to write to Discovery Channel and share it with them.

I've gotta run for now though—I'm on my way to the drug store to stock up on Beano and Ex-Lax.

Isaiah 43:2 When you pass through the waters, I will be with you; and when you pass through the rivers, they will not sweep over you. When you walk through the fire, you will not be burned; the flames will not set you ablaze.

The flames of hell will ultimately separate us from God but He has provided us the way to flame proof our souls, to protect us from the flaming arrows of the great enemy and rest peacefully in this knowledge. Amen?

Psalm 4:8 I will lie down and sleep in peace, for you alone, O LORD, make me dwell in safety.

Stacie, Bubble Wrap And A Paper Shredder—An Amusing Combination

Stacie recently bought a new diamond cut paper shredder from Target which, not that it matters, is one of her favorite stores. It's a great shredder, capable of shredding up to 8 sheets of paper at a time, though we tested it and it took 10 without pausing. It can also shred credit cards and even CD's. She let me try the CD feature with a blank CD and it worked quietly and quickly. What fun new toy!

Stacie tells her friends if only they knew her family that it would explain so much about her. This probably explains how I could completely understand why she decided to put bubble wrap through her new shredder. She could just imagine that it would make a cool popping sound as it slid through the blades. It sounded like a great idea in theory anyway. Not only did it not make a cool popping sound, it didn't make any sound at all. Zip, zilch, not even. It did however wrap itself completely and thoroughly around the blades. She spent a good half hour yesterday sitting and pulling the pieces out bit by bit. All I could do was laugh every time I walked by her room.

I also found myself wondering if it can handle plastic credit cards and CD's how it would handle......

Deuteronomy 32:29 If only they were wise and would understand this and discern what their end will be!

Stop Right There! Don't Move!

Yesterday Ernie, Alexis, Jarod and I rode down to High Point to pick Irene up and bring her back to our home for the Thanksgiving break. Her mom has to work Thanksgiving Day so we will have our dinner on the weekend when she's off, and can drive up to join us. While there we took advantage of the much larger area and did some shopping. The kids were all happy to see each other and having fun as we shopped. Jarod was wired from the excitement, and from being in the van for the three hour trip there so was fast working this tired Nana's last nerve with his antics. It finally reached the point that I told him to "Get into this cart and don't move! Don't even breathe!" He climbed in most of the way and we continued on shopping. A couple of minutes later he quietly says "Nana?" Can I breathe now?" As irritated as I still was with him I had to bite my lips to keep from laughing, but even that didn't help because when told that he could breathe, he responded "Can I move now too?"

Somehow my nerves weren't nearly as irritated for the rest of the trip.

2 Corinthians If anyone has caused grief, he has not so much grieved me as he has grieved all of you, to some extent—not to put it too severely.

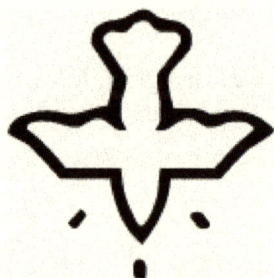

My biggest regret in raising my own children? That I didn't make time to have more fun with them along the way. I love having this second chance.

Super Nana And Little Super Hero!

God must really love us to have blessed us with little ones. They can make you laugh, keep you young and make you cry. As you know, mine make me laugh far more than cry, and oh do they keep me young!

Irene went through a period in pre-school, where we alternated between playing "fireman" and "super hero". I don't know which part I liked more. When playing fireman we had to wear bowls on our heads. She even used a flexible hose from my vacuum as the fire hose! Is she brilliant or what? Do you have any idea how difficult it is to cook, sweep and do laundry while wearing a bowl on your head? I finally fixed that problem by buying plastic firemen hats...adjustable too. The embarrassing thing is I would get so into the part that I'd forget to take the bowl/hat off after she had lost interest and had moved on. I was doing laundry one day struggling to hold that hat on while sorting when I realized she was no where around. Apparently she had gotten bored so moved to the living room to watch TV. Oh wow, this was right in front of a window too. Apparently none of my neighbors witnessed this episode though since no men in funny white coats showed up at the door. Just to be sure though I pulled all the blinds and refused to answer the doorbell for the rest of the day.

If I had to choose a favorite role to play though, I suppose it would be "Super Nana". I got to tie a cape on (it pulled double duty as a towel when not involved in super hero duties) and chase the "Little Super Hero" around the house. I have no idea why we are both super heroes, I guess she just didn't realize one is supposed to be the bad guy, and I'd like to keep it that way for as long as possible. LSH will run away taunting that SN couldn't catch her. SN can't resist such a challenge and would take off at a lumbering pace to chase her down. Little Super Hero then started giggling so hard it was difficult for her to run while Super Nana was breathing so hard that she was ready to drop, yet refusing to give up the fun.

Bad guys beware! If you come snooping around this house you're as likely to be run down as you are to be soaked with imaginary water then tied up and tossed to the wind. Super Nana and Little Super Hero may well be on duty and we take our jobs seriously.

Genesis 6:4 The Nephilim were on the earth in those days—and also afterward—when the sons of God went to the daughters of men and had children by them. They were the heroes of old, men of renown.

Tattoos, Irene And God

There is a joke about a little girl who was shopping with her mom when they saw a heavily tattooed man. The little girl looks at her mom and says, "I'll bet his mommy took away all of his markers!" This would not be the case with our own little three year old Irene. She would march right up to him and ask if she could borrow them. This child loves to write on herself.

We frequently find her with spots all over her tummy. She calls these, "□lipped pops", as in chicken pox. We have no idea where she has even heard of them. She has sported every color of □lipped pops her marker case contains. This isn't a problem thankfully, since they're water color Crayon markers and wash off. Of course there was the time she got a hold of a permanent green marker and stuck it in her tummy button. It looked as if she had mold growing out of it for a couple of weeks.

Yesterday she gave her self a goatee. I have no idea if she knew what she was doing but she did a great job. Except it was purple which is not my favorite color and it sort of looked like a bruise. I was going to say it made me think of the time my sister and three boy cousins put electrical tape on our chins and pretended we were Mitch Miller, but that would date me so I won't go there.

She is quite the little artist and loves to color and draw on other things besides herself, though she does seem to spend more and more time doing this. I halfway expect to see her on display in a New York art museum some day as a living art exhibition. Either that or making a living as a tattoo artist in some swanky parlor. No sleazy business for my grandkid.

I might even be a customer. I'll bet you didn't know I have a secret desire. Of course you don't because then it wouldn't be a secret. I'll tell you what it is but don't tell anyone else, they may think I'm weird. I've always wanted to have an ankle bracelet tattoo. Yup, it's true. I'd even go one step further and have my eye liner tattooed on but that sounds painful just saying it.

There are only two things that keep me from following through and that would be fear of God followed closely by fear of P*A*I*N. First I'm afraid of ticking God off. I mean, if He had intended us to have tattoos wouldn't he have designed us with paint by number pictures on our skin? Anyway I've never found any biblical passage to back me up on this but I just have a strong feeling that He doesn't like us to mess too much with what he's given us. However if you have any insight or proof that it's ok, let me know won't you?

Of course it wouldn't matter if it were ok with the Big Boss or not because I also fear pain and infections. I have always heard the tattoo process is especially painful on less fatty parts of the body. Wouldn't you know the only non-fat parts on my body are my hands, knees and ankles? And we've all seen and heard what sleaze pits tattoo parlors are supposed to be. Even if I could convince myself that antibiotics would cure the infection I'm convinced God would zap me with, I just can't get past the idea of the P*A*I*N. I'm a real sissy when it comes to P*A*I*N. I can't even tweeze my own eyebrows. I tried to once and spent so much time jumping up and down and wiping tears from my eyes so I could see that it took me nearly an hour, and that was for three hairs.

So Irene will never be a Tattoo Artist. I can live with that. Actually I'm thinking she may have more of a future as a surgeon or an upholsterer considering the tremendous job she did carving up our living room chair with a steak knife recently.

Whatever career she decides on will no doubt be colorful. And hey, there's still the living art display to look forward to.

Oh wow, look what I found.

Leviticus 19:28 Do not cut your bodies for the dead or put tattoo marks on yourselves. I am the LORD.

The Funny Things Kids Say

As you've no doubt figured out by now, I think my grandkids are funny. Many days I want to give them away but I love them dearly and find them to be endlessly entertaining, which is about the only thing that saves them from actually being given away much of the time. What would I do for free entertainment if I did? Irene has always been especially funny with her innocent and perfectly serious comments.

We went to Cracker Barrel for dinner last night and 5 year old Irene, who loves the place, was so excited to the point that she couldn't pronounce it correctly. This restaurant will now be forever known by this family as "Crackle Barrow".

I was recently helping her shower when she reminded me that she needed to "wash her underpits". I will never be able to apply deodorant to my underarm or armpits again. From now I will be deodorizing the underpits.

Last night brought the most recent and by far most hysterical new term. Stacie, Brooke and I somehow got all three children to calm down and watch TV with us before bed. I suspect the satisfying meal that we had just enjoyed at Crackle Barrow had sedated them. Of course the 30 minute wait that involved everyone in a constant game of "catch me if you can" with a hungry and wired Jarod helped. At any rate we were all settled comfortably in chairs with kids sprawled all over us while we watched "The Count of Monte Christo", a movie I highly recommend if you haven't seen it yet. Without giving away the plot I'll just say there came a point in time that the young hero was sporting a long beard and moustache. Irene started talking to her mom but being engrossed in the movie I didn't pay much attention until I heard "nose beard". Brooke started laughing and asked if she meant moustache. We were all laughing then, so hard in fact that I nearly dropped a sleeping Jarod off of my lap.

NOSE BEARD?! I now have a new personal favorite. That one may even have earned her a lifetime pass on being given away. I seriously doubt that even Irene can top that one but only time will tell. In the meantime Jarod is coming on fast and has shown a knack for getting himself into predicaments that offer up some great laughs so who knows what the entertainment future holds.

Stay tuned. We never know what this house full of young comedians will say or do next but it's almost guaranteed to be side splitting laughing funny. At least *we* think so.

PS Ernie is in Georgia for his annual deer-hunting trip with his dad (also known as hunt for Bambi's mom by those of us who won't eat venison) and I can't wait to tell him that he wears a nose beard.

Deuteronomy 29:29 The secret things belong to the LORD our God, but the things revealed belong to us and to our children forever, that we may follow all the words of this law.

The Never Ending Humiliation

As you may recall (I know *I'll* never forget!) I managed to totally embarrass myself with our regular mailman recently, when I had to make the mad half-naked dash past my open front door. He had to deliver mail to my door about a week later and when I answered, he was already facing the street in anticipation. Neither of us made eye contact with the other. My face still burns if I dwell on the memory for too long so moving on.....

I must also tell you about how you can't fight City Hall. The city is resurfacing our street and somehow the street crew broke our mailbox. The city representative insisted that they would replace it even as I assured him it wasn't a problem; I had wanted Ernie to build me a new one anyway. He still insisted so I relented. Hey, it's free! The mailbox and broken pole are now lying on the ground waiting to be replaced.

I'm sure I've also shared with you that though it's paranoid, I feel as if every mailman in the area stares at me now. I know that when one of the substitutes has to deliver a package to my door he'll lay it on the porch, ring the doorbell and hurry back to his truck so I'm not toooo sure that it's paranoia. In fact, I'm now convinced that it's not.

The day the crew prepared a poured the new bottom portion of our driveway, they asked me to move Jimmy out into the Street. Later that same morning I was going to run some errands which included a stop at the bank. I always seem to forget to prepare my slips in advance but that day I remembered. After we all piled into Jimmy I spent a few minutes signing checks, filling out deposit slips, etc. Just before I finished, one of the workmen came up and tapped on the window. As I ran it down he started laughing and said, "You might want to come get your mail. The mailman stuffed it in the box, right where it is!" I was distracted with trying to finish my deposit information, and just figured that the mailbox was still standing but ready to fall over so sent the girls to get it for me. They came back and exclaimed, "Nana! The letters were on the ground!" Still distracted, I figured the mailbox was leaned over so far that they had fallen out. When we got home I glanced over and saw that the box was indeed lying on the ground and *not* standing as I had assumed. No wonder the guy was laughing as he told me to get the mail.

Retrieving our mail is a new daily adventure in embarrassment. Since the flow of traffic has slowed substantially due to the gravel surface (waiting for the end to resurface so they can do the entire thing at once), I try to time my trip to the curbside box between cars. If I happen to get caught I try to act nonchalant as I bend over reach into the box on the ground as if it's perfectly natural to be retrieving my mail from ground level. I feel like a total goof even when no one is around to witness. I don't know whether to laugh or cry.

Are the mail carriers lazy? Are they too spooked to come to the house? Is it some sort of revenge for humiliating one of their own? Are they hidden in the bushes, filming the totally weird woman as she bends to gather her mail from the ground? Who knows but if you happen to see a video of a large butt as some woman bends to retrieve her parcels on "America's Stupidest People Videos" please let me know. I want in on the royalties.

Ezekiel 16:63 Then, when I make atonement for you for all you have done, you will remember and be ashamed and never again open your mouth because of your humiliation, declares the Sovereign LORD.' "

The POWER Of Prayer!

I received some bad news medically in March of 2001. It wasn't urgent or currently life threatening but it still shook me to my core. I had some routine blood work done to check my chronically low blood count and an incidental finding was made of a high glucose, so I went back in to my doctor's office for a fasting test and was diagnosed as a diabetic. I cried, ranted, railed and was extremely angry and depressed to the point of barely being able to function for weeks. I was so scared! I have a horrendous family history of diabetes. My dad died recently (oldest of 7, 6 of whom have/had diabetes) and had had two heart attacks, heart by-pass surgery, his heart stopped beating once which resulted in a pacemaker and two months before passing away had a foot amputated, all due to diabetes. His next oldest brother dropped dead when his heart stopped mid-stride, again due to diabetes. Three months before my own diagnosis his youngest sister, who was also my favorite Aunt, dropped dead at her kitchen sink due to heart problems brought on by diabetes. His other sister had both legs amputated before she died, ditto diabetes. All thank God are Christians and all fight or fought very hard to maintain their glucose levels and all have/had a horrible time with it. My doctor agreed that this is a scary history but assured me that this disease does not necessarily doom me if I can get serious about taking care of myself. I'm very lucky since it was caught early. Some people go on like this for years before it's found.

I knew the risks yet continued to play Russian roulette with my weight over the years. In the back of my mind I was afraid but didn't really think it would ever happen to me. Sometimes I wonder how I can be so dumb.

All in all I spent a lot of time pretty much holding a pity party for myself. Then one day, thanks to the power of prayer the pity party was over and I started praising the Lord. How did this change come about? I was talking on the phone with Dana, my wonderful Christian neighbor about two weeks after being diagnosed and just before we were ready to hang up, she spoke a prayer for me. While she prayed two things were revealed to me; first that my joy in the Lord had returned. Praise the Lord!! It felt GOOD to feel good again! Secondly since I was being uncharacteristically quiet, God revealed to me that He had used this as an answer to a long sought prayer. I had prayed for many years that God would "help" me lose weight. He answered this prayer several years ago when I woke up one morning and said, "Let's go!" and I lost 28 pounds in a few months. Unfortunately the holidays arrived and I never got that momentum back. In a moment of total self-honesty I realized that I have been waiting for God to wave a majestic hand and take away all of my desires to overeat. As silly as that sounds it's true. I had messed around for years and not only gained the 28 pounds back but gained many more until I was at an all time high weight and very unhealthy. How many times have we all heard "Be careful what you ask for, you may get it."? How many times have we prayed for something and God answered, but in His way not ours? I have actually been guilty of wishing I could 'get a little sick' so I could lose some weight. I have prayed fervently for an answer to this eating issue. I am now diabetic (a little bit sick!) and I now have a way to control the eating issue. I'm not saying God did this to me. I did this to myself and I know that. I also know that He is there for me, always has been and would so much more have preferred that I do this the easier way. I may be slow but I am learning: There is POWER in prayer!

I have come to terms with the diabetes and I'm now a woman on a mission. I am determined to educate my family and friends on the hazards of waiting and playing games with their weight, of ignoring the real facts of how they look and how unhealthy they really are. Diabetes is epidemic in this country and when there is a family history it's just plain foolishness to play games of chance. Anyone is at risk though, family history or not if they are overweight.

I spent some time on the "Setting Captives Free" website, which offers Christian weight loss support and through them I learned "No food will satisfy my heart nor fill the emptiness in my soul. That is what Jesus Christ is for. He's the 'real meat' and the 'bread of life' and I am to feed on Him". Now THAT is power for change!

PRAISE THE LORD!! Thank you Jesus! I will be healed some day and that will be for eternity.

Isaiah 58:8 Then your light will break forth like the dawn, and your healing will quickly appear; then your righteousness will go before you, and the glory of the LORD will be your rear guard.

The Rug Of Destiny

Ernie has been doing some repair work on the tiles in our master bathroom. When the job was completed I noticed our bath rug was missing so asked about it. He admitted he had thrown it in the trash bag since it was dirty and stained after he was finished. When he saw the stricken look on my face, he went and dug it out for me to wash. It is now freshly laundered and ready to lie down on the floor again. So why am I so emotional about a *rug*? Because it has a history that goes back several years so please allow me to start at the beginning.

Before we had grandkids, we had pets. We loved those babies like children and grieved when they all passed on. One in particular captured all our hearts and brings smiles and funny stories to mind whenever we think about him. His name was Destiny and I called him my grand-cat. Though he belonged to Mistie, Ernie tried several times to change that. He was an ordinary cat, or so we all thought, that she found and bought in a pet store. Destiny was a calico colored cat, long and skinny with a long tail and satellite dish size ears. We used to accuse him of being an alien cat due to being so out of proportion. He also had the whitest fur I've ever seen on a cat, no doubt due to the seemingly endless grooming he did.

I'll never forget the first time we met. I had heard many stories about his funny personality and winning ways from my mom. Mistie and Destiny had lived with my folks in Arkansas for a few months before Brooke and I helped her move to Colorado, where we were living at the time. Brooke would switch off riding with me and Mistie and at one point, Destiny rode with me, and it seemed that all he did was groom. In fact I think he sat on a pile of stuff in the seat next to me, licking and wiping for a solid two hours. I looked over at him and told him I had no idea what everyone saw in him, that in fact he appeared to be somewhat boring. Destiny just looked at me then kept on licking and swiping.

We had two cats and a dog of our own. Lucy the dog wanted so badly to be friends with the cats but Tiger (A.K.A. Little Hitler) and Midnight made it clear long ago that they wanted NOTHING to do with her, and in fact were barely civil with each other. I had warned everyone that we would need to keep Destiny penned up for a few days to allow the other animals to get used to the idea of having him around. Destiny apparently had other ideas though and took no time at all in simply taking over the household.

Once we arrived home, we locked him in Brooke's downstairs bedroom for all of five minutes. He raised such a ruckus that we let him out and prayed for the best, suspecting that the other two cats would settle their differences and gang up on Destiny. How wrong we were. Those two were under his spell from the very first moment of introduction. Tiger, who was a lazy old bum, actually started acting like a kitten again, chasing and being chased by Destiny day and night. They would roll, swat and tussle all over that house having a grand old time. I made the unfortunate mistake of leaving my bedroom door open one day while I was at work. We had a waterbed and I had stripped the sheets before work to wash them. The cats chased each across the bed---leaving tiny little holes all over it. I didn't find them until that evening when I sat down on it while on the phone with Ernie, who was out of town. I had to make a trip to Wal Mart for a repair kit and got to sleep on the sofa sleeper that night. I never made that mistake again.

It wasn't long before we started meeting the Destiny that had won over so many hearts before us. To this day we believe the reason he had such an outgoing personality was because he was raised with dogs the first several months, and didn't know he was a cat. In fact the first time he saw another cat while still living in Arkansas, he went berserk and tried to go through a closed window after it.

Lucy adored Destiny because he would actually play with her. When he got tired of playing he would just hook his claws in Lucy's long silky ears and she, smart puppy that she was, knew it was time to back off.

Destiny had a "thing" for sitting on our shoulders while we talked on the phone or answered the door. We had no idea where he got the idea he was a parrot since he'd never been raised around them. One time he wanted to jump on the shoulder of Jean, a friend who was standing by the front door and who, even in heels was very short. Though none of us is terribly tall, he was used to judging his jumps based on our heights. He went to jump on Jean who was startled and screamed. He missed and she nearly had a heart attack! He also missed on a jump to Stacie's shoulder once. She was in the 5t^h grade then and when he jumped, landed on her head instead of her shoulders. Both stories have been re-told and laughed about many times over the years.

Destiny also had a penchant for chasing feet—especially when they were peeking out from under long winter bathrobes. You never knew when you walked across a room or up the stairs if he was going to come running from seemingly nowhere to swat at your feet with his velvet paws. He never used claws so it only tickled.

Ernie likes cats, especially when they belong to other people. But we all knew he loved our old Tiger and even Midnight, the scaredy cat who would run and hide in a kitchen cabinet every time the doorbell rang. Still he would try to get me to "give Mistie one of ours so we can keep Destiny". As if I had a chance of that even if I had been willing to give up one of mine. I did think about telling her we weren't going to allow him to move with her though.

That cat just had a way of getting under your skin with his quirky ways. He loved to sit and wait on a bar stool in the kitchen while he waited on food. He never opened his mouth to cry, always allowing the other two to do all the squalling. When Mistie and Destiny moved out, I gave that stool to Mistie so he would have a place to rest and to signal her when hunger overtook him.

One day he scared us all silly and sent an hysterical Mistie and her dad rushing to the vet with him. I had been working on some cross stitch and laid my needle and thread down. (We didn't have any little ones then) Always curious, Destiny found it and swallowed it. Ernie tried to pull it out with no luck so off they went. Ernie's folks were visiting us and I doubt they will ever forget the terror that day. It was such tremendous relief when the vet called and said he was ok.

The one piece of memorabilia I have left of dear old Destiny is that rug I mentioned earlier. We actually had two but have long since lost the other one. We used this rug to lay between the kitchen and dining room threshold. Destiny could not stand to see that rug lie flat and would whoop the tar out of it every time he saw it straight. He could be asleep in a chair nearby (or so I would think) and as soon as I turned my back he would attack the rug, not qutting until it was a rumpled, balled up mess again. Many times this turned into a game with us. I still get a case of the giggles when I go to straighten it in the bathroom floor.

Poor baby Destiny was never allowed to be an outdoor cat for his own safety. However it came to pass after Mistie married that he had to live outdoors with a person who had several cats himself. None of these cats had ever been vaccinated against feline leukemia and we feel sure this is what killed him. The only comfort we have is that he had many playmates before he went quickly, and that he didn't suffer for long.

We still miss all of our pets. Lucy was our non-problem child, Midnight was our special needs baby and Tiger was my special boy. Destiny however holds a special spot in all our hearts. I don't believe there is another cat alive before or since who had the personality of that silly, mixed up, original cat/dog. That rug will stay with me now until it falls apart. Then I'll just pack it away in a safe place to hand down to the next generation in hopes of keeping his memory alive.

1 Thessalonians 3:6 But Timothy has just now come to us from you and has brought good news about your faith and love. He has told us that you always have pleasant memories of us and that you long to see us, just as we also long to see you.

The Weirdest Herd You Ever Saw

If you haven't seen the movie "Ice Age" yet then I have three words for you; "Go! Go! Go!" This wonderful movie is refreshingly clean with not one dirty word or scene in the entire movie.

Brooke gave me a certificate for dinner and a movie for my birthday opted for lunch instead, at a local seafood restaurant and suggested a movie this evening. Since it was a family oriented movie I suggested we all go, including the two little girls. We arrived early and got popcorn and sodas then went to find our seats, which was easy since we were first to arrive. This theater has stadium seating, which is tiered seating. I've never seen this and really like it. We took the front row on the top tier, spacing it so that no one would sit beside us. Irene immediately settled in to entertain us by throwing popcorn at the seats below. Fortunately no one was sitting there yet but it didn't keep her from getting in trouble with her Mommy and Bapa. Of course Nana laughed at her antics so her feelings were saved.

Ernie and I went to the movies last week and sat through at least twenty minutes of previews before the movie started. Amazingly there were only two or three tonight. I think I really like this theater. One of the previews was for "Hey Arnold!" the movie. I am so psyched. I didn't even know there was a movie in the planning for Hey Arnold, which is one of my favorite cartoons. Too bad for me, the kids don't like it so I don't get to watch it very often. When it's released I think I'll go see it and leave them at home.

The movie started and we settled back in our seats. I had Alexis crawl up in my lap since she was having trouble seeing over the waist high wall in front of us. We all giggled and chuckled from the opening scene where the squirrel is trying to bury his nut and causes a near disaster. Before long we were laughing as much at the woman up behind us as we were the movie. She had one of the funniest and most uninhibited laughs I've ever heard and it was fun just listening to her.

Mistie doesn't "do" movie theaters (I don't normally either, unless it's an exceptional movie or I just can't wait for the DVD version) so she stayed home with Jarod. We all thought about him every time Pinky, the human baby laughed. Pinky laughed and squealed all through the movie, except for one scene when he needed his britches changed and some food. I swear he was modeled after our own happy little Jarod.

There was one scene near the end that was sad and when we looked down at Alexis, saw her wiping tears. The characters in the movie are funny with such great personalities that after a while you forget they aren't real so it was rough when Diego…. Well, I won't ruin it for you.

My favorite passage in the movie was when Sid said, "I don't know about you guys, but we're the weirdest looking herd I've ever seen". I kind of feel like that about my own family but as with Sid the Sloth, Diego the Sabre Toothed Tiger, Manny the Mammoth and Pinky, we make it work. This is one movie I'm glad I got to go see with part of my herd and I urge you to take your own to go see it too. I don't think you'll regret it.

Genesis 45:10 You shall live in the region of Goshen and be near me—you, your children and grandchildren, your flocks and herds, and all you have.

They Call Me A Heroic Snake Wrangler

The girls brought friends home from 4-H camp again today and of course all wanted to go swimming. They had just gone out when Roberta came running to the door and yelled in the much dreaded frantic voice "Mrs. Nagy! Come quick, Alexis wants you!" I jumped up, ran to the door and as I ran out asked what the emergency was, barely able to speak at all with my heart in my throat and all. On the run I heard them all yell "There's a snake in the pool!" Oh geeeeeeeeeeeeeeee...I nearly came to a screeching halt as I flashed back to the story a neighbor of ours in Alabama told us once, about a young girl who reached up from inside the pool to pull an air mattress in and flipped a copper head into the pool with it and her. My heart was pounding but I took off on the run and bravely called "Where is it?" to which they all responded "THERE!" as they pointed and said it was trying to climb the walls. (YIKES!) Finally I spotted the monster—it must have been 8 feet long and a good 3 feet around; a veritable boa constrictor and those kids were terrified. Someone mentioned that it was alive and I said "Not for long because I'm going to kill it!!" as I grabbed the nearest item which happened to be a net for scooping debris out of the pool. I tried to grab it with the net, but it just swam frantically away and into one of the filter buckets. How in the world a snake that big fit is still a mystery! We tried to poke it with a stick to make it leave but it was stuck. In the meantime Alexis and Roberta are yelling "Don't kill it! It didn't do anything to deserve to die!" While Irene and her friend Pooja are urging me "Yes kill it! Kill it good!"

After poking it around for a while I finally turned the pump off so that we could see clearly and managed to force it back out of the bucket and into the water where I scooped the mighty monster snake into the net where it promptly fell onto the cement beside the pool. Taking a stick I held it down so that it couldn't get away and told Alexis to carefully place the net beside the snake while I'd attempt to push it into the net. No way was it going to cooperate. EEEK this meant I was going to have to TOUCH the thing with those cold, beady, black eyes. Irene and Pooja are nearly in hysterics and urge me to be careful as I grab it by the tail and toss it on the net. Off it slithers right back onto the pavement. Uuuuuugh Heart pounding, I grab it again and toss it and once again it slides right off. I have to wait for him to look around since I don't want it to see my hand within striking distance, then grab him once more and toss the slimy thing into the net and this time he stays! Everyone started cheering as Roberta took off with the net and I.......spared its life and let go.

OK here are the facts of the story. Everything but the size of the snake is true.

It was actually about 8 INCHES long, red and as big around as a pencil but the way those kids were carrying on, and with my heart pounding you'd have thought it was 8 feet long and 3 feet around. My grandkid's tendency to exaggerate is no doubt genetically inherited, especially where snakes and spiders are concerned. The best part is I'm now Irene's hero, which she declared along with a hug.

Personally, I'm just thankful that the neighbors weren't home to see us toss the snake over the fence into their driveway.

Mark 16:18 They will pick up snakes with their hands;

Timber!!!!

The mighty oak has fallen and I almost feel sorry for it. That tree put up a fight that would have made any prizefighter proud. If only I had thought to grab the video camera instead of the digital camera, we might even have won money for the documentary of the tree that wouldn't give up.

Our front yard is (was) crowded with oak trees. They not only block sunlight from the yard, but they are proliferate acorn manufacturers as well. We have never seen such huge acorns. Walking under those giants while the acorns dropped felt like walking through a hailstorm and you put yourself at risk of a head injury. Some of those trees simply had to go.

We've taken a couple of the other oaks in the front yard, out and they went down as smooth as soft butter on hot toast. Brooke pulled on a rope while Ernie cut with the chain saw and I would run out into the street where I'd jump in front of traffic, forcing the drivers to stop or be squashed by the falling tree. Well maybe not squashed since it never went that far into the street, but certainly their cars would have been scratched by the limbs. Last weekend one couple in a car stopped just in time. As soon as the tree hit the ground we all jumped to it and started dragging limbs to the curb as Ernie cut. The husband/driver beeped his horn at us his wife waved, hollered and clapped in appreciation of a job well done. For a fleeting moment I felt like a true lumberjack.

Today I had a feeling this one wasn't going to go down as neatly due to the very tallness of the tree. Little did any of us know the fight that hardwood had in it.

Ernie started cutting with the chainsaw which dull as it is, was only moderately more effective than cutting with a steak knife, or so it seemed. He finally got a notch cut and still it stood tall, straight and regal. Ernie ran over to help Brooke pull on the rope while I bossed the traffic in the street.

Suddenly we heard it start making a cracking sound as it started to lean---the completely opposite direction we had intended. I started screaming "MOOOOOOOOVE!!!!!!!!" but Brooke screamed back, NOOOOOOOOO!!!" because it was headed straight for her less than 1 year old canvas top Jeep TJ, which was sitting in the driveway. She and Ernie pulled with everything they had in them but the tree was headed dead on for her Jeep. I think we all stopped breathing as we watched it slowly fall over. We breathed a collective sigh of relief as it leaned over, hit and snagged in a tree on the other side of the sidewalk, slipped off of the stump and onto our brick sidewalk where it drove one of the bricks two inches into the ground.

That crazy tree was now being supported by a smaller oak, tangled up so much it was difficult to tell which branch belonged to which tree. Brooke took off running to her precious Jeep and moved it to a neighbor's driveway well out of harms way.

Little did any of us know though that the hilarity had only just begun.

Ernie (AKA Paul but not Bunyon) surveyed the situation then propped a ladder against the grounded oak, climbed it with a rope over his shoulder, then tied himself to the smaller one. He started cutting limbs but apparently none that would allow the tree to fall. It was totally snared by the other one. He was so high up at this point that we worried that the tree would go down with him tangled in it. I reminded him that tomorrow is my birthday, and that my being in the hospital with a heart attack from watching him fall and probably breaking his neck and back would not be a good present. Alexis, who was standing at a safe distance hollered over and asked him, "Bapa are you scared?" He just looked at her and shook his head no but I shouted, "I AM!"

He finally came back down to the ground and started cutting the trunk about four feet up from the ground. It was about this time that the tree grabbed hold of that chain saw and bit down. The chain saw was now good and stuck, just hanging between the sections. He gave the tree a shove and it started to fall but as before it just scooted off the new stump and planted itself firmly on the ground 10 feet away and now next to the other oak. Unreal! It now stood unsupported, about 20 feet away from the original starting point and showing no signs of giving up. It looked for all the world as if it were growing from this spot except for the branches that "grew" two feet above the ground.

I was snapping pictures like crazy wishing the entire time that I had grabbed the video camera. This was just too comical, and more like something from a cartoon than real life. Ernie had cut several sections from the tree, each weighing at least 400 pounds and it had simply "walked" its way across the yard with each cut. In the meantime people driving by were slowing down to watch the spectacle while the kids were running around the yard safely out of the area, and excited by all the drama. Jarod the toddler, managed to roll one of those humongous sections onto his feet where he was securely stuck in place. He started screaming so Bapa rescued him and rolled it off. We all watched and chuckled as he walked on his tip toes for a while looking at his feet as if he couldn't believe they were still there.

Dinner was waiting in the house and we were all getting a little impatient as well as weirded out by the behavior of this thing. Ernie had had enough so took the rope and tied it to another tree then started pulling. Timberrrrrr! The tree finally gave up the fight and went down over 3 ½ hours after the first cut. We all cheered, I snapped some more pictures then we went inside to eat dinner.

Ernie went back out as soon as he finished eating and using the now freed chain saw, cut the beast into firewood then cleaned up the debris. There's a huge stack of limbs waiting at curb side for the next round of yard debris pick-up by the city.

The strangest thing of all is that the center of the tree trunk was rotten. The thing wasn't even healthy, yet it fought with all it was worth to stay standing. All that's left now though is a stump, rope burns on Brooke's palms and the memories of a tree that refused to go down gracefully.

Job 41:12 I will not fail to speak of his limbs, his strength and his graceful form.

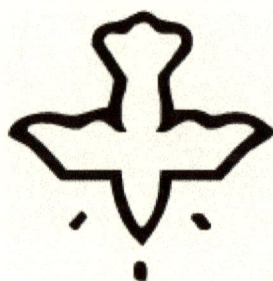

Toxic Moving Day Adventures

Anyone who knows me knows that I'm useless during times of emergencies. Just ask anyone who has needed me and they'll tell you; I either fold under the pressure or I laugh. Sometimes I do both. You should probably add helping move to the "Don't ask Jayne for help" list unless of course you're in the need of aggravation tempered by the occasional good laugh.

I'm offering the following as a fine example of why you should avoid calling me at all costs when it's time to re-locate. Middle daughter Brooke is trying to get the last of her household moved down to High Point from her home in Halifax, and asked me to help her on a recent trip home. She assured me it wouldn't take long; she just needed me to finish packing her kitchen, sweep and mop the floor and clean the bathroom. Oh, and of course help moving a dresser to the street. I had previously worked on packing her kitchen so really all that needed was sweeping and mopping. In true Tom Sawyer form (which Alexis is now reading) I made the mopping look like such fun that she begged me to let her do it. What could I do but let the deluded but excited child have her way? While she slaved away at the floor I tackled the bathroom which wasn't all that bad, so was clean and orderly in short order. Brooke in the meantime, was outside slowly mowing the wet grass so I decided to take the dresser outside for her.

It's a heavy dresser so I grabbed two drawers at a time and carried them to the street. I should add here that by this point we had piled up so much trash and cast off household items for trash pick-up that Alexis and I ran inside to hide when we heard the trash truck coming, being too embarrassed to face the sanitation workers. They were just finishing up when I carried the first of the drawers out and one of them went to reach for them. "No" I said, "These are to a fairly good shape dresser so I'm just going to stack them here with the dresser in case someone wants it". Thank you Jesus for allowing good sense to prevail..... After all of the drawers were out at the street I pushed and drug the dresser from the bedroom to the front door where Alexis jumped in and volunteered to help me get it out the door and down the stairs. (I love Tom Sawyer) Once on the sidewalk, I grabbed it and waddle-walked it to the street. I had just sat down to rest and admire my handy work and reflect on how pleased Brooke would be that one more chore was taken care of when I hear "Mom WHY did you bring Irene's dresser out to the street?! I'm keeping it! I meant the dresser in MY room!" Doi. Is it any wonder my kids and now my grandkids have so much trouble listening to me? Apparently it's a talent they learned from me. Alexis hurried to take the drawers back inside the house two by two while Brooke and I lugged the dresser back inside as we heard the trash truck coming back our direction.....

Next we move to the back yard to carry clutter from her deck to the street for the next pick-up. Then it appears we're done and as promised, it didn't take us long. But wait! There is a red and white Coleman cooler sitting between the house and driveway so I ask Brooke "What do you plan to do with this cooler?" She chuckles and tells me that under no circumstances should I open it. Well of course that made me curious and again she says "Do NOT open it!" Turns out it's full of food and rain water and has been sitting there all summer. Oh gross. She has been commuting back to Halifax and home from High Point where she works, on her days off for the past 2 ½ years (which is why she's moving, she's tired of the commutes) and would take care of her yard on these trips home. She had never had problems with theft or vandalism so got into the habit of leaving her lawnmower on the outside of her fenced back yard, next to the cooler which had seemingly turned invisible over the months. (How else to explain it sitting there for so long?) Sure enough on one of her jaunts home she discovered that her mower had been stolen. Now she laughingly tells me that when it was stolen the person obviously had tried to take the cooler as well, because she found it open. I told her they probably took the mower as an act of revenge.

So being forewarned to not open that cooler under ANY circumstances I try to move it. Wow it's heavy. What kind of food does she have in there anyway, pound cakes and cheese wheels maybe?? While this is going on Alexis, who heard the conversation about the toxic contents, ran across the street to hide in my car with her hand over her mouth in lieu of a gas mask. We decide the only thing left to do is to put it inside her huge rolling trash can, so holler over to ask Alexis to bring it to us. She responds by vigorously shaking her head "NO!" We assure her it's safe so she drags it over and runs back to the relative safety of the car. Ha the joke was on her; I was driving the Miatia and had the top down. She could sit there with her hand over her mouth all day but if that cooler opened the fumes were potentially going to kill all life forms within a mile radius. So we tip the trash can on its side and I pull by one handle while Brooke stands behind the cooler pushing it into the trash can with a broom handle. It's working when suddenly it hits a bump in the can and before we could realize what was happening, the lid flew open and unbelievably foul smelling liquid sludge splashed out and alllll over my left foot. Oh dear Lord---and I mean that sincerely—I started screaming like a little girl (something I haven't done since I was a little girl), jumped up and down and screamed "Where's the water?!! Where's the water?!!" Brooke who immediately started laughing so hard she was nearly choking (probably from those fumes) said, "Mom! It's at the back of the house!" So I took off running as fast as I could in my squishy, gushy, slimy sandal to the patio and over to the outdoor faucet. I turned it on as quickly as possible then my panic turned to hysteria as a tiny trickle ran out. Where's the water?!! Where's the water??!! I continued to scream as

Brooke, who was laughing so hard she was staggering came running up to help. I must insert here that her laughter was quite annoying but this was not the right time for a motherly lecture on respect. My very foot was possibly being rotted away and needed immediate attention. She has one of those splitters that allow two hoses to be attached with a little lever on each that controls water flow, and after about an eternity she got the water streaming. I stuck my foot with sandal still on, into the water flow and let it wash over them until my foot no longer felt gooey. Being the brave mom that I am, I followed Brooke back to the cooler (slipping and sliding every step in my mushy sandal which was still on my possibly rotting foot) where we once again attempted to get that cooler inside the trash can. What a stench! A several months previously, hard boiled egg had plopped out onto the ground when the lid plunked open and laid there daring us to pick it up. We're not that brave so held our breath as we flipped the trash can over to a side without a hump in it, and slid the container inside. Now we had a new problem. We realized that when we set it up it was going to fall open again. Ugh. So we each grabbed a side, tilted the can up, jumped back as fast and as far as we could then ran away. Sadly, I was exhausted by my run to the faucet *and* still wearing a smushy sandal so I couldn't run fast enough to miss some of the stench billowing out from the can. Following in Alexis' example we held our breath as we drug the can over to the street. Man those poor sanitation workers are going to hate her next week.

The moment I got home, I ran to the bathroom shower to detoxify my foot and shoe. I sprayed both liberally with an industrial strength toxin slayer then jumped into the shower, shoe and all to wash it away in hot, hot water.

I'm pleased to say that my foot has almost quit glowing in the dark and has plumped back out nearly to its former size and resembles the right foot more each day.

In closing I'll say if ever you're tempted to ask me for help moving, please refer to this story and call Two Maniacs in a Mini-bus or even your lazy brother-in-law. You'll be far better off, believe me.

Ecclesiastes 10:1 As dead flies give perfume a bad smell, so a little folly outweighs wisdom and honor.

Twenty Four Years And Counting Towards Fifty At Least

Ernie and I celebrated our 24th wedding anniversary this past weekend. We find this incredible—24 years! Where have the years gone? They've simply flown by for both of us.

We celebrated by driving down to Rocky Mount (a short 30 minute drive) to shop some fireplace stores followed by dinner at Outback. One of the stores was defunct, another was already closed and we never did find the third one. We always have a good time together though, so we still enjoyed our evening together as we shopped several other stores after a wonderful and quiet prime rib dinner.

I had time on the drive down to Rocky Mount to reminisce with him about our meeting, wedding and wedding eve. The memories are still fresh and bright so I thought I'd share them with you.

Most of you know that I was married before and rather unhappily at that. You can't love someone that you don't like and that had always been my situation. I married far too young and paid for it for the next nine years. For many of those years I had dreamed of my perfect man. He had a dark complexion, dark hair, wore a moustache and was of average build. I knew without a doubt that I'd meet this man some day, and that is exactly what happened the day Ernie was invited home to dinner. I wasn't struck by lightening bolts nor was it love at first sight but was more of a gradual melding. Having just been stationed at Ft. Hood, TX, he was looking for a place to live so looked at a duplex across the street and moved in a few days later. I probably started to fall for him about the third time I saw him. He was just so sweet and gentle with my daughters who were 4 and 7 at the time. He was and still is the most handsome man I've ever known and has a smile and sense of humor that knocks me over to this day. All of this combined was too much to resist so I didn't even try, and just happily fell deliriously and head over heels in love where I remain today. Lucky for me he fell for me as well.

I'll never forget the first time he called me his baby nor the first time he told me he loved me. His proposal was less that and more of a discussion of what kind of wedding we'd like. I don't think I've known a happier moment in my life—as happy yes but none happier. We went right out and bought our wedding bands and though plain and slim, they remain the most beautiful wedding rings in the world as far as I'm concerned. We then purchased "wedding dresses" for Mistie and Brooke. Ernie and the girls together chose beautiful white lace and navy velvet dresses that looked made just for them. We then sent out the invitations. He hadn't told his folks about us yet so calculated how long it would take their invitation to arrive, and planned to call before they had a chance to check the mail, wanting to be on the phone with them when they opened it. Unfortunately he forgot to take into account that he had also mailed invitations to family friends, Gail Kahn in particular, whom his mom was temporarily helping in her family owned business. His mom was in the office the day her invitation was due to arrive, when Gail received her own. I can only try to imagine the shock of seeing their friend receive the news of her son announcing his impending marriage to a woman his folks had never met nor even heard of. His family took the news well though, and made their plans to travel from Georgia to Texas for our wedding. As good fortune would have it his sister Gail and Mike, one of his college buddies was also able to attend so drove out with them.

I had dreamed about this man and this day for so long that I was afraid it was still just that; a dream. I'd walk across the street to Ernie's place just to look at the wedding bands and assure myself that my dream was actually going to become reality. At times I thought it never would but November 6th, 1981 had finally arrived. Ernie planned to leave work to come to my apartment in time to meet his parents and Mike, who were due in early that afternoon. Having an extra driver they made better time than expected and made their appearance well ahead of time. I'll never forget the butterflies in my stomach! I was trying put on make-up and had yet to change into decent "meet-the-new-parents" clothes when I heard them pull up outside our ground floor 4-plex apartment. I ran to the phone to call Ernie and frantically told him that his family had arrived early. He calmly told me to let them in, and he'd be there as quickly as possible. They were all still getting out of the car so I rushed back to the bathroom to try and quickly finish hair, etc. I could hear Brooke talking through the door telling them that she wasn't allowed to open doors for strangers so ran out, took a deep breath and opened the door......

Thank goodness for kids! Brooke, five years old at the time, had never met a stranger (She still hasn't) so she helped break the ice while we made introductions. Ernie was good to his word and showed up just a short time later and I could finally relax. Mistie came home from school right after that and things just got easier from there. To a point. His dad walked over with Ernie to his place, ostensibly to Ernie could show his dad his house. While there his dad asked him if he was sure this was what he wanted to do and Ernie assured him that he had no doubts. Ernie told me about this conversation later but has since forgotten about it. I'm rather grateful to his dad though. Who can blame the man? They hadn't known I existed until a few short weeks before. By asking him about his decision, Ernie was able to reassure his folks and in doing so confirm his feelings for me.

We had our wedding rehearsal that evening followed by a spaghetti dinner and several fun UNO games with our wedding party. We had a good scare before we ever got out of the apartment complex for the rehearsal though. Brooke had gone missing and we couldn't find her anywhere. We were anxiously calling her name and worried that something had happened to her in all of the confusion of getting ready to leave. Someone finally thought to check Ernie's place, and this is where we found her, sitting and watching TV with Mike. The scare was soon forgotten as we practiced our ceremony. I was calm but happy beyond words—my dream was finally coming true and I was on the eve of becoming Mrs. Ernie Nagy.

November 6th—our wedding day! Ernie, being a junior officer in the Army went to work for a few hours. We were catering our own small reception at his best man's home so his folks came to my apartment to help prepare the food. His mom carved out a cabbage and filled it with dip which was served with lots of raw veggies. She also made a huge batch of those fabulous cocktail meatballs and among other foods, pounds and pounds of steamed and peeled shrimp. This is how we all learned a valuable lesson— pounds and pounds of steamed shrimp shells will clog a sink disposer quite thoroughly, requiring a plumber to unplug it.

I had arranged for Mistie and Brooke to get haircuts while I got my own hair done and eye brows waxed. Unfortunately the hairdresser I was using didn't have slots for the girls, so I sent them to another shop where the hair dresser assured me that she knew exactly what I was talking about when I described their "mushroom cuts" which they had been wearing and which looked darling on them both. Off they went to their appointment while I went to mine. Ernie came to get me in a couple of hours and was upset—the hairdresser had ruined their haircuts and they in no way resembled what I had described. In fact he said "they ruined my babies' hair!" Still they looked adorable and since there was nothing we could do about it, we just accepted it. My hairdresser was running late so Ernie left his car for me and caught a ride home to get his clothes, then on to the chapel on post. I was starting to feel stressed since I hadn't realized how late it was getting—I had an hour to get to the chapel! The hair dresser swiped some wax on my eyebrows then she got on one side, another lady was positioned on the other and telling me to take a deep breath, they stripped them off at the same time! I needed to get going so didn't give the pain much thought—just paid her and took off.

I rushed back to my apartment where I quickly put on my make-up and grabbed my dress and shoes. Martha, who was my maid of honor, lived upstairs, had my two as well as her three kids ready to go so I hollered up, and told them to roll. We all piled into Ernie's car and took off. I used to have this annoying habit of coughing when nervous and had had a coughing fit while standing as a bride's maid in my twin sister's wedding years before, so stopped at a convenience store for cough drops on the way. This was almost my undoing. Ernie's car had a bad habit of stalling at the most inconvenient times and chose to do just that two blocks from the chapel! If only I hadn't stopped for the cough drops we'd have been there. I was nearly hysterical as I tried to start it over and over. I told Martha that if it didn't start soon, I'd jump out and run the rest of the way and she could follow with the kids. Saying a quick prayer I tried to start it again and God heard my prayer—it turned right over. We tore up the street, sped into the parking lot, parked and we all tumbled out. I ran into the church, found the dressing area and though a little self conscious with his mom and sister there, started tearing off clothes and changing into my dress. His sister even managed to get a picture of me putting on my panty hose. That's one for the memory books—not. I asked his mom if Ernie had arrived and she assured me he had so I could relax. She also told me that he was holding up great and that was all that I needed to hear. He didn't have any doubts and was ready to marry me. ME! I was just moments from becoming his wife and spending the next at least fifty years by his side.

We're almost half way there and have had a great ride. We've had ups and downs, hard times of military separations, illnesses and unhappy moves but most of our memories are good ones—great even. We tell each other that time flies when you're having fun and we're having a ball so that explains why it feels like just last week we were picking out wedding rings, choosing dresses, sending surprising invitations........

As of this editing we've now been married for twenty five years and eight days and fifteen hours. We're still having fun and we're still looking forward to our fiftieth wedding anniversary at least.

Psalm 68:3 But may the righteous be glad and rejoice before God; may they be happy and joyful.

Two Cute Boys, One Pretty Girl

Christian author and humorist Liz Curtis Higgs wisely advises us to look for the funny in each day. It has been my experience that I don't need to look far nor hard to find the funny. In fact it's usually right in front of me, as with the two cute boys and one cute girl that I used to see every school morning. When Alexis was in first grade, I would drive her to school each morning and just down the hill, before our turn into the school I started noticing two cute young teenage boys and one pretty, teenage girl standing together in one of the yards as they waited on their bus. All looked sleepy but happy most mornings. One morning however, I noticed that the cute blonde boy was standing alone in his own yard, while the dark haired cute boy and the pretty girl stood at the usual spot. They looked happy while the cute lone boy looked put out. Each school day I would pass them and the lone boy would look more miserable as the days went on. The other boy and the girl looked quite content, smiling with arms around each other. This went on for several weeks and though the unfolding drama made me smile, I was really starting to feel sorry for lone boy.

Then one morning as I drove up the hill to school, I noticed that the cute lone boy didn't look so sad. In fact he was almost smirking. I glanced ahead and there stood the other cute boy, standing alone and now looking rather unhappy himself. As I drove on up the street, I spotted pretty girl walking up to another group of kids. She was smiling, perky and seemingly unaware of the broken hearts standing by the side of the street back behind her.

Psalm 69:20 Scorn has broken my heart and has left me helpless; I looked for sympathy, but there was none, for comforters, but I found none.

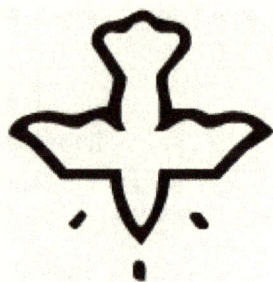

Very Important Question Of The Day

It has been a while since Irene and I spent time alone in the car. I have always looked forward to time alone with her since I never know what sort of deep conversation we might enter into, as we tended to do when I drove her to pre-school back when we still lived in High Point. She started Kindergarten here and it has been rush, rush every morning trying to get her and Alexis ready, then out the door to the car. Most of the short drives to school are spent confirming book bags, signed papers, clean faces etc.

Alexis and Jarod had spent the night at home the night before with their Mom, who had been working in Virginia the past week meaning Mistie would take Alexis, so Irene and I had a nice leisurely morning and a pleasant drive to school (after a mad dash home to retrieve her forgotten book bag). Irene appeared to be deep in thought as we sat in line waiting for our turn to drop-off at the gate. It wasn't long before she decided to share her deep thoughts with me which I am now sharing with you:

"Nana... how do chickens go to the bathroom when they're sitting on their eggs?" ?????!!!!!

My paternal grandparents had a farm as I was growing up, and though they did raise chickens for a while and later 20,000 plus turkeys, I'm afraid I missed out on the answer to this question. I wish I'd had more foresight back then; I would have paid far more attention so that I could now answer that oh so important question.

1 Kings 10:3 Solomon answered all her questions; nothing was too hard for the king to explain to her.

We're All Wacky But We're Family

There just isn't anything that can compare to family. Especially mine. Sometimes we're fairly normal but much of the time I wonder if there are other's like us. Our grandkids keep us giggling and laughing though so who cares if we're "normal"? We wouldn't have nearly as much fun if we were.

Permit me to fill you in on a little background. Irene has a "boyfriend" named Will. When they were in the same pre-school class last year they were almost inseparable, sitting together, arms around each other during chapel and playing on the playground. Will even announced their engagement to the hairdresser while getting a haircut before going to Irene's birthday party. They aren't in the same class this year so they don't see each other often, but Irene still loves him. She even has an invisible Will who takes showers with her, rides in the car (always wearing a seatbelt) and gets his hair dried when she does. Brooke saw Will's mom at the school picnic last week and it turns out he still loves Irene. It's cute how it never occurs to Irene to think that he doesn't. I am still going to insist if they grow up and get married however, that he takes Irene's name though. Irene Adele Meisenheimer is just too hard to say.

It was dinnertime a few days ago and Irene didn't like what I had fixed. That's not unusual since she's 5 years old and as picky as her mom is. Nothing we said or threatened was going to make this child eat and just as I decided the only thing left to do was ignore her, she pulled a famous "what Reenee did" and had us all laughing. Amidst threats of no dessert she suddenly laid her head in her arms on the table, started sighing, and declared in a teary voice, "Leave me alone! I'm missing my boyfriend Will!" As funny as we all found it, unfortunately for her it still didn't get her any dessert.

Irene attends Child Enrichment at the First United Methodist Church here in town and yesterday was CE day during church services, so we attended. Mistie and Alexis went with us and we were rushing around as usual trying to get out the door on time. I was sitting in a chair with Alexis standing in front of me, facing away so that I could brush her hair. Jarod has gotten into the habit of pulling chunks of her hair out and had pulled some out just minutes before. I told her that she was going to need to wash her hair since it was full of loose hair. I guess I mumble more than I realize or she just didn't understand because she turned around and said, "Hey! I am NOT a moose and I don't have moose hair!" I chuckled all day over that one. Kids can be wonderful stress relievers, at least when they're not *causing* the stress.

It has been a while since I had a reason to wear pantyhose. Yay!

Recently I decided to buy something a little different while shopping at one of the local closing K Mart's—thigh high nylons. I thought this was a great concept so bought a couple of pairs, and wore a pair to church yesterday. Ladies, please take my advice and do not try them. I can't describe how weird feeling these things are. Making matters worse was the fact that they would creep down every time we stood. Even though I'm not affiliated with them now I did grow up in a Methodist church, but I had forgotten how much standing and sitting they do. Every time we stood I would try to give a discreet little tug to the tops of those silly thigh highs. Afterwards on the way to the education building to pick the little girls up (who had gone to children's church after CE's program) I told Mistie that I was going to completely embarrass myself if we didn't get out of there soon. I could feel those things slooooowly inching down my thighs and we still had to walk the very public sidewalk to the parking lot. Fortunately I made it all the way home and inside the house before the left one finally let go and slid down past my knee. I promptly ripped those babies off and threw them in the trashcan. I'll stick with the traditional style panty hose or go bare legged from now on.

Jarod who is our little doll man, hasn't felt good for a few days and hasn't eaten much. Normally he has a great appetite and we have yet to find anything he won't eat. Today though, we may have done that as he was picking at his dinner. At one point he picked up a piece of broccoli from his plate and started eating it. He got a funny look on his face, threw it down and said "Yeck!" (He's a 1-year old food critic) Later he was sitting on his Bapa's lap, still at the table, when his Aunt Brooke handed him some more broccoli thinking she was being funny. He (Jarod not Bapa) nibbled at it, rubbed it on the table nibbled some more then rubbed it on the table again before finishing it off. Brooke laughed and said he was "adding table flavor".

Certain people (don't worry Brooke, I won't mention you by name) are picky eaters and with the characters in this family I won't be a bit surprised if I see them rubbing their food on the table to pick up a little table flavor of their own. After all I know it can't be my cooking that turns them off. I'm a good cook. Honest. I just have a wacky family.

1 Timothy 3:4 He must manage his own family well and see that his children obey him with proper respect.

We Are the Griswold's AKA the National Lampoon's Poster Family

Our family rarely takes a vacation, moves or pretty much travels in a car together without something happening. Mistie has always thought it was her bringing bad mojo on us. I sometimes think it's me but now realize it's all of us. We're dysfunctional travelers and movers. Or then again maybe we're subconsciously living up to Christian humorist Liz Curtis Higgs advice to "look for the humor in each day". I certainly found plenty of that in "the adventures of moving with Stacie" this week. What a wonderful learning adventure it was too.

The wheels on the truck go round and round

Our adventure started out Tuesday morning at approximately 9:30 AM as we entered I-95; Stacie was driving her dad's pick-up with me, Alexis and Jarod as her passengers for this planned day trip. Nothing exciting happened, it was just the road to Stacie's apartment in Carrboro and in fact the road trip down (a little over 1 ½ hours) was actually quite uneventful. We couldn't pick the trailer up until 1PM or later so we had it all planned—arrive in town around 11:00 and do some shopping that I can only do down in that area and finish up in time to go get the trailer. Oh what foolish people we are to think that we could ever stick to a planned schedule. Our first stop in town was at the Earth Fare Market for some almond milk which they had on sale. I have decided that I really like this and will never drink milk again as long as I have a supply of this on hand, and the only way to have this supply was to stop and buy some. I had never been to Earth Fare so of course had to check it out—and what a neat store it is. Very organic and earthy—hence the name. Brooke and Stacie both have a love of the fancier, upscale, yuppie stores and this one fit that description. I used to feel funny and all out of place following along behind them when we'd visit places such as Fresh Market, but I'm finding that I feel more comfortable as time goes on so was having a great time looking around. Their bulk spice offering is awesome, and incredibly cheap for a fancy, upscale, yuppie kind of store. I knew we were on a tight schedule though so hurried through and checked out with my milk (4 boxes) and organic veggie tortillas (2 bags).

I hadn't eaten breakfast and all of that shopping and browsing had made me hungry so I looked at my watch and seeing it was noon, suggested lunch. Stacie is on a far different schedule than most normal people so wasn't really ready for lunch (which for her is more like 2 or 3 in the afternoon) but could tell from the determined and hungry look on my face that it was useless to try and argue so we set off in search of a place to eat. We're talking the Chapel Hill area which is a University town, so there are tons of unique places. We finally agreed on a little Indian restaurant on Franklin

Street which she assured Alexis, who wanted a buffet, that it had a lunch buffet. Turns out this was wrong so we promised her a Chinese buffet for dinner on the way out of town, after we got done loading Stacie's apartment. Wow—what a great lunch! This was my first experience with Indian food and I was hooked from the first bite. Yummy. Of course I can't remember the names of the foods that I ordered now other than the onion Nan, which is flat bread that is cooked in a tandoori oven. Whatever the name, the vegetable balls in a medium hot sauce were perfect with the Basmati rice. In fact everything was wonderful. Alexis so thoroughly enjoyed her chicken that I have to ask Stacie for the name so that I can look up a recipe to make it for her. Stacie has long told me how good Indian cuisine is and I learned that as usual, she hadn't steered me wrong.

It's now after 1 PM as we leave the Indian restaurant and head to Whole Foods, another wonderful healthy, organic, earthy type of store but much larger than Earth Fare. We made a quick run through to see if I needed anything but I passed. When I am there I try to buy organic milk which is the same price per gallon as the hormone laced milk that every other store carries. However since I have discovered almond milk I didn't feel the need to buy any. Good thing too—our afternoon was far from over.

After Whole Foods we were off to Southern Seasons for a bag of Chai Tea. I love a good, hot cup of Chai in the fall and winter then a tall, cold glass of Chai latte in the summer. Since that was all that I needed, Stacie ran in for me while Alexis, Jarod and I waited in the truck. Next stop was a place called "3 Cups" for a chocolate treat. Stacie once again ran in alone to buy some 100% Ecuadorian chocolate bars, one of them sugar free for me. She's so good to take care of mom's diabetic need for sugar free and had bought me some fabulous sugar free chocolate bars from Southern Seasons once. It was the best I had ever had so I was looking forward to trying this new one. I tore into it as she started driving to our next destination, which was the Asian market that we always visit on trips down there. She knows the owner who always sends her regards to us when she sees Stacie. Anyway, the kids were anxious to try my chocolate so I broke a piece off for all of us. The moment I bit into it I knew we were in trouble. Almost simultaneously we all grimace and Jarod, who is in the back seat softly said "I really hate this". I started laughing so hard that it was hard not to drool down my chin while trying to laugh and keep this vile stuff in my mouth until I could spit it out. Alexis followed with "Sometimes 100% chocolate doesn't mean 100% tasty". That was it for me but fortunately we were now in the parking lot of the Asian market so I rolled out of the truck and started spitting this stuff into the bushes, while laughing hysterically with Alexis behind me trying to scrape her tongue off with her hands. I can only imagine what people driving by must have thought when they saw us. This is how we discovered that sometimes sugar free means just that—as in baking chocolate sugar free. Packaging it as a candy bar is apparently someone's idea of a cruel joke. By the way the regular version Ecuadorian candy bar was excellent. We forgot all about the nasty candy bar while inside the store shopping and visiting with Joanne, the sincerely pleasant owner.

Next stop a little middle (literally) of the street place called "The Spotted Dog". While shopping one of the stores Stacie remembered that we had forgotten to bring my Dyson vacuum cleaner with us. Great—her vacuum only blew dirt back out so we had planned to take mine. Her friend Laura works at "The Dog" so we stopped in to ask if we could borrow her vacuum. Sure thing she said, but it has a problem with stopping randomly. Still it's better than nothing, especially since Stacie's cat loves to attack and destroy unsuspecting rolls of toilet paper when left to her own bored devices as she often was. She always made sure she spread the mess everywhere, and I do mean everywhere. To be such a shy cat she sure has fun making a mess. So we make a quick run to Laura's apartment for the vacuum then back to The Dog to return her key.

At last! Time to go get the trailer

It's now heading on towards 3 PM and we're finally ready to go get the trailer. If we hurry we might be able to load her stuff and be back on the road by 7 or 8 PM. We get the trailer (which went surprisingly quick and painless) and head for her apartment. We get there and find that there aren't enough open spaces to park near her apartment so she drove around and around the parking lot, at one point having to leave the complex completely so that we can come in at a different angle, to try and park in a row up the hill from her apartment. She had never parked while pulling a trailer before and was kind of nervous. She finally just pulled in parallel and we started to get out at last when she stopped in her tracks and yelled **"OH NO!!"** **"OH NO!!"** is not something you want to hear after a long day and a much longer evening facing you. Oh no—she had forgotten her apartment key back here at home. Not to worry though, her friend Shrav has a spare. She called Shrav at work and sure enough she has it—at her apartment in Durham. **Ooooh nooooo.** The kids are bored out of their minds from so much in and out time in the truck that I tell her to go meet Shrav at work on campus, then drive to Durham and get the key while we stay there. We had yet to figure out how in the world to park, remove and secure it so off she went dragging that trailer behind her. The apartment complex has a playground area where the kids could play while I sat and rested from all of my own in and out of the truck time. Unfortunately there were no benches so my resting was done while sitting on the steps to the slide in the full sun. The kids got bored and I was hot so we moved to the stairs at her apartment, which was in the shade at least. It wasn't long before I started smelling something really unpleasant. I knew that I had been sweating heavily but sure didn't expect to smell *that* bad. I was busy trying to discreetly sniff inside my blouse when Alexis clears everything up with "Jarod stinks!" Well thank goodness it wasn't coming from me but now we had a whole new problem. Jarod had been having a terrible time with sudden onsets of tummy aches for several days which, judging from the smell, was bowel related. Or this could have been brought on by the three small cups of organic and earthy apple juice at Earth Fare followed by the Indian chicken dish at lunch. Whatever the cause, he had had an accident. Being locked out of the apartment we had to walk over to the leasing office across the street and ask to use their facilities. Oh dear—we get in there and find just how awful the accident is. Jarod was 4 years old and hasn't had an accident since shortly after potty training so I felt bad for him. I admit that I felt bad for myself too, as I tried to clean him up. I called Stacie, caught her before she left Durham, and asked her to stop somewhere and buy him some clean underwear and pants since we hadn't brought changes of clothes, having foolishly planned on this being a day trip. Thankfully she hadn't gone far yet so was able to stop at Wal Mart. Unfortunately, by this time it was almost 5 PM so she had to fight that traffic into and out of the already difficult to get into and out of Wal Mart shopping center, and find a parking place in a tight shopping center parking lot with a trailer in tow. After that she got to fight the 5 PM traffic on the ride back to her apartment. She would have been entitled to be a little crabby but wasn't since she was afraid that I was crabby from all the disasters. So neither of us was too terribly ill-tempered, but then again the fun had only just begun.

Round and round we go

Somewhere during this two hour fiasco, I had decided that it was probably going to be in the best interest of all of us if we just spent the night to get a fresh start in the morning. Stacie was somewhat relieved when I made this suggestion after she finally arrived back at the apartment. We still planned to start carrying some of her stuff down stairs so needed a lock. Great—we had to get back in the truck and head to the nearest Lowes, still dragging the trailer. We had again tried to take it off but couldn't get it loose. We had already put on quite a show for some guys in the complex who had inexplicably decided to sit outside as we drove around (and around and around) trying to park the thing and now we struggled to figure out how to take it off. We were getting desperate so decided to leave it on while we ran to Lowes and oh by the way, deliver some odds and end items that she didn't need, to someone who had claimed them from her Craig's List posting. FYI (www.craigslist.org) acts as a virtual community bulletin board for unwanted/needed items that someone else may want. It's getting late, we're all tired and frustrated but at least we no longer have the pressure to finish up in time for a late evening drive home. I'm irritated with Lowes and my husband by the way. A Lowes employee suggested that we have a 2x4 cut into segments to use as wheel blocks since they didn't have anything specifically for that purpose. We wasted a lot of time waiting for someone to come do that for us. My husband irritated me further the next day when he told us that he had a lock in the glove box all that time (It didn't occur to us to look there) and he made it worse when he suggested we should have just bought a couple of bricks. What a smart-aleck. Finally we're en route to the house to drop the Craig's List listed odds and ends. Stacie is driving along watching for the house number, talking on her phone and laughing about how she really thinks this is the same house where she had gotten some chairs that had been Craig's List listed. I was in a daze by this point but perked up fast when I realized several heartbeats after entering the street that a sign at the beginning said "No Outlet". "Wait!" I yell as my stomach □lipped over, "this street has no outlet! HOW are we going to get turned around?" Stacie who is more her father's daughter than she is mine, calmly hung up the phone and pulled into the first driveway. I jumped out and ran back to make sure that she stayed straight because her dad had already terrorized me with the admonition to be sure she didn't jack knife the trailer and tear up his truck while we were using it. GREAT now I had to worry about jack knifing while getting her backed out of this driveway, knowing that all earlier attempts to back up had failed and required just going forward and around in circles. Each attempt to back resulted in her needing to pull forward further into the driveway to get straight (that was kind of scary being it was actually a parking area for a run down apartment building, surrounded by bushes on a no outlet street in a rundown neighborhood). I'm standing in the street waving her backwards, to the right, to the left and just offering encouraging arm signals in general when Stacie stops, pokes her head out the window and say's, "Mom your hand signals make no sense at all so stop it!" Well geeeee I was just trying to help. Finally something clicks and she's able to back that puppy right out of the driveway and into the street without even coming close to jack knifing. I jump into the truck, giddy with relief and ride back up the hill to the house where yep, she had gotten her chairs from the Craig's List of unwanted/needed items. We laughed about the coincidence as we walked up the driveway to lay the items on the porch for the owners who weren't home.

Grub time

It is getting late now and going on 7 PM. We had eaten lunch around noon and I for one was getting hungry again. All of that exercise getting in and out of the truck, coupled with the arm exercises worked up an appetite. We're feeling emboldened by her successful backing out of the driveway feat so we return to the apartment complex to once again attempt to park and remove the trailer. We give up quickly on parking and simply take several spaces up the hill to parallel park. This time we are successful in removing the trailer and find that it's surprisingly easy and light to move when empty, so set it towards the curb where it can't roll away and pray that no one steals it while we're at dinner. We had promised Alexis her buffet Chinese for dinner so headed to a great little place with a huge buffet in Chapel Hill, called a not very Chinese-ie Gourmet Kingdom. We had to park across the street from it in an almost full and tightly packed parking lot. (If you've ever been in a university town then you know how parking is always at a premium) As we drove in I commented that I sure was glad that we hadn't needed to drag that trailer behind us. As I made this remark we turned a corner and were face to face with a big SUV pulling a U-Haul trailer. We laughed and agreed that he was in for a bad time. We got parked and started walking to the corner, and looked over to see him backing that thing into a tight spot as if he did this every day. Stacie muttered something about hating him then decided that he probably does do this often since it looked as if they might be part of the band that was playing in concert in one of the stores located there. We were glad we don't have to do that so often we get good at it.

Dinner was wonderful as always at Gourmet Kingdom with their hibachi grill, sushi bar and huge selection of yummy food selection. I did as I always do in places like this—try to sample everything and get too full too fast to finish it. It's nearly 9 by this point and I'm feeling groggy and ready for bed. But wait, we're still not done......

Suds and Duds

We drive back to the apartment and prepare to go in when we remember that the kids need something to do (watch) while we work on moving stuff, so back out of the complex we go, climb back into the truck and drive to the video store where we rent "Babe" for $1 and head back at last. Stacie pointed out an interesting observation about this shopping center as we passed through. They have a recently re-named Laundromat with a full bar that serves $1 drafts on Friday nights while you do laundry. What a ridiculous idea—get people soaked in beer suds while they soak their duds in soap suds. I can just imagine the confusion if they forget which is which. I don't recall the new name of the drink and wear place but rather prefer the original name of Suds and Duds.

I think we're finally ready to go back to the apartment get down to some actual work.

Home at last

We finally arrive back at the apartment for the last time that night around 9:30 PM. We had left home 12 hours before for the less than 2 hour drive to Carrboro and still hadn't moved so much as a box of glasses. We decide now that we're simply going to move the few things that she has left to move (she had been moving stuff home for the past few weeks and truly is a sort of minimalist person anyway) to the front room for quicker loading in the morning, after a good night's rest. First though we need to put the trailer back on the truck so that we don't need to worry about anyone borrowing it. Great--- new problem—we can't get the trailer hitch to drop back down onto the ball. This is tricky too since it could take some fingers off if it suddenly does decide to drop into place while we fumble in the dark. Stacie grabbed a flashlight, crawled underneath it in her good GAP jeans no less, and quickly figured out the problem. Success! We now had it in place, tightened it down and were free to….. go start moving stuff. The first thing we moved was the queen size mattress and box springs to the front room floor so we'd have a place to sleep. We then moved her dresser and nightstand, followed by the few boxes she had into the dining room. Anything not in a box was just stacked.

I fell onto the mattress at 10:15 while the kids, who were still going strong, watched Babe. I woke up about two hours later and the kids were asleep at last. Stacie was sitting in one of the chairs communing with her cat Desdemona. When I woke up at some point after that she was on the other side of the mattress bed. Even later I woke up and saw her in the floor. She told me the next day that Alexis, who is a tiny thing, had pushed her off by moving ever closer to her until she gave up and rolled to the floor. I completely sympathized. On the rare occasion that her Bapa is gone and she gets to sleep with me, she crowds me over too, but I have a lot further to fall to the floor from my bed so I push back.

A proud moment

I woke up at 6:15 AM but decided to allow them all a little more time to sleep so sat in one of the chairs and dozed until nearly 7, when I got up and cleaned a few spots visible on the wall in the daylight. Stacie and the kids got up shortly after and we decided to get busy with the move at last. Stacie went to get the truck to move it closer to her apartment. A spot in front opened as she went so it made her job of parking even easier. I stood and watched while resisting the urge to assist with encouraging arm movements. Jarod on the other hand offered words of encouragement such as "That's good! That's good! Keep going! That's good!" It was a proud moment for both me as mom and her as a novice trailer backer-upper when she backed that thing straight in and squarely between the lines of the parking space. I still puff with motherly pride when I think about it.

Before we can get very far though, we decide that we need breakfast and especially coffee for me. We look like a motley crew in our wrinkled, sweaty clothes that we had now been wearing for almost 24 hours but hunger and need for coffee is a powerful urge so we decided to brave the stares and, dragging our little trailer once again, head to Burger King.

Back at the apartment, renewed with a huge coffee (when you order a large coffee at Burger King you'd better *mean* large) and a little bit of breakfast Stacie once again backs into a parking space and we finally at long last start the process of moving stuff downstairs to the trailer. There were a couple of apartment maintenance men across the hall working on that empty apartment and I wasn't about to let them think I was too old for this job. Let me tell you, there is little else that I can think of doing that will energize you and make you feel young quite like trudging up and down stairs to and from a second floor apartment, moving boxes and such in front of a couple of men watching you and making comments about how hot it is. Stacie even commented that we weren't doing too badly for twenty three and fifty one year old women. (Puffing with pride once again). At the end of the day there is little else I can think of that will make you feel every bit of your age quite like moving, especially while trying to show others how young you are. Eureka we have the last box, chest, and lamp in the trailer with room to spare. Now we get to.....

Stupid vacuum cleaner

Stacie opted to sweep and mop while I started vacuuming with the borrowed, wheezy Dirt Devil Jaguar. What a stupid name for a vacuum. Then again I hate all vacuums unless someone else is pushing it around so there is no such thing as a good name. I had already gone around and swept the edges of the room since I suspected, correctly, that the Jaguar wouldn't begin to clean them, and was making good progress all things considered and was seeing light at the end of the move when it suddenly quit. Just stopped running. So Laura had told the truth when she said it sometimes just randomly quits. I mentally apologized for thinking she actually said this in hopes we wouldn't borrow it. It became obvious that it wasn't going to start again any time soon so I started sweeping the carpet. This was actually doing a better job than the stupidly named Jaguar but wow, sweeping carpet is hard work. Up until that point the living room hadn't looked all that big; now it appeared to be cavernous. I swept until my back ached. Stacie grabbed a broom and started helping me move stuff towards the front door and when my back screamed that it could not handle another sweeping stroke I decided to try the vacuum again. It worked! I quickly finished up before it could expire on us again, and at long last we were DONE. We locked the apartment door and walked out to the truck one last time.

On the road again

We had to make a couple of stops on the way out of town including dropping off the Jaguar and the video. A quick stop for gas, drinks and snacks (I was so zombied out that I completely forgot that Stacie has been a vegetarian since the New Year and bought a bag of salt and vinegar pork rinds to share with her. Ugh) and we're on the road by 12:30. The trip home was kind of anti-climactic,,but that's a pleasant thing trust me. I even managed to stay awake (for the most part) for the entire trip. I did start to doze about 30 minutes from home, so it's a good thing I wasn't driving.

Stacie called this our learning trip and she is so right about this. Here are a few of the things that we learned along the way:

Next time this family goes somewhere either as a whole or just a few of us even if it's only supposed to be for a few hours, we need to do as the Gilligan's Island group did and pack enough changes of clothes, toiletries, etc for a several months stay

To always read signs no matter how tired or distracted you may be. Otherwise it could be an eye opening, heart thudding event

It feels good to sweat when you've earned that sweat

23 and 51 year old women can accomplish a lot more than they ever realized

At least one of us learned the fine art of how to back up with a trailer

Both of us learned we hope we never have to do the directly above again

With effort carpets can be swept (painfully) cleaner with a broom than with some vacuums

Dresser drawers work great for packing when you don't have enough boxes

When mom is needed and kept moving she can actually make it through a day without a nap

Indian cuisine is really tasty

To never say you'll never move again. I said this when we moved here three years ago but please, from my mouth to God's ears—no more moves in this world

And the most important lesson of all?

That sometimes 100% chocolate doesn't mean 100% tasty

Genesis 43:10 As it is, if we had not delayed, we could have gone and returned twice.

Weirdo

Ernie, Jarod and I enjoyed a nice leisurely meal of meatloaf and mashed potatoes for dinner this evening. Jarod said it was the best meatloaf and mashed potatoes I've ever made by the way. His Aunt Brooke will be jealous because she loves my meatloaves. During dinner, I was telling Ernie about my day which involved me attempting to catch an abandoned cat at one of the parks to take him for shots. (I had plans to have him neutered then find him a home later this month). Sadly the kitty was having nothing to do with me stuffing him in a bag, so we're going to set a trap for him tomorrow night. But I digress. Jarod jumped into the conversation and informed us that we need another cat in this house. (A discussion that his Bapa and I have had with Ernie flatly refusing to allow it) His Bapa said "Only if Nana wants to be a widow". I chuckled and Jarod said in all seriousness, "Yeah she's a weirdo". I of course laughed harder to which he responded, "Still a weirdo".

He may be right too. Alexis wasn't at dinner with us since she had her Wednesday night church youth function to attend. She asked me to pick her up in the Miata, top down of course and since it was such a pretty evening, I happily obliged. As I backed out of the driveway I realized something; I've never driven the Miata at night. I don't know how to turn the headlights on! So I'm sitting in the street twisting this and flipping that and decide it's best to pull back into the driveway while I figure this thing out. I would have gone to get Ernie, who was working on a wood project in the garage but I knew he'd probably tell me that if I couldn't find the lights then I had no business driving it. So I kept fiddling until I finally happened on the right combination. Off I go into the dark night with headlights, but now I don't have dash lights. Thank goodness for frequent street lights which I used to keep track of my speed. I get to the church driving blind so to speak, park then step out of the car while I wait for Alexis. Fiddling some more I find the dial to turn my dash lights on so now we're set to go as I give a small whoop of victory. But wait. NOW my seat cover light isn't working. (Brooke bought her dad a set of car seat covers last Christmas that light up. They're really cool too.) The passenger seat lights up but I can't get the drivers seat turned on. Ah well, at least the important lights are on.

Alexis runs out, makes a running jump over the door and lands inside the car (I warn her that her Bapa had better never see her do that) and we take off down Roanoke Avenue or "the ave" as we call it around these parts. Yes sir, we're having a great time in the 20 mph downtown speed zone, the wind barely blowing our hair and the radio blasting out Christian music. We are jammin' now.

It's far too nice an evening and Alexis is having way too much fun to go straight home so off we go, cruising around town, taking the longest way home we can find, enjoying the gorgeous evening, top down and the sounds of Jesus worshiping blasting from our radio. It's just Alexis and her weirdo Nana and we had a fabulous time. I just hope I can get that seat cover light working before we do this again.

Psalm 100:2 Worship the LORD with gladness; come before him with joyful songs.

Preface: For many years, all of my daughter's lives in fact, it was well known how much I detested peanut butter. I bought only good brands for the family but couldn't stand even the smell of it when a jar was opened. A few days after being diagnosed diabetic and not yet having met with the nutritionist but being desperate for something to eat for breakfast, I decided to experiment with peanut butter on toast and was hooked from the first bite. I ate this every morning 365 days a year for the next two years and even carried a jar with me when we traveled. I still enjoy it frequently on some crunchy, grainy whole wheat toast. For the longest time my family would watch me while shaking their heads in disbelief, knowing how strongly I had previously disliked the stuff and how much I now thoroughly enjoy it.

Where's My Peanut Butter?!

Ok, someone thinks they're being funny.

I was shopping at Food Lion last week and happily discovered that they had Peter Pan peanut butter on sale so I bought three jars of the Low Fat crunchy and one of the creamy and once home, stored them in the pantry, stacked one on another in pairs. They looked so lovely sitting in there too, real comfort food. I opened the jar of creamy yesterday to make Irene and Alexis a PB&J sandwich. All were there at the time. I went to get a jar of the crunchy out this morning and three of the jars were gone, including the newly opened creamy!!! No one in this house is admitting to thievery and in fact has helped look high and low for them. Brooke, who swears they were there two nights ago when she put her soup away, accused me of walking in my sleep and taking them to bed with me. This is preposterous. I haven't walked in my sleep since I was a teenager and even I couldn't eat that much peanut butter without getting sick. Besides I've already patted down the bed covers so I know they aren't there.

Jarod loves to play with the spice jars on the pantry door but can't reach the shelves where the food is stored. Just to be sure though, I checked his diaper bag but didn't find the missing loot.

My neighbor Dana recently admitted to being as big a Peter Pan low fat peanut butter addict as I am, but I can rule her out since she hasn't been here to visit in a while.

I think one of the kids thought they were being funny and hid the jars but are afraid to admit it now after seeing the crazed look in my eyes. If they did they should be afraid, very afraid. I'm on my way to the phone to call the police and report this heinous crime right now. Don't be surprised if I show up at your door with a police escort asking to see your pantry. I'm not saying you took it but when it comes to my peanut butter, you're *all* suspects.

Exodus 20:15 You shall not steal.

Nope, we never did find those jars of peanut butter. It remains an unsolved family mystery

Who Would You Give A Volvo To?

I'm sure you've all seen the Volvo commercials asking who you'd give one to. Our favorite is the one with the little girl who is chattering non-stop as her dad tries to buckle her in after picking her up at school.

We've really missed Irene since her move, but are delighted to know that she is happy down in High Point with her mom. They've had a period of adjustment but both are happy to be together full time once again. She has made new friends and still talks to her old friends up here on occasion. A few weeks ago she got to come home for a weekend visit. Her mom drove her to her Aunt Stacie's (in Durham) who then drove her to Zebulon to meet us. This is the half way point between Durham and us so it worked out nicely. We chatted with Stacie for a few minutes at the meeting point then we all headed home.

Irene was seated in the front seat of the pick-up truck between me and her Bapa. She started chattering from the moment she buckled her seatbelt, filling us in on her life at school, home and with friends. We're not too sure she took breaks to breathe, since she chatted non-stop. Her Bapa eventually looked at me over the top of her head and asked, "Who would you give a Volvo to?" I laughed and told him I was thinking the exact same thing. What a delightful trip home. It was great to see her again, and a wonderfully secure feeling to hear in her own words just how happy she is and that she still misses us as much as we miss her.

Psalm 16:5 LORD, you have assigned me my portion and my cup; you have made my lot secure.

http://www.youtube.com/watch?v=n3fjp3kYf3Q

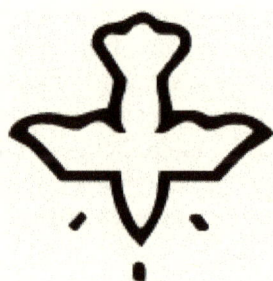

Whoooooosh Goes The Wind

Have you ever felt like such a spectacle that you were glad that you'd never have to see the people around you again? In other words have you ever felt like a total fool? I recall one particular occasion like that, that still makes me cringe in embarrassment.

I had recently had a second surgery on one of my feet, and had complications causing my foot to swell which required me to wear a soft cast and for the next six weeks I had to make weekly trips to my surgeon's office for treatment and cast changes. I worked at a hospital in Baltimore and would take those afternoons off to make the 45-minute drive to his office in Laurel. Upon arrival I would stick my foot in a warm whirlpool bath, sometimes have x-rays taken and receive an ultrasound treatment that felt so good I wanted to take the machine home with me, followed by the new cast. All in all most visits were very pleasant, partly because they got me out of work early.

One particular Friday afternoon I was driving home via I-95. If you've ever traveled I-95 in the Baltimore area around 4 on a Friday afternoon, then you know how heavy the traffic flow is. Keep that in mind as you read.

I was zipping along with the traffic flow somewhere between 65 an 70 MPH, just enjoying the after effects of the ultrasound treatment and rejoicing in a beautiful Friday afternoon that also happened to be an extremely windy day.

Suddenly I caught sight of a large brown object blowing towards the interstate from my right. Before I could even think of getting out of its path a GIGANTIC cardboard box flew into my car. There I was just one of *many* cars on the road that day, moving along at 65 MPH with a huge box plastered to my right front fender......I felt like an utter idiot.

I tried slowing down to see if it would come loose but that box wouldn't budge. I feared being run over so had to speed up again and just keep going. I couldn't pull over on the shoulder because I was afraid I'd never get back on the road again in the heavy traffic, so I drove on with that stupid piece of cardboard stuck to my car. I knew there was a tollbooth ahead so I drove the next 5 miles trying to act as if nothing was amiss, but I could see other people staring and laughing as they passed me and my big box.

I thought I would never reach that toll booth but after what felt like eternity my box-car and I did arrive. I started to slow down and it was looking as if that box still wasn't going to let go, but as I tossed my coins in the basket it slid off of my hood and onto the pavement. Red faced but relieved, I drove on home.

I still shudder with embarrassment when I think about that box and can only hope that anyone who saw the totally embarrassed woman driving along I-95 between Baltimore and Laurel, MD over 10 years ago has long forgotten what a spectacle I made. I remember it well enough for all of us. It sort of reminds me of the time I came out of the store on another very windy day and my full-skirted dress flew up over my head in front of a person parked at the curb. But that's another story all together.

Job 30:15 Terrors overwhelm me; my dignity is driven away as by the wind, my safety vanishes like a cloud.

Wonderful-Awful Places

Once upon a time in a strange but not so far away land called Maryland, lived a typical military family. They had an officer type Captain dad (who though now retired still keeps close watch on the family and runs a tight office), a mom and three lovely daughters. They also had a dog and two cats. They were a very "normal" military family living in a not so normal place, but they endured since they knew being military it was also temporary. Of all the places they lived up to that point, this was their least favorite assignment because the state of Maryland is a strange land.

Everyone settled in and adjusted to the surroundings. The daughters all went to school now so Mom decided to go back to work. At first she worked in an awful-wonderful place called *** Nursing Center. Mom was afraid it would be depressing working there but soon found the residents to be precious, making it a wonderful experience. Some of the administration and staff were a totally different story though. Mom never really knew what was expected of her other than when the nursing staff paged her, seemingly endlessly to run errands for them. Apparently no one had ever explained to this staff just what a Unit Clerk's job is *supposed* to be. Still the nurses were all compassionate and caring people who sincerely appreciated having their new go-fer, so Mom tried to be happy there. Occasionally, being required to be there at 6:30 in the morning, she would get to field crazy calls since the receptionist reported for work much later. One morning she answered the phone to the heavy breathing of a pervert on the other end who said, "I want to suck your toes!" to which Mom responded "Come on over! We have hundreds of toes to suck on!" Alas she never did see anyone going room to room sucking toes though she did make rounds with the podiatrist soon after. You can bet she kept a close watch to see if he did any toe nibbling during his rounds.

Mom worked every other weekend and this was her favorite times. The pace was slower, and the sincerely funny head nurse on the first station had time to tell stories to Mom and the medicine nurse while preparing for the day. One time she (the nurse not MOM!) told a hysterical story on herself about dreaming she was in a tree with rising flood waters around her. Just as the flood waters reached her toes her husband woke her up to tell her she had wet the bed!! Mom and the nurses laughed and laughed over that story, especially when she quipped "I told him he should be thankful I wasn't dreaming about standing in mud!"

Mom also got to sit with the smoking patients to supervise them twice a day. She was only supposed to allow them one cigarette each but always looked the other way for numbers two and even three. After all they were paying for them. The patients loved Mom and she loved them. One patient who was 104 years old took a grand liking to Mom but hated the nurse's aids, something no one could ever explain but they were happy to roll her wheelchair near the desk so that she could watch Mom work, making things easier for the aids. Mom didn't mind since she loved the patient. Yes there were some very good times in the *** Nursing Center.

Unfortunately the management made the job too awful to endure. Mom never knew what the Administrator expected of her but she always seemed angry with Mom. Even the Director of Nurses was befuddled by her commands to tell Mom that she was doing some job such as the call-in record wrong without explaining what her expectations were. Evil Director Woman (AKA EDW) as Mom still calls her had many loyal puppets on her staff. However though Director of Nurses was loyal she wasn't a puppet so she would call Mom in to her office and explain what she was apparently doing wrong, then apologize for not knowing the correct way herself. Once EDW even came running out of her office swinging her arms and raising her voice very loudly in the lobby in front of patients and visitors to YELL at Mom for not reading minds and telling someone she needed supplies before the secretary went to the supply store. There was no mention of the secretary not asking anyone if they needed supplies before she left on the unannounced trip however. Oh nooooo.

The final straw for Mom came the day she was chatting with Mr. Maintenance Manager and she mentioned that the cord on the station one phone needed replacing. The phone cord had been acting up for a few days and was starting to cut people off. Mr. Maintenance Man offered to buy a new cord on his daily trip to the hardware store (where it was widely assumed he went just so he could get away from EDW) and Mom told him that would be great if he thought it would be OK. So Mr. Maintenance Man good to his word, came back to the awful work place with a shiny new $3 and change phone cord. Mom replaced the bad one and the phone worked just fine once again. Little did she know this was to be the proverbial straw for her and EDW. Lucky for Mom, she had been to a job interview at Franklin Square Hospital's Medical Records Department a few days before.

Janet the nice receptionist who disliked EDW but who also knew who signed her pay checks, made a quick trip to station one later that morning to let Mom know that EDW was on the war path because Mom had "taken it upon herself to order a new $3 and change phone cord!" Mom sort of blew up and said, "I have GOT to find a new job!" And literally before the sentence was completed the phone with the shiny new cord rang and it was FRANKLIN SQUARE HOSPITAL offering her a job with a substantial raise in pay and NO weekend duties! By this point Mom would have taken the job even if it were a pay cut as long as Evil Director Woman wasn't going too. Mom happily accepted the job offer, and with a new spring in her step and with great joy in her heart went to inform EDW that she had only a week left in her employment. EDW hatefully said "Fine" but sure was grouchy when Mom informed her so she figured EDW was upset that she would have to find some new victim to torture.

Mom had already planned (and surprisingly been granted by EDW) vacation time for the following week so put in her last week with a renewed spirit knowing she had a week off before starting the new job. It was also a sad time for Mom since the staff and patients made it obvious they would miss her very much. The employees threw a big going away party where they presented her with a beautiful inscribed Cross pen and pencil set and even money for Mom to buy new clothes since she would no longer have to wear the hideous white skirt, white stockings, white nursing shoes and pink blouses to work each day. Mom had only been working there for eight months but she felt very blessed to have met so many hard working and dedicated people, and was sad to leave them. But not EDW; she was happy to leave her.

Happily the happy ending just goes on and on. EDW had already lost several other employees to Franklin Square so she and her puppets started referring to the nursing home as the training ground for Franklin Square. Happily Mom wasn't the last person to leave for greener pastures, bigger paychecks and happier work places at FS. If EDW is still there after all these bitter years, then they no doubt continue to be training grounds for any number of other employers. Hopefully though EDW got her just desserts and the owners finally realized just who was running their employees off to better environments.

***name deleted to protect the names of the innocent including Mom and all who went before and after her while in the employment of Evil Director Woman.

Exodus 1:14 They made their lives bitter with hard labor in brick and mortar and with all kinds of work in the fields; in all their hard labor the Egyptians used them ruthlessly.

Wonderful-Fun Places

Mom left the employment of EDW and went to work in Medical Records Land at Franklin Square Hospital in Baltimore. This job was so much better than working for EDW, that Mom even forgave EDW. Forgave yes but never forgot.

Mom certainly had days at FSH that made her want nothing more than to go home at the end of the day and never return, but most days she enjoyed her job and within a few months was promoted from a clerical position to an outpatient coder. She especially enjoyed that job and was very good at it indeed.

Mom was a fun person to be around but also a reliable, hard working and "go to" kind of employee so it wasn't long before she was tasked for extra duties. She enjoyed helping "the big coders" who were also known as inpatient coders, by making phone calls to doctor's offices for final dismissal diagnosis and checking for chart completion. Mom enjoyed learning about other areas in her department and her job. But she didn't like some of the classes that she was required to take. Medical Terminology and her coding classes were fun and easy "A's" but she did not like Anatomy and Physiology. Oh no, that was not a fun time. That class was harder than any bad day at work. She did find one thing funny about that course though. Her teacher kept a large plastic cup filled with fat, colored chalk and each subject that he wrote about on the opposing chalk boards had its own assigned color. He would go back and forth between the chalk boards (and was he fast!) yet never lose track of which color chalk he needed. Since Mom likes to look for the fun in her days and was especially desperate for something amusing in this class, she found this entertaining and even fascinating.

Being a fun to work with person, Mom was soon unofficially in charge of moral. She had two fun assistants who helped make sure that life never got too dull in Medical Records Land. They had lots of fun arranging frequent pot luck lunches and even a lasagna cook-off, the winner of which received a $25 gift certificate to an Italian Restaurant in the Little Italy section of Baltimore, owned by one the very oh so generous and nice doctors on staff. He was cute too.

One Halloween Mom, co-worker Margie and older and tiny Jean all agreed to dress up as (good of course) witches for the day since they knew kids from the pediatric floor would be coming by to trick or treat in Medical Records Land. Oh but Margie chickened out and showed up in regular clothes! So tiny Jean played Mother to Mom and together they made everyone laugh with a spontaneous skit about Margie being the ugly step daughter and Mom being Mother's favorite daughter. Director Woman

Connie (who could be moody but who was nothing like EDW) was so delighted that she took all three to the administration office to put on their spontaneous skit where they made everyone laugh and laugh.

Then one day word came in that the hospital had a multimillion dollar fund raising project underway. Soon several departments were competing to raise the most money for the fund. Oh boy oh boy, this was right up Mom's alley and the contest was underway. Mom was excited and delighted to join in on the fun and after a phone call, arranged for a donation of valuable and quite tasty bushel of Grade A, Number 1 crabs to be raffled. Soon most of Medical Records Land employees were selling tickets for a raffle at $1 a chance. But how were they going to promote the raffle within the hospital? Idea! Mom and co-worker Mary would dress up as giant Grade A, Number 1 crabs themselves, complete with antenna and Styrofoam eyeballs and sell tickets in the cafeteria hallway to other employees and visitors! Red felt, red tights and black leotards made sense for the costumes—until Mom put hers on and stood in front of a mirror. She looked at her reflection and said "I can't believe I'm going out in public in something this short" to which conservative Captain (promotable to Major) Dad responded "Forget short, I can't believe you're going out in public dressed like a crab". Go out she did and oh what fun it was. Mom and Mary got to spend many hours standing in the hallway laughing along with lots of laughing and pointing hospital co-workers and visitors, selling tickets, playing and having fun. At the end of the raffle a winner's name was drawn for the Grade A, Number 1 Crabs (the tasty ones, not Mom and Mary) and Medical Records Land had taken the lead as top contributors to the multimillion dollar building fund with $1, 647 in raised funds.

Mom left Franklin Square Hospital's employment not long after when Captain (promotable) Dad was transferred to the glorious land of Colorado. Even though she didn't really like Baltimore, she still has fond memories of her play for pay days while working there. Another department no doubt eventually took the lead but everyone in Medical Records Land got to bask in the joy and glory of being Grade A, Number 1 fund raisers for a while at least.

Mom was excited about going to live in the exotic place called Colorado, but oh how she would miss her playmates in Franklin Square Hospital Medical Records Land! To this day mom smiles when she thinks about her moral boosting duties, the enjoyment of her "real" job and especially her crabby assignment but marvels most of all that they actually paid her to play.

Ecclesiastes 8:15 So I commend the enjoyment of life, because nothing is better for a man under the sun than to eat and drink and be glad. Then joy will accompany him in his work all the days of the life God has given him under the sun.

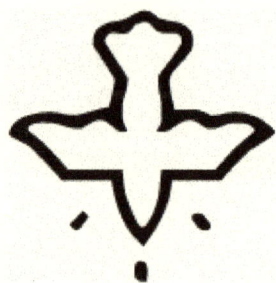

Work Place Jollies

I am a fun person to work with, even if I say so myself. It's true. When I was still a member of the work force outside of home, I was a great person to play with. I spent a good deal of time as one of three (the other two were fun people too) unofficial "moral booster hostesses" when I worked at Franklin Square in Baltimore. We organized everything from monthly themed luncheons to a lasagna cook-off in our department with official judges. One of the judges just happened to be a doctor who owned an Italian restaurant in the Little Italy area of Baltimore. His was the deciding vote and I'll always believe he voted for the girl who won because she's the one who asked him to donate a $25 gift certificate to the contest, which he gladly did. That's the only way she could have won because my lasagna was ever so much better than hers. Truly.

Of course I'll never forget the time I dressed up in a red crab costume and paraded around that same hospital selling raffle tickets for a bushel of Grade A #1 crabs to raise money for the hospital building fund. This was well after the cooking contest so I know that wasn't why I lost. Though I'm sure another department overtook the lead, I was tickled that our department was way ahead in the fund raising contest when I left.

An especially funny memory from my Colorado Springs Memorial Hospital days involves a personal female matter. (So if any guys are reading you are forewarned—take this time to avert your eyes until you get to the next paragraph). Even in those days I had horrific times of the month. My crabbiness was only increased by a young woman whom I sincerely liked, but who could work my nerves like a piano player. Being that horrific time of month she was playing a concerto with my nerves that day, so I grabbed my "you know what in the overnight size" and having no pockets in the dress that I was wearing that day and not wanting to carry it in plain sight, stuffed it under my bra strap long enough to get to the ladies room. Betty, one of my work playmates was sitting at the front desk as I passed so I stopped to vent. I had just started with "You won't believe what Ding Dong did this time...!" when Betty looked up and saw that not so well concealed as I had thought "you know what in the overnight size" poking out of the neckline of my dress. Her mouth fell open, and then she pointed at it and started to laugh. Hysterically. That was all that I needed to brighten my day as I wiped tears of laughter for the rest of the afternoon.

When I left that job, my supervisor wrote me a letter of recommendation and stated that I was something of a "goodwill ambassador in the department". That still makes me smile when I read it.

Rich Rowand of Recipe du Jour e-zine fame once again sparked a lovely memory for me this morning when he wrote about his usual morning routine of getting to work early and drinking coffee, etc. This instantly transported me back to my play for money job in Colorado. Once again it involved my playmate Betty and our other play time friend, Kathy. Each morning we would meet at the coffee maker in our department about thirty minutes early to drink coffee, chat, vent and just get our moods on straight for a day of non-stop fun. Kathy and I thought we'd surely blown it one day as we chatted about our interim director also named Kathy. She was a nice person but not very effective being an interim person. None of the supervisors ever came in early so we felt safe discussing almost anything and anyone. This particular morning we discussed Kathy-the-Interim and how we all believed she probably hoped to be offered the job as director and how we wished she would but feared she wouldn't since she spent all of her time in the inner office drinking coffee and talking to the supervisors. Did I mention that since it was usually just us and the one night person we didn't worry about how loud we were? Wouldn't you know that Kathy (the interim not my play time friend) came walking out of her office sipping on a cup of coffee just minutes after one of us (probably me) had made this observation? We giggled all day long and half way feared that we'd need a box to clear our desks before the day ended. We never were called into the office and as feared, Kathy (the interim, not my play mate) didn't get the promotion. A nice man named Jim did, but I digress.

All three of us would attempt to be first there to make the coffee each morning since Kathy and I both liked it strong and Betty liked it weak. Many a morning started with playful bickering on the strength of the coffee, depending on who got there first. One morning after listening to Betty gripe about the strong coffee, Kathy muttered "You want weak coffee? I'll give you weak coffee" and the fun began. She and I got our heads together (easy to do since we worked in a tiny room together inside the department) and cooked up plans for a special pot of coffee. I volunteered to go to the Chinese restaurant that my family liked, to buy some Jasmine tea after work. The plans were to make her a pot of Jasmine tea in place of her coffee. We had a ball planning and plotting my extra early arrival the next morning to make it. I got up early and arrived about fifteen minutes earlier than normal to make the special "coffee", chortling and snickering the entire time. The only problem was the tea was so weak that even Betty wouldn't have wanted any. Sooooo I grabbed a pot of old and cold coffee from the night shift and dumped it in. Perfect! It now looked like a pot of weak coffee. I then made another pot of "real" coffee, poured a cup for myself and Kathy then set the pot behind the Bunn coffee maker, just as Betty walked in and set her purse down at her desk. Kathy was right behind her so we all gathered at the coffee machine where I greeted them both, smiling and giving a slight nod to Kathy to signal that I had done the deed as we started putting creamer and theirs YUCK) sugar into mugs. Kathy and I held our breath as we waited to see if Betty would notice a difference in the way the coffee smelled. Nope—she continued to chat as she took her first sip of the brew. She didn't say a word but did give her coffee mug a funny look. By this point I was ready to absolutely burst a seam from holding back the laughs. In fact, I had to turn away for a moment so that I could smile and release the pressure. Kathy kept giving me "don't you do it!" looks which didn't help me at all. So we continue to chat and Betty continues to give her coffee funny looks when she finally say's "Weird coffee!" That was it for me, there was no holding back. I burst into gales of laughter and was nearly in the floor as I pulled the good coffee from behind the machine and told her what I had done. Kathy was irritated with me because she had hoped to drag it out longer but I couldn't hold it in. It was just too much! Betty, being a good play mate laughed and said "I'm going to get you for this!" Don't you know that this set me and Kathy off on another plan? We spent the day giggling and plotting our next move. All day Betty would chuckle and say "I'm not forgetting this!" and we'd just laugh because we knew she'd never get us for you see, we were making plans to keep an eye on her.

I stopped after play for pay time at another popular with the family restaurant (Red Top—home of quite literally dinner plate sized hamburgers) to buy some gumballs that looked like eyeballs. Later that evening I went to Wal Mart where I purchased plastic headbands and the biggest assortment of bugs that I could find—including a tiny VW Beetle car. I glued the gumballs to the headbands then played with the bugs for a while. The next morning I once again got up early and met Kathy at Betty's desk a good twenty minutes before she arrived. We placed bugs all over her desk and put the VW Beetle (that was such a special touch and Betty's favorite) on top of her computer monitor then went to get our coffee while we waited. Betty arrived but was in a hurry to get to her coffee so just tossed her stuff down on her desk, failing to notice the bugs. At first. As our co-workers arrived, we wandered to our work areas and waited for her to find them. It didn't take long before she started laughing hysterically. We sauntered over to explain that she'd never get even with us because we had bugged her work area so we'd know every plan she devised now. It was one of the funniest moments in work history ever, with what happened next being the topper. Betty was the person who took care of requests for copies of medical records for the hospital and was helping a lady who was there with her twenty something son, fill out forms when Kathy and I decided to wander by with our headbands with eyeballs affixed to the backs of our heads.. We casually mentioned that "Oh yeah, we now have eyeballs in the backs of our heads so don't get any ideas!" That was it for Betty. I thought we'd have to pick her up out of the floor. The people waiting thought it was pretty funny too, especially when we pointed out the bugged work space. Those bugs stayed there for months. Surprisingly the supervisors didn't make her remove them until we had an inspection looming. Every now and then I wonder if she still has those bugs.

Sometimes I miss playing for pay. If you hear of anyone in need of a department moral booster hostess/goodwill ambassador let me know, won't you? I can give lessons if nothing else. Resume with references available upon request.

Leviticus 23:31 You shall do no work at all. This is to be a lasting ordinance for the generations to come, wherever you live.

Recipe du Jour link: Archives are at http://www.topica.com/lists/rdj/read

You Just Put Hand Lotion On Didn't You Mom?!

I can't begin to tell you how many times I've heard the above question over the years. As a hand lotion addict though, I can tell you that it has been many, many times.

I have very dry hands that feel tight and awful when they get wet so once dry, I simply *must* put lotion on them. I have bottles of the stuff all over the house and tubes of it in my purse. Of course there is always a bottle in the kitchen, ready for duty the moment I dry my hands after cooking or washing. So it stands to reason that at just about any given moment while in the kitchen, I will likely have put lotion on recently. You'd think my family would learn this and either quit asking for my assistance with ice for their drinks, or at least get used to the taste. Oh so many times over their lifetimes, I have heard them bitterly complain about the taste of lotion in their drinks. Now the grandkids even complain. I'm *sorry*! My hands feel like drawn up claws if I don't wear lotion, okay?

Stacie called to chat a few minutes ago and while talking, I grabbed some bagged salad and a bottle of Ken's Steak House Light Caesar salad dressing, my favorite, which was sitting next to a bottle of light creamy poppy seed dressing, my next favorite, from the fridge door. I set everything on the counter and preparing to make a salad for my lunch, saw a spot of creamy poppy seed dressing on my hand. Naturally since I love the stuff, I licked it off my hand.

Oh gross! It wasn't creamy poppy seed dressing at all! It was hand lotion and at long last I had a taste of my own medicine. When I told Stacie (who was asking why I was yelling Gross!) she started laughing. Hard. Harder than I've heard her laugh in many years. She was positively delighted that I had finally tasted my own lifelong torment. In fact, she said if I don't tell her sisters then she will. I suspect she already has.

I myself laughed so hard my stomach hurt. That stuff really is *nasty* tasting and as Stacie pointed out, I finally know the taste that they had to live with in their mouths while growing up.

Best of all I was feeling a bit blue when she called and she was feeling stressed from a work related problem, but we both felt better when we hung up!

I've learned a great lesson too; Let everyone get their own ice for their drinks from now on.

2 Samuel 12:20 Then David got up from the ground. After he had washed, put on lotions and changed his clothes, he went into the house of the LORD and worshiped. Then he went to his own house, and at his request they served him food, and he ate.

In Closing

I hope you have enjoyed your trip down memory lane with me and that, at least in some small way, you have been blessed. I am preparing to start on another book very soon. That book will contain letters written to God. I welcome letters from women, men and children. If you would like more information on submitting or simply want to offer feedback on this book, please e-mail me at:

Mrs.Footinmouth@gmail.com or write me at:

Mrs. Jayne Nagy
232 Old Farm Road
Roanoke Rapids, NC 27870

I look forward to hearing from you!

As The Deer

As the deer panteth for the water
So my soul longeth after thee
You alone are my hearts desire
And I long to worship you
You alone are my strength, my shield
To You alone may my spirit yield
You alone are my hearts desire
And I long to worship you
Oh how He loves you and me
Oh, how He loves you and me,
Oh, how He loves you and me.
He gave His life, what more could He give;
Oh, how He loves you, Oh, how He loves me,
Oh, how He loves you and me.
Jesus to Calv'ry did go,
His love for mankind to show.
What He did there brought hope from despair.
Oh, how He loves you, Oh, how He loves me,
Oh how He loves you and me.
Oh, how He loves you and me,
Oh, how He loves you and me.
He gave His life, what more could He give;
Oh, how He loves you, Oh, how He loves me,
Oh, how He loves you and me.

www.ingramcontent.com/pod-product-compliance
Lightning Source LLC
Chambersburg PA
CBHW031825090426
42741CB00005B/131